Brandeis on Democracy

Brandeis on Democracy

EDITED BY PHILIPPA STRUM

UNIVERSITY PRESS OF KANSAS

Frontispiece courtesy of the Library of Congress

Published by the University Press of Kansas (Lawrence, Kansas 66049), which was organized by the Kansas Board of Regents and is operated and funded by Emporia State University, Fort Hays State University, Kansas State University, Pittsburg State University, the University of Kansas, and Wichita State University

Library of Congress Cataloging-in-Publication Data

Brandeis, Louis Dembitz, 1856–1941.
    Brandeis on democracy / edited by Philippa Strum.
      p. cm.
    Includes bibliographical references and index.
    ISBN 0-7006-0678-5 (cloth) ISBN 0-7006-0679-3 (pbk.)
    1. Brandeis, Louis Dembitz, 1856–1941—Views on democracy.
    2. Judges—United States—Biography. I. Strum, Philippa.
    II. Title.
    KF8745.B67A4 1994
    347.73'2634—dc20
    [347.3073534]   94-21125

British Library Cataloguing in Publication Data is available.

Printed in the United States of America

10 9 8 7 6 5 4 3 2 1

The paper used in this publication meets the minimum requirements of the American National Standard for Permanence of Paper for Printed Library Materials Z39.48-1984.

For David W. Levy and Melvin I. Urofsky

Contents

Illustrations

Acknowledgments

As with every such project, I am extremely grateful to the large number of people who contributed to the making of this book.

Grayson Williams spent hours running documents through a scanner that seemed unable to perform its job as well as he did his, exercised his patience and research skills in tracking down sources of documents published decades ago, and managed to make both endeavors seem like fun. My thanks go to him and to the many people who were so helpful with sources and permissions: Judith Mellins and David de Lorenzo of the Manuscripts and Archives Division of the Harvard Law School Library; Janet Hodgson, of the University of Louisville Archives, who has been aiding me in one way or another for more years than either of us can remember; Franz Jantzen, of the Office of the Curator, Supreme Court of the United States; Jessica Kaz, of the Jewish Historical Society, Washington, D.C.; and the staff of the Prints and Photographs Division of the Library of Congress.

Alice Brandeis Popkin has treated me to memories and hours of good conversation and laughter in addition to her grandfather's letters, and she has my warm thanks.

The staff of the University Press of Kansas is an author's dream. I would like, once again, to thank Fred Woodward, its director; Susan McRory, senior production editor; and Susan Schott, marketing manager.

David W. Levy and Melvin I. Urofsky are deservedly well known for the now-classic volumes of Brandeis letters they meticulously unearthed, transcribed, edited, and annotated. They learned so much about Brandeis in the process that I cannot imagine publishing anything about him without showing it to them first. They each worked their way through this volume, repeating what they had done for my earlier study, *Brandeis: Beyond Progressivism*, commenting copiously, correcting my more egregious factual, grammatical, and stylistic errors, and making the kind of helpful suggestions that can come only from experts. That does not mean that they agree with my choice of documents or everything I have written. Their time and effort reflected a devotion to scholarship and a sense of collegial community that has been enormously important to me and equally available to other Brandeis scholars.

They have fulfilled the tasks I have inflicted upon them with great good humor—some of their comments, in fact, are better left unprinted—and we have become friends in the process. Dedicating this book to them is an insufficient but heartfelt expression of my gratitude.

1 / Introduction

The vice-president of a major corporation is accused of diverting company money to pay for his gardener, expensive dinners for influential people, and the cost of maintaining his overseas estates. Concerned citizens turn to a public-spirited lawyer, who meticulously examines reports and statements issued by the company and others in the industry and discovers that they have contributed huge sums to the campaign of a presidential candidate and have maintained a secret fund to pay off state legislators considering regulatory statutes. A public scandal follows. So do reforms.

The players could be Michael Milken or Ralph Nader or Richard Nixon. But they were not. The high-living vice-president, who quickly sold his stock to a friend when the scandal erupted, was milking the New York–based Equitable Assurance Company. The Equitable Assurance was collaborating with the New York Life Insurance Company, which contributed $48,702.50 to Theodore Roosevelt's campaign of 1904. The concerned citizens were Bostonians who had paid almost a million dollars per year in premiums to the Equitable and some of whom worriedly organized the New England Policy-Holders' Protective Committee. The attorney to whom they turned in 1905 was Louis Dembitz Brandeis, then practicing law in Boston. After giving himself a crash course in the insurance industry, Brandeis created an entirely new approach to insurance that was enacted into law by the Massachusetts legislature. Brandeis's invention was savings bank life insurance, which freed workers from the necessity of dealing with corrupt insurance companies and which Brandeis later called his life's greatest achievement.

A year earlier, he had been asked by activists in the Public Franchise League to investigate the Boston Consolidated Gas Company, which was about to refinance itself by issuing worthless stock. Brandeis had then immersed himself in the arcane world of public utility rates and the clash between stockholders and consumers. He found three areas of concern. The monopolistic company was being run far from efficiently, he wanted consumer rates to be as low as possible, and he considered it legitimate for stockholders to get a fair return for their investment. He soon came up with a novel idea that would satisfy all the competing interests while promoting efficiency: the company would be permitted to increase dividends to its shareholders only to the extent that it simultaneously lowered the rates charged customers. Brandeis manipulated the carrot of high dividends and the stick of punitive legislation so well that he actually convinced the Consolidated's skeptical president of the wisdom of the plan. With both men's support, it was passed by the Massachusetts legislature. Brandeis then got the company to calculate the worth of dividends paid to stockholders and to give employees who chose to participate in his novel plan the equivalent value in shares of stocks as "dividends" on their wages. The employees not only became owners as well as workers but quickly developed an interest in efficiency, as did the company. Efficiency brought lower rates, which in turn led to greater sales; the greater sales resulted in even lower rates; and the sliding-scale system promised that for every reduction of five cents in rates, the company could increase its stock dividend by one percent. The system worked well until it was faced with the inflationary pressures of World War I.

Life insurance and public utilities were only two of the areas that Brandeis tackled and in which he came up with innovative solutions that changed the way business was done. An observer, watching him argue a case before the Supreme Court some years later, wrote to Felix Frankfurter that Brandeis "not only reached the Court, but he dwarfed the Court." Brandeis had a way of dwarfing everyone around him, and the number of activities to which he brought his brilliant and tirelessly creative mind was enormous. During a life that lasted from 1856 to 1941, he took part in almost every major social movement: trade unionism, trust-busting, women's suffrage, conservation, labor legislation, and Progressivism. He virtually wrote presidential candidate Woodrow Wilson's New Freedom platform and advised Wilson as well as President Franklin Delano Roosevelt while they were in office. A much-sought-out attorney, he invented a new method of arguing constitutional cases and adapted it for the use of judges when he sat on the Supreme Court from 1916 to 1939. While still in private practice he gradually turned over half of his time to public causes, becoming known as the "people's attorney." In addition, he led American Zionism from

1914 through the 1930s—and he enjoyed a rich and full existence as husband, father of two daughters, grandfather, and friend.

He is not simply a historical figure worthy of study, however. The problems he faced and the answers he fashioned are as much a matter of concern toward the end of the twentieth century as they were early in it. He wrote and spoke about the nature of democracy, the way to protect majority rule without violating individual rights, the limits of permissible speech, the right of privacy, the importance of education, the causes of and possible solutions for poverty, the tendency of concentrated and unaccountable power to corrupt those who hold it, the relationship between the lawyer and the public, the most efficient and just way to run a workplace, the lessons that socialism might hold for a capitalistic society, the way to balance power in the United States between the federal government and the states, gender equality, and the responsibility of citizens to their community.

Every one of those matters is on the public agenda today, and what Brandeis had to say about them is still as relevant as it is provocative.

Louis David Brandeis was born on November 13, 1856, to a prosperous Louisville, Kentucky, merchant and his wife. They were members of three related families that had immigrated from Prague after the failure of the 1848 democratic revolution in the Austro-Hungarian Empire. The financial success of Brandeis's father indicated that he had found the land of economic opportunity he had been seeking. Equally important to the decision of the families to immigrate to the United States, however, was the individual liberty and concern for human dignity that they had understood to be part of the American ethos. Brandeis's family was strongly abolitionist during the Civil War in spite of their neighbors' disapproval, and his earliest memories were of his mother taking food and coffee to the Union soldiers on their street and of his father moving the family across the river to Indiana when the fighting came too close.

The dominant figure in Brandeis's early life besides his parents was his uncle Lewis Naphtali Dembitz. Dembitz was an attorney with a plethora of interests who participated actively in public life and wrote authoritatively about Kentucky law and jurisprudence. A highly respected figure in Louisville, he gave one of the nominating speeches for Abraham Lincoln at the Republican party convention of 1860, read a dozen languages, and was an expert astronomer and mathematician.

Brandeis was originally named Louis David, but he changed his middle name to Dembitz as a young man out of admiration for his uncle's intellectual interests and high standards of morality. Dembitz's orthodox Judaism was of no interest to the secular Brandeises, but it would affect Louis Brandeis dramatically later in his life.

Brandeis's early education was in the Louisville schools. After the Civil War, his family went on an extended European trip, and the sixteen-year-old Brandeis enrolled in the Dresden Annen-Realschule. He was as outstanding a student there as he had been in Louisville, studying Latin, French, German, literature, mineralogy, geography, physics, chemistry, and mathematics. Upon the family's return to the United States, he became a member of the Harvard Law School class of 1878, where he studied the new case method introduced by Dean Christopher Columbus Langdell and earned the highest grades the school had ever seen.

Brandeis seems to have loved the law from the moment he began classes at Harvard. "I am pleased with everything that pertains to the law," he wrote to his cousin and future brother-in-law, a lawyer, in March 1976. "Law schools are splendid institutions," he enthused. "Aside from the instruction there received, being able continually to associate with young men who have the same interest and ambition, who are determined to make as great progress as possible in their studies and devote all their time to the same—must alone be of inestimable advantages. Add to this the instruction of consummate lawyers, who devote their whole time to *you*, and a complete law-library of over fifteen thousand volumes . . . A lecture alone is little better than the reading of textbooks, but such lectures as we have here in connection with our other work are quite different things." He added, "Our law-clubs are grand institutions, a great incentive to labor and the work for them is a pleasant change," and then went on for several pages about a recent case the club had discussed, several "admirable" textbooks, and professors he particularly admired.

His father's business had foundered before Brandeis entered law school, and Brandeis, determined to remain at Harvard for a year's graduate work, enabled himself to do so by tutoring fellow students and proctoring examinations. A few months with a St. Louis law firm convinced him that Boston was a much more exciting place, and he returned there in 1879 to go into partnership with his law school classmate Samuel Warren, a member of a prominent Boston family.

The firm's almost immediate success resulted from a combination of

Warren's connections, referrals by Harvard faculty members, the business of Boston's prosperous German-Jewish community, and Brandeis's burgeoning reputation as a brilliant lawyer. By 1890, when 75 percent of the country's lawyers had an income of less than $5,000, he was earning more than $50,000 a year. His earnings continued to rise. He and his wife Alice, a second cousin whom he married in 1891, lived frugally with their two daughters, and Brandeis invested his surplus income in low-paying but safe bonds. He was a millionaire by 1907, a millionaire twice over when he joined the Supreme Court in 1916, and in spite of substantial charitable contributions, he left an estate worth over $3,000,000 in 1941.

He did not, however, develop the values such a fortune might imply, and one reason may have been his immersion in public causes and the occasional course he taught at the Harvard Law School and at M.I.T. In 1892, while he was preparing a course on business law for M.I.T., violence erupted at the Carnegie steel works in Homestead, Pennsylvania. The company had decided not to renew the workers' contract and refused to deal with a union. It erected walls with apertures for guns around the steel mill grounds. The workers went out on strike. Pinkerton guards, hired by the company to protect strikebreakers but denied entry by the strikers, opened fire with their Winchesters. The workers suffered most of the casualties in the ensuing battle, and Brandeis never forgot the horror with which he heard the news. He later told an interviewer, "I saw at once that the common law, built up under simpler conditions of living, gave an inadequate basis for the adjustment of the complex relations of the modern factory system. I threw away my notes and approached my theme from new angles. Those talks at Tech marked an epoch in my own career." The lessons he learned during his early years as a practicing attorney, a public activist, and a teacher had a lasting effect on his thinking about the law and about the American economy. So did his own first-hand encounter with a strike.

The strike at the McElwain shoe factory in 1902, which he describes in "Business—a Profession" (p. 119), brought him into contact with the workers' union and reinforced the belief he had begun to have in 1892 that unions were crucial if employers were not to have unlimited power. He worked out a system by which McElwain could spread his shoe factory's work out over the year rather than paying his workers only when a big contract was in hand. The irregularity of their employment was what had sent the workers out on strike, and the need for regularity of employment became a major tenet of Brandeis's creed. Even more telling was his discovery that union officials were reasonable people with whom he could discuss matters rationally. He went on to mediate other strikes and, after having settled one in Syracuse in 1907, wrote to his brother, "I am experiencing a growing conviction that the labor men are the most congenial company. The intense materialism and luxuriousness of most of our other people makes their company quite irksome."

A combination of the teaching he had experienced at Harvard about law as resulting from changing circumstances and his own unending intellectual curiosity had already led him to enunciate a theory of lawyering that emphasized morality and a knowledge of real-life circumstances as much as law. An early memorandum in his handwriting, entitled "The Practice of the Law," says in part, "Broad Scope of Opportunity . . . Question—how a man handles it . . . Broad interests—Excitements—where Else can you find Such. Thoroughness in law—Know not only specific Q. but whole subject. Can't otherwise Know the facts. Know thoroughly each fact. Don't believe client witness—Examine Documents. Draw on the imagination. Know the whole Subject. Know bookkeeping the Universal language of business. Know Each Subject . . . Know about persons . . . Persistency—Courage. Devotion. You may become master. Don't have personal interest. Advise client what he should have—not what he wants . . . Know not only those facts which bear on Direct controversy. but Know all facts that Surround."

He expanded on these themes in his 1893 letter to William Dunbar (p. 48). Brandeis extolled the days when the local lawyer was the wise adviser thoroughly cognizant of his clients' affairs and therefore able to see their legal problems in a larger context. An adviser needed facts, which Brandeis saw as the key to knowledge in all spheres, not only law. He credited his own exposure to facts with gradually changing his thinking about the supposedly equal relationship between employer and employee and the evil of labor unions that he had formerly taken for granted.

Brandeis's vision of the ideal lawyer, as well as his deeply felt need to be free to represent only clients whose cases he considered legitimate, led him to scorn attorneys who made themselves servants of corporations, thereby not only confining themselves to a knowledge of nothing more than their clients' wishes but, far worse, bargaining away their freedom in exchange for large salaries and hurting society in the process. Many lawyers, as he charged in his speech on "The Living Law"

(p. 59), were becoming hired hands for the ever-growing corporations that became hallmarks of the early twentieth century in the United States. Addressing the Harvard Ethical Society in 1905 on "The Opportunity in the Law" (p. 52), he reminded his listeners that in the early United States, "nearly every great lawyer was . . . a statesman; and nearly every statesman, great or small, was a lawyer." Now, he lamented, attorneys no longer held "a position of independence, between the wealthy and the people, prepared to curb the excesses of either." Too many lawyers in the early twentieth century had turned their backs on the people in order "to become adjuncts of great corporations."

It was extremely unusual in 1905 to find a lawyer condemning other practitioners for becoming adjuncts of corporations. Brandeis's speech reflected the distinction he had begun to make between "the people" and corporations, between the average person and the wealthy. He was gradually reaching the conclusion that wealthy corporations were not good for "the people" and that lawyers had a particular responsibility to do something about the situation.

Public service was one of the values he had learned from his family, and his growing reputation combined with the prominent position of the people he represented resulted in his being called to participate in Boston's civic life almost as soon as he began practicing law there. By 1884 he was lecturing to a Unitarian Sunday school class about the necessity for taxation, to a state insurance committee about the need to value policies uniformly for tax purposes, and to another state legislative committee against women's suffrage—a position that he would soon reverse. He also spoke out that year against a proposed temperance law that he considered unenforceable, in favor of a law that would have limited the impact of lobbies on the Massachusetts legislature, and for better treatment of Boston's poor people.

Brandeis later said that "my important public work" began only in 1893. The occasion was his successful battle against the attempt of the Boston Elevated Railway to acquire a monopoly over Boston's transportation system. His continuing interest in public transportation would lead him into a years-long and ultimately successful battle against J. P. Morgan and the monopolistic New Haven Railroad that Morgan controlled. In 1902, when the fight over the Boston Elevated had been won, he declined to accept the fee offered for his services by the Boston Board of Trade that had been his "client." His friend Edward Filene reported that Brandeis said "he never made a charge for public service of this kind; that it was his duty as it was mine to help protect the public rights; and . . . that he resolved early in life to give at least one hour a day to public service, and later on he hoped to give fully half his time." The fame he won in his various battles on behalf of the public, always without remuneration, set an example for what was at first a handful but decades later became a small flood of lawyers willing to follow it. As he reported in his interview with the *American Cloak and Suit Review* (p. 35), he considered public service a joy as well as a duty.

It also fit his view of democracy, which was one of citizens making intelligent choices about matters affecting their joint lives and then working in the public arena to ensure the effectuation of those choices. He considered politics too important to be left to politicians. It was "obvious" to him that democratic government could not work without citizen participation. "It is customary for people to berate politicians," he noted. "But after all, the politicians, even if their motives are not of the purest, come much nearer performing their duties as citizens than the so-called 'good' citizens who stay at home." Citizens could participate effectively in public life only if they were educated, he told the New England Civic Federation in 1906 (p. 32). This meant that "the citizen should be able to comprehend, among other things, the many great and difficult problems of industry, commerce, and finance, which with us necessarily become political questions." An education and mental development that citizens "gained only from their attendance at the common school" would not suffice. "It is essential that the education shall be continuous throughout life" and consist of reading and discussion with other citizens as well as formal classes. Remembering the development of his own views about business and labor, Brandeis emphasized experience as the great teacher.

His law practice led him to appear before legislative bodies on behalf of paper manufacturers who were fighting unsuccessfully against a municipally created monopoly over disinfecting the rags that were used in making paper, and as the representative of various clients opposing a national protective tariff. He relished his roles as a private attorney and as an occasional actor in the public sphere, performing his civic duty to help prevent greedy or uninformed people from attempting to misuse the political or the economic system. He also assumed that there was nothing intrinsically wrong with either system; law and twentieth-century capitalism were both good and complementary.

These beliefs were unsurprising for the son of a relatively affluent businessman, who had grown up with a belief in laissez-faire economic theory. They were echoed by the world of Boston Brahminism, which welcomed him warmly while he was a student at Harvard. But the ideas of the Brahmins remained the same when Brandeis's began to change, particularly as his experiences made him more and more friendly to unions.

By the beginning of the twentieth century, Brandeis had come to fear big business, believing that it was stifling the American economy. The rapidly expanding trusts, he thought, inevitably were inefficient, because any economic or political institution so big that the human being supposedly in charge of it could neither understand nor control its operations simply could not be run rationally. Managers did not perceive or care about either the wastefulness of their enterprises or the damage their personnel policies were doing to the human beings who depended upon their jobs for their livelihood. In addition, he deplored the corruption and undemocratic power gained in legislatures by the huge concentrations of capital that big businesses were amassing for the first time in American history. Giant corporations were able to end competition by buying up smaller firms and creating oligopolies or monopolies that charged the public unfair prices and wasted much of their ill-gained profits through inefficiency. The trusts' sale of stock to millions of "little" Americans who knew nothing about the trusts' policies gave the trusts too much unbridled power, as did their close relationships with the banks that funded and profited from them and with the politicians influenced by their money. The destruction of competition minimized the impetus to seek better products, better services, and greater efficiency: bigness was bad for creativity. It was also inconceivable that employees could exercise any creativity while working inhumanely long hours at repetitive tasks, and their exhaustion made it impossible for them to find fulfillment after working hours or to participate in the political process. Thus bigness was threatening the very fabric of American democracy.

He was horrified by acts such as that of James and Joseph McNamara, who dynamited the *Los Angeles Times* building, killing twenty-one workers, because of the antiunion stance of the *Times*'s publisher. It was "well-founded unrest; reasoned unrest; but the manifestations of which are often unintelligent and sometimes criminal," he told the Senate Committee on Interstate Commerce in 1911. But he understood the violence of workers even as he condemned it, and he saw the trusts and their refusal to grant workers justice through their unions as the real culprits. As long as men like the McNamaras believed that their only recourse was to dynamite, there would be violence. He had considered and rejected the option of socialism because it would depend upon huge governmental bureaucracies. He could nonetheless comprehend its appeal to workers. "It seems to me," he wrote to an attorney who had asked if social reform might stave off socialism, "that the prevailing discontent is due perhaps less to dissatisfaction with the material conditions, as to the denial of participation in management, and that the only way to avoid Socialism is to develop cooperation in its broadest sense."

A number of the selections included in this book (and the reader is asked to note that they are excerpts; for those interested, full citations appear in the Notes) reflect Brandeis's support for unions as a way to balance employer power and provide for laborers' needs—a support he conditions on unions acting responsibly. Long hours and low wages constituted exploitation of the workers, and as he came to appreciate the enormous power of big business, he realized that the unions alone could not balance it: the government would have to enact legal constraints on employers. In addition, as he considered the impact of industrialization on the American economy and the workplace, he began to wonder why employers should enjoy so great a share of the fruits of their workers' labor. This led him to call for profit-sharing and, ultimately, worker-management.

His theory of law as responsive to communal needs and his interest in the problems of labor came together in 1908, when he worked with his sister-in-law Josephine Goldmark and the National Consumers' League on what became the famous "Brandeis brief" in *Muller* v. *Oregon* (1908). Submitted to the United States Supreme Court on behalf of an Oregon law setting maximum hours of work for women, it devoted only two pages to legal precedent and over a hundred pages to sociological data demonstrating that overly long work days had negative effects on women and their families. It persuaded a Court, then inclined to strike down such welfare legislation, to uphold the law, and earned Brandeis the rare distinction of being named in the Court's opinion. The view that law must reflect societal conditions, articulated largely by Justice Oliver Wendell Holmes, Dean Roscoe Pound of the Harvard Law School, and Brandeis, has since become the basic American approach to law.

Brandeis went on to argue for maximum hours legislation for men as well as women and, ultimately, for minimum wage laws. His fear of centralized power, whether in private industry or government, however, re-

HOW TO TRIP
UP WITNESSES

"The successful cross-examiner must possess a knowledge of the case which is greater than the sum of the knowledge possessed by all of the witnesses.

"You can represent the knowledge of the witnesses by a cluster of dots. One witness will know one dot on the edge of the cluster, one in the centre, etc. Another will know a row of dots along one edge. Each witness knows, too, the line or lines connecting his dots.

"But the knowledge of the cross-examiner who is successful will be represented by the circle drawn around all the dots.

"Then, a witness may attempt to connect a dot within the circle to one without. Or he may attempt to draw a line tangent to the circle.

"It is when he makes these attempts that he is tripped up in cross-examination."

Brandeis, 1910, during his days as a litigator in Boston. The accompanying text suggests the careful preparation that made him a respected lawyer and is in keeping with his emphasis on facts. (Boston Traveler, University of Louisville Archives)

sulted in his preference for private agreements over governmental statutes. And when he began reading the English Fabians, particularly Beatrice Webb, around 1914, he took his thinking beyond hour and wage agreements and even past profit sharing. He began talking about an economic system in which "labor will hire capital, instead of capital hiring labor," with workers owning and managing their own enterprises cooperatively and consumers also combining in cooperatives (p. 103).

In 1912, when the Democratic party nominated Woodrow Wilson as its candidate for president, Brandeis wrote to Wilson in the hope that he would include Brandeis's ideas in his campaign. The two men first met on August 28, 1912. Brandeis gradually spelled out for Wilson the dangers of bigness and the way the government ought to go about destroying the trusts. At the same time, Brandeis was writing the articles for *Collier's Magazine* that were later incorporated into his book *Other People's Money*. Wilson read the articles, jotted comments in the margins, and took most of them to heart; indeed, they became the basis for his "New Freedom." After Wilson's election, Brandeis became an informal but highly influential adviser to the new president and to members of his cabinet. By 1914, however, various political considerations led Wilson to stray from what Brandeis considered to be the path of political virtue. Brandeis remained an unofficial adviser to Wilson and other officials of the Wilson administration but began to spend more of his time on a new interest, Zionism, as reflected in the speeches in chapter 6. Two years later Woodrow Wilson implicitly endorsed Brandeis's ideas about the economy and his approach to law by naming him to the United States Supreme Court.

Brandeis, his former law clerk Dean Acheson commented, was an "incurable optimist." In spite of what he viewed as Wilson's failures as president, Brandeis did not give up his hopes that an informed government might yet enact policies more to his liking. He was filled with enthusiasm when Franklin Roosevelt was elected in 1932, believing that the New Deal might finally turn Brandeisian beliefs into public policies. His prescriptions for the administration are detailed in the memorandum of Harry Shulman's conversation with Brandeis and in Brandeis's letter to his economist daughter Elizabeth (pp. 193–94). Earlier in his career, he had served as counsel for *Collier's Weekly* during the Pinchot-Ballinger hearings. They grew out of the decision of President William Howard Taft's secretary of the interior to sell government-owned lands in Alaska to private commercial interests. When the deal was made public, Taft became part of a scheme to hide the transaction, and Congress decided to hold hearings about both the sale and the cover-up. Brandeis's ability to immerse himself in a new subject and master it was now employed in his study of land use and government ownership of land and other natural resources. He soon formulated a proposal for government ownership of land that would be leased to individuals or groups and that would be overseen by local community groups. He sketched out his ideas in his letter of July 29, 1911, to Robert

LaFollette (p. 43). These became the basis for the land policy mentioned in his letter to Elizabeth (p. 193) and in his plans for the Zionist community in Palestine (p. 178).

Brandeis had not been raised as an observant Jew. His parents practiced a secular humanism based on what they believed to be the high ethical standards implicit in Judaism. There is nothing in the first fifty-four years of Brandeis's life to suggest that being Jewish was of any significance in it. He and his wife were married in an Ethical Culture Society ceremony, and he approved of the marriage of his daughter Elizabeth to the son of a prominent Protestant theologian. He never became religious, but in the second decade of the twentieth century he threw himself into the Zionist cause.

The first event that was to lead him in this direction came in 1910, when he was asked to mediate the New York garment workers' strike. He had already written widely of his fervent belief in political and economic democracy. He was still uncertain whether the early twentieth-century industrial working class, which he had read about but had very little to do with in person, could achieve the heights of knowledge and responsibility crucial to democracy. That changed when he met the Eastern European Jews who constituted most of the workers as well as the employers in the garment trade. The workers in particular astonished him with their intelligence, rationality, openness to democratic procedures, tolerance for each other's viewpoints, sense of equality, and knowledge. He spent his days negotiating a settlement and his evenings excitedly exchanging ideas with the workers. Brandeis had found the citizens of his ideal democracy. The experience, central though it proved to his subsequent activities, did not immediately move him to embrace Zionism. A reporter for the *American Hebrew* asked his opinion of the Zionist movement, and Brandeis promptly replied that while he had a "great deal of sympathy" for it, "there is no place for . . . hyphenated Americans" who thought of themselves as members of particular ethnic groups rather than as Americans. "The opportunities for members of my people are greater here than in any other country," he declared.

Shortly thereafter, Brandeis was interviewed by journalist Jacob de-Haas, former secretary to Theodor Herzl, the father of modern Zionism. DeHaas asked Brandeis if he was related to Lewis Dembitz, a "noble Jew" devoted to Zionism. Brandeis, who had considered his uncle a role model as a lawyer of integrity but had known nothing about his Zionism, listened enthralled to deHaas's explanation of the movement to build a Jewish homeland in Palestine and the reasons for Dembitz's interest in it. Two years later Brandeis heard a talk by Aaron Aaronsohn, who had adapted a strain of wild wheat so that it could grow in the rocky soil of Palestine. "The talk was the most thrillingly interesting I have ever heard," Brandeis exclaimed, urging his brother to send for the U.S. Agriculture Department bulletin written by Aaronsohn. Brandeis himself was too busy with his practice and with his work for Wilson to do more than join a few Zionist organizations. During the summer of 1914, however, he retreated to Chatham, Massachusetts, for his yearly vacation, and spent much of his time there reading extensively in Zionism. When war broke out and he was invited to an emergency meeting called by American Zionists, he surprised its organizers by attending, by accepting what they had thought would be the nominal position of chairman of the Provisional Executive Committee for General Zionist Affairs designed by the conference to help endangered European Jews, and by then asking them to remain after the meeting to "educate" him further about Zionism so that he could perform his duties effectively. He jumped into organizational work with his usual enthusiasm and, within months, was the acknowledged leader of American Zionism, drawing in members and donations and organizing the movement so that it reflected his own efficiency and flair for generating excitement. During the next years he founded the American Jewish Congress, the Palestine Endowment Fund, and the Palestine Co-operative Company, all incorporating the thinking about democratic decisionmaking and institutional accountability that had evolved from his experiences in American public life.

As his Zionist speeches indicate, he saw the Jewish settlements in Palestine as embodying the best of American Progressivism and of Periclean Athens, which he considered to be the acme of democratic civilization. The confluence of the two were apparent in his statement that his Uncle Dembitz "reminded one of the Athenians." He made a triumphal tour of the Jewish settlements in Palestine in 1919, his ecstatic letters home reflecting the renewed commitment it generated in him to a Jewish homeland. Palestine became a kind of laboratory for Brandeis's ideas about worker ownership, universal education, land management, and natural resources and utilities. If he was overly sanguine in his partial acceptance of the Zionist insistence that Palestine was "an empty land for a homeless people," he was equally insistent that the Arab inhabitants of the land be treated fairly. His statement to that effect in the Pittsburgh Platform (p. 178) was heartfelt. One of the last of his many charitable contributions to Palestine was for playgrounds specifically designated for the use of Jewish, Muslim, and Christian children.

Woodrow Wilson nominated Brandeis to the Supreme Court on January 28, 1916. A friend wrote to former president William Howard Taft, "When Brandeis' nomination came in yesterday, the Senate simply gasped," and the next few months were filled with what Mrs. Brandeis called "fireworks." The battle over the nomination was one of interests and ideologies, although the fact that Brandeis was the first Jewish American named to the Court made an element of anti-Semitism almost inevitable. Much of the opposition was centered in Massachusetts, and Senator Thomas J. Walsh of Montana, a Brandeis supporter on the Senate Judiciary subcommittee that considered the nomination, commented, "The real crime of which this man is guilty is that he has exposed the iniquities of men in high places in our financial system. He has not stood in awe of the majesty of wealth." Reverend A. A. Berle added that the Brahmin community "simply cannot realize" the fallacy of its belief "that whoever is not approved by them is ipso facto a person who is either 'dangerous' or lacking in 'judicial temperament' "—both charges hurled at the nominee. Brandeis played no public role in the fight but directed it from behind the scenes with his usual success, and on June 5, 1919, he took his seat on the Supreme Court.

He went to the Court with a fully developed philosophy of democracy and law. His fear of bigness, his emphasis on facts as the key to knowledge and good law-making, and his belief in experimentation as central to progress came together in his judicial opinions. The best place for experimentation was the states, which were still the small laboratories suitable to experimentation that Jefferson had envisaged. Experiments could be dangerous because "Man is weak and his judgment is at best fallible." But human fallibility was everywhere, even on the Supreme Court, and so the wisest and most democratic approach was to minimize judicial limitations on reasonable experimentation. His close friend Norman Hapgood commented to Brandeis, "I think . . . that if the chances of being right seem to be represented by eighty percent, that is justification enough for working to bring something about." "Sixty percent would usually be enough," was the justice's reply, and he held the states to an even lower ratio. If they could show that legislation embodied a reasonable approach to a societal need, he would vote to sustain it, even if he disagreed that the approach was the best one possible or doubted its chance of success. Felix Frankfurter commented that Brandeis believed that the Constitution "provided for the future partly by not forecasting it and partly by the generality of its language." The Constitution, in Brandeis's eyes, was designed to be flexible. It was as amenable to legislative experimentation as to judicial imagination, and Brandeis frequently reminded his colleagues of Chief Justice John Marshall's statement that "we must never forget that it is a constitution we are expounding." By this Marshall, and Brandeis, meant that their responsibility was to interpret a generalized statement of principles designed to be interpreted in light of the needs of society at differing historical moments, rather than to promulgate a static legal code.

The way to demonstrate the relationship between societal need and legislative enactment was through a summary of the relevant facts— the technique Brandeis had created for *Muller* v. *Oregon*. But as a justice he discovered that not enough lawyers practicing before the Court were fashioning "Brandeis briefs" and that their arguments contained too little factual information. So his theory of attorney responsibility was broadened to include a theory of judicial responsibility. When attorneys failed to include the factual data he felt explained the rationality behind various legislative experiments, not only to the Court but to the public, he had his clerks seek it out and then placed it in his opinions. He regretted the unwillingness of the other justices to do the same. In *Jay Burns Baking Co.* v. *Bryan* (1924) the Court was asked to determine the constitutionality of a Nebraska consumer protection law that set weight standards, including maximum weight limits, for commercially sold loaves of bread. It found the statute to violate the due process clause of the Fourteenth Amendment. Disagreeing, Brandeis chastised the Court for not examining the relevant facts, saying that all the brethren had to do in this instance was "merely to acquaint ourselves with the art of breadmaking and the usages of the trade; with the devices by which buyers of bread are imposed upon and honest bakers or dealers are subjected by their dishonest fellows to unfair competition; with the problems which have confronted public officials charged with the enforcement of the laws prohibiting short weights, and with their experience in administering those laws." He fulfilled this "mere" task by presenting the Court with fifteen pages of information about the baking industry, most of it in massive footnotes.

His penchant for documenting all his statements, to the point that many pages of his opinions consist of a few lines of text and many more of footnotes, was not meant to make the opinions inaccessible to the concerned layperson—quite the contrary. He tried to write in plain English, not legalese, and he drafted and redrafted opinions so that an interested citizen would understand why Brandeis voted as he had. The Court was part of a democratic political system and therefore had an obligation to explain itself to the sovereign people. Theodore Roosevelt had called the presidency a "bully pulpit." Brandeis would have used different language but he felt the same way about the Supreme Court. Judicial opinions were a fine mechanism for educating the public and lawmakers alike. One of his clerks recalled working on what seemed endless revisions of an opinion. Finally, when the clerk was certain no more could be done, he heard Brandeis ask, "Now I think the opinion is persuasive, but what can we do to make it more instructive?" The comment about opinions he made to another clerk was, "The whole purpose, and the only one, is to educate the country." A third clerk noted that Brandeis made sixty changes in one draft of a ten-page opinion. On those occasions when Brandeis delivered an opinion orally and without notes, he reportedly knew every word so well that journalists sitting in the courtroom followed the written text to see if they could catch him in a mistake. They never did.

He was the first Supreme Court justice to cite law reviews and developed a symbiotic relationship with them, privately suggesting current topics for articles to law school professors such as Felix Frankfurter and then referring to the resultant articles in his opinions. But he did not favor judicial policymaking, except when the majority threatened the rights of a minority. Judicial restraint was a key element of his sociological jurisprudence. When Arizona sued to prevent the construction of the Boulder Dam and the possible diversion of water to California, for example, Brandeis pointed out that construction of the dam had not yet begun and so there was no need for the Court to decide whether waters that might never be taken from Arizona could legitimately be diverted. If a party based its case on a right new to American law, as happened when the Associated Press claimed that it had a property right in its dispatches, Brandeis, in dissent, objected to the Court's usurpation of the legislative function by creating and legitimizing a largely undefined right. Similarly, he dissented from the Court's declaration that stock dividends were a category of untaxable property; that was up to a legislature to decide. In *Ashwander* v. *TVA* (p. 191) he spelled out many of the rules that continue to be used in deciding whether it is appropriate for the Court to deal with constitutional issues. He repeatedly emphasized the importance of state independence. His seminal opinion for the Court in *Erie Railroad* v. *Tompkins* held that federal courts had to be bound in matters of state law by the decisions issued by each state's highest court. He was wary of federal power, dissenting in *Myers* v. *United States* (p. 187), when the Court permitted a president unilaterally to fire a civil servant even though a statute required Senate advice and consent before such a removal, and joining the Court whenever, as in the landmark case of *Schechter* v. *United States* (1935), it struck down what he felt was a level of governmental assumption of power not contemplated by the Constitution or consistent with democracy.

Schechter spelled the end of Franklin Roosevelt's National Industrial Recovery Act of 1933, which Brandeis believed delegated an unconstitutional amount of power to the president. The NIRA exempted industries from antitrust laws if they adopted codes providing for specific wages, hours, conditions of employment, and prices. The act provided no guidelines for the codes, however, giving the president total power to approve or disapprove them. Brandeis feared that the NIRA fostered unaccountable power and bigness, even though the statute was designed by Franklin Roosevelt, of whom Brandeis approved, during a moment of national emergency and was considered by Roosevelt to be a key element of his design for recovery. Brandeis's views were signaled during oral argument in two earlier cases resulting from the prosecution of oil company officials for ignoring the code Roosevelt had promulgated. One company's attorney asserted during oral argument that his client had not known the code existed and that the only copy he knew of was in the "hip pocket of a government agent sent down to Texas from Washington." Brandeis turned to the government's lawyer and demanded, "Who promulgates these orders and codes that have the force of law?" The lawyer replied that as they were promulgated by the president, "I assume they are on record at the State Department." This was insufficient. "Is there any official or general publication of these executive orders?" Brandeis pressed further. "Not that I know of," came the answer, with the lawyer finally admitting lamely that "I think it would be difficult, but it is possible to get certified copies of the executive orders and codes from the NIRA." Brandeis joined seven of his colleagues in striking down this particular use of the NIRA. When *Schech-*

ter sounded the death knell of the NIRA, on the same day that the Court handed down a number of other decisions negating legislation favored by Roosevelt, Brandeis spoke sharply to top Roosevelt adviser Thomas G. Corcoran. "I want you to go back and tell the President," Brandeis directed Corcoran, "that we're not going to let this government centralize everything." Bigness in government could be every bit as oppressive as bigness in business, and Brandeis would have no part of it.

Brandeis's emphasis on the facts led him to focus on the way real human beings and the institutions important to them would be affected by Supreme Court decisions. When the Court overturned an Arizona law forbidding its courts to issue injunctions against strikes and picketing, Chief Justice Taft wrote about the equal protection and due process clauses of the Fourteenth Amendment. Brandeis, dissenting, described the factual situation (*Truax* v. *Corrigan* [p. 78]).

Brandeis's influence went beyond cases in the economic sphere. He was a major force in creating today's law of speech and of privacy (see chapters 8 and 9). Both pitted the government against the individual; both were central to his thinking about human dignity and democracy.

It is difficult to divide Brandeis's writings and speeches into neat compartments, because his activities at any given moment were so diverse and his ideas, as another former law clerk said, were "of one piece." In May 1905 alone, he was mediating a labor conflict for the Boston Symphony Orchestra, delivering "The Opportunity in the Law" to the Harvard Ethical Society, working with the Industrial League, and beginning his membership on the Advisory Committee of the National Municipal League's Municipal Taxation Committee. In July, in addition to writing letters reflecting his interest in and reading about London's improvement of streets in working-class areas, a meeting of Chinese-Americans about American policy toward China, domestic unrest in Russia, temperance in England, the proposed Panama Canal, immigration, Massachusetts' cranberry industry, street railways, Boston gas company rates, and the end of the Russo-Japanese War, he corresponded with relevant Massachusetts officials about prison conditions, charities, treatment of the insane, Boston's acquisition of land for parks, and the collection of labor statistics. The chronology that follows this introduction is an attempt to indicate the variety of his interests, particularly as they are reflected in this volume, and the way they complemented each other. One theme did underlie and unify his multitudinous activities, however: his insistent belief in the dignity of all human beings.

He was a democrat because democracy was the best protection for dignity. He cared about the kind of political system in effect because the community in which people lived affected their ability to retain their dignity and to educate and fulfill themselves. Democracy could not work without an educated electorate; neither could uneducated people explore their own possibilities. Human beings were fallible, and while it was better than any other political system, democracy was no guarantor of perfection. The populace and its government had to be open to constant experimentation. Because Brandeis learned from experience, he assumed everyone else would do so as well. Experience had to be of ideas as well as of events. It was crucial that the free flow of ideas be maintained so that people could have access to all possible policies. The position that Brandeis the jurist maintained on free speech, a position that gave communication of ideas the widest possible latitude and made government interference with them illegitimate except in the most extreme emergency, flowed from his belief that democracy was dependent on knowledge. The people had to be free to try out ideas, and because the weight of society usually lay behind whatever ideas were popular at the moment, people had to have the privacy in which to explore thinking that was different. Government had to be kept out of the home as much as possible to protect both individual dignity and individual thought.

Experimentation, creativity, and human dignity would suffer when institutions became too big. Individual voices would go unheard. People with great power tended to believe that they were right because they were powerful and to close their ears to other ideas. They could not know what those in the institutions they governed were doing or how the individuals who worked in them were faring. Policies, whether of corporations or of political bodies, that engendered poverty were wrong: they violated human dignity and prevented the popular participation in the political process central to a democratic state. Democracy depended on responsiveness and therefore on smallness. It was possible for a country as large as the United States to maintain a democracy, assuming always that institutions were kept to a reasonable size. The federal government could not be the ultimate problem solver, because in order to do so it would have to become so big as to constitute a problem itself. The states had to be nurtured as a way of balancing the power of the federal government and to provide small-scale laboratories for experimentation with new policies. Presidential power had to be balanced by congressional power. Judges had to check legislatures and executives if they interfered with communication of ideas, but judges also had an obligation to interpret the Constitution so as to give wide latitude to legislative and executive experimentation with policies appropriate to the conditions of the day. There was no situation in which power could safely be left unbalanced or unchecked. Ultimately, concentration of private power would be avoided only if capital and labor were joined in institutions owned by their workers. There would then be no fear of unbridled power, but there would be infinite possibilities for creativity and individual fulfillment.

Democracy as a ceaseless process rather than an end, education, civic responsibility, ideas, decentralization of power, experimentation: these were Brandeis's constant focus. One colleague called him a "serenely implacable democrat." Another noted that to Brandeis, "democracy is not a political program. It is a religion." It was the concept that illuminated his life.

CHRONOLOGY

1856, November 13	Born in Louisville, Kentucky
1875–1878	Student and graduate student, Harvard Law School
1878–1879	Law practice in St. Louis, Missouri
1879–1916	Law practice in Boston, Massachusetts
1881 July	First law review article, "Liability of Trust-Estates on Contracts Made for Their Benefit"
1882–1883	Teacher of Evidence at Harvard Law School
1887	Helps found *Harvard Law Review*
1890	"The Right to Privacy" with Samuel D. Warren
1891	Marriage to Alice Goldmark
1892–1894	Teacher of Business Law at Massachusetts Institute of Technology
1893	Letter to William H. Dunbar
1893–1902	Boston subway system fight
1897 January	First appearance before a congressional body,

	the House Ways and Means Committee, testifying against a tariff act
1902 December	Debate, ''The Incorporation of Trades Unions''
1903 April	Article on ''Experience of Massachusetts in Street Railways''
1903 December	Speech to the Good Government Association
1904 April	Address, ''The Employer and Trades Unions''
1904–1906	Involvement with Boston gas rates issue
1905–1907	Creation of savings bank life insurance system
1905–1913	Fight with New Haven Railroad
1905 May	Address, ''The Opportunity in the Law''
1906 January	Address, ''Hours of Labor''
1906 December	Article, ''The Greatest Life Insurance Wrong''
1908 January	Oral argument in *Muller* v. *Oregon* before Supreme Court
1908	''The New England Transportation Monopoly,'' address to New England Dry Good Association (Boston)
1910 January–May	Involvement in Pinchot-Ballinger hearings
1910 July–September	Arbitrator, New York City garment workers' strike
1910–1911	Testimony before Interstate Commerce Commission on proposed increase in railroad freight rates and scientific management
1911 December	Testimony, Senate Committee on Interstate Commerce hearings, supporting the La Follette-Stanley antitrust bill, written in part by LDB
1912 January	Testimony before special congressional committee investigating the Steel Trust
1912 February	Address, ''Big Business and Industrial Liberty''
1912 May	Testimony before House Committee on Patents
1912 June	Address, ''Business-the New Profession''
1912 August–November	Advises and campaigns for presidential

	candidate Woodrow Wilson, creating "New Freedom" program
1912 September	Article, "Trusts, Efficiency and the New Party"
1912 December	Articles, "The New England Railroad Situation"; "Interlocking Directorates"
1913 August–January 1914	Publication in *Harper's Weekly* of articles about the Money Trust ("Banker Management," "Breaking the Money Trust," "How the Combiners Combine," "Interlocking Directorates," "Where the Banker is Superfluous," etc.), later reprinted as *Other People's Money and How the Bankers Use It*
1913 August–May 1914	Special counsel to Interstate Commerce Commission on question of whether railroads should be allowed a rate increase
1913–1914	Informal adviser to President Woodrow Wilson
1914	Publication of *Other People's Money and How the Bankers Use It*
1914 April	Testimony before U.S. Commission on Industrial Relations
1914 June	Testimony before Senate Interstate Commerce Committee on antitrust legislation
1914 August	Accepts leadership of American Zionist movement
1914 November	Article, "Efficiency and Social Ideas"
1914 December	Oral argument in *Stettler* v. *O'Hara*
1915 January	Testimony before U.S. Commission on Industrial Relations; statement before House Committee on Interstate and Foreign Commerce concerning regulation of prices
1915 January	Address, "A Call to the Educated Jew"
1915 February	Address, "An Essential of Lasting Peace"; interview, "Laborers as Directors"
1915 April	Address, "The Jewish Problem"
1915 April	Statement on trusts before Federal Trade Commission
1915 July 4	Address, "True Americanism"

2 / Democracy and Public Service

Brandeis's ideas of democracy were expressed far more eloquently by him than the summary in the Introduction to this volume might suggest. Its elements—liberty, creative participation in political and economic life, access to education, social insurance, balanced power, the free expression of ideas—are elaborated upon in the speeches included in this chapter. As he repeated over and over again to general audiences and to groups of lawyers, democracy was impossible unless citizens possessed and acted upon a sense of civic responsibility. His personal contribution was the public service that came to occupy half of his time as a lawyer, and it can be asserted that his professional training and his idea of citizenship finally came together completely when he joined the Supreme Court. There was no democracy without public service, which is why his statements about the two are combined in this chapter.

"TRUE AMERICANISM," 1915

Brandeis was extended the honor of being asked to deliver the annual Fourth of July oration at Boston's Faneuil Hall, and in a rather ironic meeting of the anticorruption forces and the people they were fighting, he was introduced by Mayor James Michael Curley, against whom Brandeis had campaigned when Curley was an alderman (see next selection). His speech articulated the themes basic to his democratic faith, which by 1915 and his accession to the leadership of the American Zionist movement included a strong belief in cultural pluralism.

E pluribus unum, Out of many one, was the motto adopted by the founders of the Republic when they formed a union of the thirteen states. To these we have added, from time to time, thirty-five more. The founders were convinced, as we are, that a strong nation could be built through federation. They were also convinced, as we are, that in America, under a free government, many peoples would make one nation. Throughout all these years we have admitted to our country and to citizenship immigrants from the diverse lands of Europe. We had faith that thereby we would best serve ourselves and mankind. This faith has been justified. The United States has grown great. The immigrants and their immediate descendants have proved themselves as loyal as any citizens of the country. Liberty has knit us closely together as Americans. Note the common devotion to our country's emblem expressed at the recent Flag Day celebration in New York by boys and girls representing more than twenty different nationalities warring abroad. On the nation's birthday it is customary for us to gather together for the purpose of considering how we may better serve our country. This year we are asked to address ourselves to the newcomers and to make this Fourth of July what has been termed Americanization Day.

What is Americanization? It manifests itself, in a superficial way, when the immigrant adopts the clothes, the manners and the customs generally prevailing here. Far more important is the manifestation presented when he substitutes for his mother tongue the English language as the common medium of speech. But the adoption of our language, manners and customs is only a small part of the process. To become Americanized the change wrought must be fundamental. However great his outward conformity, the immigrant is not Americanized unless his interests and affections have become deeply rooted here. And we properly demand of the immigrant even more than this. He must be brought into complete harmony with our ideals and aspirations and co-operate with us for their attainment. Only when this has been done will he possess the national consciousness of an American.

I say "he must be brought into complete harmony." But let us not forget that many a poor immigrant comes to us from distant lands, ignorant of our language, strange in tattered clothes and with jarring manners, who is already truly American in this most important sense; who has long shared our ideals and who, oppressed and persecuted abroad, has yearned for our land of liberty and for the opportunity of aiding in the realization of its aims.

What are the American ideals? They are the development of the individual for his own and the common good; the development of the individual through liberty, and the attainment of the common good through democracy and social justice.

Our form of government, as well as humanity, compels us to strive for the development of the individual man. Under universal suffrage (soon to be extended to women) every voter is a part ruler of the state. Unless the rulers have, in the main, education and character, and are free men, our great experiment in democracy must fail. It devolves upon the state, therefore, to fit its rulers for their task. It must provide not only facilities for development but the opportunity of using them. It must not only provide opportunity, it must stimulate the desire to avail of it. Thus we are compelled to insist upon the observance of what we somewhat vaguely term the American standard of living; we become necessarily our brothers' keepers.

What does this standard imply? In substance, the exercise of those rights which our Constitution guarantees, the right to life, liberty and the pursuit of happiness. Life, in this connection, means living, not existing; liberty, freedom in things industrial as well as political; happiness includes, among other things, that satisfaction which can come only through the full development and utilization of one's faculties. In order that men may live and not merely exist, in order that men may develop their faculties, they must have a reasonable income; they must have health and leisure. High wages will not meet the workers' need unless employment be regular. The best of wages will not compensate for excessively long working hours which undermine health. And working conditions may be so bad as to nullify the good effects of high wages and short hours. The essentials of American citizenship are not satisfied by supplying merely the material needs or even the wants of the worker.

Every citizen must have education, broad and continuous. This essential of citizenship is not met by an education which ends at the age of fourteen, or even at eighteen or twenty-two. Education must continue throughout life. A country cannot be governed well by rulers whose education and mental development are gained only from their attendance at the common school. Whether the education of the citizen in later years is to be given in classes or from the public platform, or is to be supplied through discussion in the lodges and the trade unions, or is to be gained from the reading of papers, periodicals and books, in any case, freshness of mind is indispensable to its attainment. And to the preservation of freshness of mind a short workday is as essential as adequate food and proper conditions of working and of living. The worker must, in other words, have leisure. But leisure does not imply idleness. It means ability to work not less but more, ability to work at something besides breadwinning, ability to work harder while working at breadwinning, and ability to work more years at breadwinning. Leisure, so defined, is an essential of successful democracy.

Furthermore, the citizen in a successful democracy must not only have education, he must be free. Men are not free if dependent industrially upon the arbitrary will of another. Industrial liberty on the part of the worker cannot, therefore, exist if there be overweening industrial power. Some curb must be placed upon capitalistic combination. Nor will even this curb be effective unless the workers cooperate, as in trade unions. Control and cooperation are both essential to industrial liberty.

And if the American is to be fitted for his task as ruler, he must have besides education and industrial liberty also some degree of financial independence. Our existing industrial system is converting an ever increasing percentage of the population into wage-earners; and experience teaches us that a large part of these become at some time financial dependents, by reason of sickness, accident, invalidity, superannuation, unemployment or premature death of the breadwinner of the family. Contingencies like these, which are generally referred to in the individual case as misfortunes, are now recognized as ordinary incidents in the life of the wage-earner. The need of providing indemnity against financial losses from such ordinary contingencies in the workingman's life has become apparent and is already being supplied in other countries. The standard worthy to be called American implies some system of social insurance.

And since the child is the father of the man, we must bear constantly in mind that the American standard of living cannot be attained or preserved unless the child is not only well fed but well born; unless he lives under conditions wholesome morally as well as physically; unless he is given education adequate both in quantity and in character to fit him for life's work.

Such are our ideals and the standard of living we have erected for ourselves. But what is there in these ideals which is peculiarly American? Many nations seek to develop the individual man for himself and for the common good. Some are as liberty-loving as we. Some pride themselves upon institutions more democratic than our own. Still others, less conspicuous for liberty or democracy, claim to be more successful in attaining social justice. And we are not the only nation which combines love of liberty with the practice of democracy and a longing for social justice. But there is one feature in our ideals and practices which is peculiarly American—it is inclusive brotherhood.

Other countries, while developing the individual man, have assumed that their common good would be attained only if the privileges of their citizenship should be limited practically to natives or to persons of a particular nationality. America, on the other hand, has always declared herself for equality of nationalities as well as for equality of individuals. It recognizes racial equality as an essential of full human liberty and true brotherhood, and that racial equality is the complement of democracy. America has, therefore, given like welcome to all the peoples of Europe.

Democracy rests upon two pillars: one, the principle that all men are equally entitled to life, liberty and the pursuit of happiness; and the other, the conviction that such equal opportunity will most advance civilization. Aristocracy, on the other hand, denies both these postulates. It rests upon the principle of the superman. It willingly subordinates the many to the few, and seeks to justify sacrificing the individual by insisting that civilization will be advanced by such sacrifices.

The struggles of the eighteenth and nineteenth centuries both in peace and in war were devoted largely to overcoming the aristocratic position as applied to individuals. In establishing the equal right of every person to development it became clear that equal opportunity for all involves this necessary limitation: each man may develop himself so far, but only so far, as his doing so will not interfere with the exercise of a like right by all others. Thus liberty came to mean the right to enjoy life, to acquire property, to pursue happiness in such manner and to such extent only as the exercise of the right in each is consistent with the exercise of a like right by every other of our fellow citizens. Liberty thus defined underlies twentieth-century democracy. Liberty thus defined exists in a large part of the western world. And even where this equal right of each individual has not yet been accepted as a political right, its ethical claim is gaining recognition.

America, dedicated to liberty and the brotherhood of man, rejected the aristocratic principle of the superman as applied to peoples as it rejected the principle when applied to individuals. America has believed that each race had something of peculiar value which it can contribute to the attainment of those high ideals for which it is striving. America has believed that we must not only give to the immigrant the best that we have, but must preserve for America the good that is in the immigrant and develop in him the best of which he is capable. America has believed that in differentiation, not in uniformity, lies the path of progress. It acted on this belief; it has advanced human happiness, and it has prospered.

On the other hand, the aristocratic theory as applied to peoples survived generally throughout Europe. It was there assumed by the stronger countries that the full development of one people necessarily involved its domination over another, and that only by such domination would civilization advance. Strong nationalities, assuming their own superiority, came to believe that they possessed the divine right to subject other peoples to their sway; and the belief in the existence of such a right ripened into a conviction that there was also a duty to exercise it. The Russianizing of Finland, the Prussianizing of Poland and Alsace, the Magyarizing of Croatia, the persecution of the Jews in Russia and Roumania, are the fruits of this arrogant claim of superiority; and that claim is also the underlying cause of the present war.

The movements of the last century have proved that whole peoples have individuality no less marked than that of the single person; that the individuality of a people is irrepressible, and that the misnamed internationalism which seeks the obliteration of nationalities or peoples is unattainable. The new nationalism adopted by America proclaims that each race or people, like each individual, has the right and duty to develop, and that only through such differentiated development will high civilization be attained. Not until these principles of nationalism, like those of democracy, are generally accepted will liberty be fully attained and minorities be secure in their rights. Not until then can the foundation be laid for a lasting peace among the nations.

The world longs for an end of this war, and even more for a peace that will endure. It turns anxiously to the United States, the one great neutral country, and bids us point the way. And may we not answer: Go the way of liberty and justice, led by democracy and the new nationalism. Without these, international congresses and supreme courts will prove vain and disarmament "The Great Illusion."

And let us remember the poor parson of whom Chaucer says:

"But Criste's loore, and his Apostles twelve,
He taughte, but first he followed it hymselve."

SPEECH TO THE GOOD GOVERNMENT ASSOCIATION,
1903

Brandeis's sense of civic responsibility led him to lecture before and join a multiplicity of civic organizations. During his years in Boston he was a founder, cofounder, or active participant in groups such as the Election Laws League, the Public Franchise League, the Good Government Association and its Aldermanic Association, the Municipal Transportation League, the Savings Bank Insurance League, the Industrial League, the Advisory Committee of the National Municipal League's Municipal Taxation Committee, the Civic Federation of New England, the National Committee of Economic Clubs, and the People's Lobby. A particular concern was citizen responsibility which, among other things, was necessary if the corruption that seemed endemic to Boston and the Massachusetts legislature was to be eliminated. Unfortunately, citizen participation did not always achieve desirable results: Curley won his race for alderman in spite of his conviction for defrauding the government.

You are gathered together not as businessmen, but as citizens of Boston . . . as men of honor, you cannot submit meekly to be represented and to be governed by men criminal or inefficient. As men of honor, you cannot without a struggle permit the City of Boston, around which cluster the noblest and most sacred memories of American history,— the City of Boston which you love, and whose fair name and welfare are now entrusted to your care, to be disgraced by the election to high office of men whose criminal practices are not only known but have been established after full hearing by legally constituted tribunals.

Think of the effrontery of this man [James M.] Curley—standing before the people of Boston as the nominee of a great political party within three months of the day when he was convicted by a jury of the crime of conspiracy to defraud the government of the United States.

The waste and theft of public monies which result from having such men in office is bad enough; but a hundred times worse is the demoralization of our people which results. Nothing breeds faster than corruption. Every criminal in the public service is a plague spot spreading contagion on every hand. Think what a heritage we shall leave to your children if corruption is allowed to stalk about unstayed. The ships which carry the products of our rich country to other lands come back freighted with thousands of men and women and children who, fleeing from the oppression or the hopelessness of their old homes, seek this as the land of liberty and of opportunity. Shall we permit these, our fellow-citizens—perhaps our future rulers—to be taught that in Boston liberty means license to loot the public treasury—that in Boston opportunity means the chance for graft . . . You must have good government because it is a disgrace in a free country to submit to the government of the bad; and if you do strive,—strive earnestly, persistently—you will not fail.

ADDRESS TO THE NEW ENGLAND CIVIC FEDERATION,
1906

Because it was impossible to maintain a democracy without an educated electorate, Brandeis argued that education had to continue long after formal schooling had ended. His interest in education would lead him to undertake a major effort in the 1920s and 1930s to build up the University of Louisville, to which he eventually left the bulk of his papers, and to applaud the establishment of the Hebrew University as a major step in the development of the Jewish homeland in Palestine. But he was equally concerned with citizens who did not have access to a university education as well as with the continuing education, long after college, of those who did. His interest in the need for leisure time during which to educate oneself and his fear that governmental corruption was inevitable if citizens were not educated became themes that he would articulate repeatedly.

The educational standard required for a democracy is obviously high. The citizen should be able to comprehend, among other things, the many great and difficult problems of industry, commerce, and finance, which with us necessarily become political questions. He must learn about men as well as things. In this way can the commonwealth be saved from the pitfalls of financial schemers on the one hand and ambitious demagogues on the other.

But for the attainment of such an education, such mental development, it is essential that the education shall be continuous throughout life, and an essential condition of such continuous education is free time; that is, leisure; and leisure does not merely imply time for rest, but free time when body and mind are sufficiently fresh to permit of mental effort.

"EFFICIENCY AND SOCIAL IDEAS," 1914

Although this selection might well have been included in the section on labor, it is included here as an indication of the way Brandeis defined democracy to apply to the economic as well as to the political sphere. The work place was yet another area in which to attain the goals of democracy: liberty, justice, and fulfillment of the individual.

Efficiency is the hope of democracy. Efficiency means greater production with less effort and at less cost, through the elimination of unnecessary waste, human and material. How else can we hope to attain our social ideals?

The "right to life" guaranteed by our Constitution is now being interpreted according to demands of social justice and of democracy as the right to live, and not merely to exist. In order to live men must have the opportunity of developing their faculties; and they must live under conditions in which their faculties may develop naturally and healthily.

In the first place, there must be abolition of child labor, shorter hours of labor, and regular days of rest, so that men and women may conserve health, may fit themselves to be citizens of a free country, and may perform their duties as citizens. In other words, men and women must have leisure, which the Athenians called "freedom" of liberty. In the second place, the earnings of men and women must be greater, so that they may live under conditions conducive to health and to mental and moral development.

Our American ideals cannot be attained unless an end is put to the misery due to poverty.

These demands for shorter working time, for higher earnings and for better conditions cannot conceivably be met unless the productivity of man is increased. No mere redistribution of the profits of industry could greatly improve the condition of the working classes. Indeed, the principal gain that can be expected from any such redistribution of profits is that it may remove the existing sense of injustice and discontent, which are the greatest obstacles to efficiency.

LETTER TO ROBERT W. BRUERE, FEBRUARY 25, 1922

After Brandeis spoke informally to a group connected with the Department of Research and Education of the Federal Council of Churches in America, Robert Bruere, who had organized the meeting, asked the justice to put his thoughts in writing. It is a cogent statement about democracy, individual responsibility, human dignity, experimentation,

the collection of facts, and eventual ownership of businesses by work-
ers. Brandeis's first biographer called the letter a statement of Bran-
deis's "creed."

Refuse to accept as inevitable any evil in business (*e.g.*, irregularity of
employment). Refuse to tolerate any immoral practice (*e.g.*, espionage). But do not believe that you can find a universal remedy for evil
conditions or immoral practices in effecting a fundamental change in
society (as by State Socialism). And do not pin too much faith in legislation. Remedial institutions are apt to fall under the control of the enemy and to become instruments of oppression.

Seek for betterment within the broad lines of existing institutions.
Do so by attacking evil in situ; and proceed from the individual to the
general. Remember that progress is necessarily slow; that remedies are
necessarily tentative; that because of varying conditions there must be
much and constant inquiry into facts . . . and much experimentation;
and that always and everywhere the intellectual, moral, and spiritual
development of those concerned will remain an essential—and the
main factor—in real betterment.

This development of the individual is, thus, both a necessary means
and the end sought. For our objective is the making of men and women
who shall be free, self-respecting members of a democracy—and who
shall be worthy of respect. Improvement in material conditions of the
worker and ease are the incidents of better conditions—valuable
mainly as they may ever increase opportunities for development.

The great developer is responsibility. Hence no remedy can be hopeful which does not devolve upon the workers participation in responsibility for the conduct of business; and their aim should be the eventual
assumption of full responsibility—as in co-operative enterprises. This
participation in and eventual control of industry is likewise an essential of obtaining justice in distributing the fruits of industry.

But democracy in any sphere is a serious undertaking. It substitutes
self-restraint for external restraint. It is more difficult to maintain than
to achieve. It demands continuous sacrifice by the individual and more
exigent obedience to the moral law than any other form of government.
Success in any democratic undertaking must proceed from the individual. It is possible only where the process of perfecting the individual is
pursued. His development is attained mainly in the processes of com-

mon living. Hence the industrial struggle is essentially an affair of the church and its imperative task.

PUBLIC SERVICE: TWO INTERVIEWS

Brandeis's devotion to public service became legendary. To him, it was a logical extension of civic responsibility, but the oddity of a well-known attorney devoting himself to the public good (see next chapter) led to his being queried about it repeatedly. His participation in public life was never half-hearted. As soon as he became interested in a cause, he learned everything he could about it and began generating a stream of mail urging everyone he could think of to join him and to spread the word. He corresponded regularly with newspapers and journals, sending them letters to the editor and exhortations to print articles about the matters he deemed important.

Interview with American Cloak and Suit Review, *1911*

Some men buy diamonds and rare works of art, others delight in automobiles and yachts. My luxury is to invest my surplus effort, beyond that required for the proper support of my family, to the pleasure of taking up a problem and solving, or helping to solve it, for the people without receiving any compensation. Your yachtsman or automobilist would lose much of his enjoyment if he were obliged to do for pay what he is doing for the love of the thing itself. So I should lose much of my satisfaction if I were paid in connection with public services of this kind.

Interview in the New York Times Annalist, *1913*

''Think of the great work that has been done in the world by men who had no thought of money reward. No; money is not worth a great man's time. It is unworthy of greatness to strive for that alone. What then? Power? That isn't much better, if you mean the kind of power that springs from money. Is it the game? You hear that now-a-days—the game! It sounds too frivolous. To me the word is Service. Money-making will become incidental to Service. The man of the future will think more of giving Service than of making money, no matter what particular kind of Service it happens to be. It will become a distinction worth striving for to give the best Service, whether you are conducting a retail shop or a great railroad. It naturally follows that those who give the best Service will make money, because success must be profitable, yet Service, and not money-making, will be the end. Though the work of the greatest artists may command the highest prices, their incentive has not been money. It has been the desire to achieve professional success. That will be the spirit of business in the future . . .''

"*How came you by your democracy? You were not bred to it?*" "No; my early associations were such as to give me greater reverence than I now have for the things that are because they are. I recall that when I began to practice law I thought it awkward, stupid, and vulgar that a jury of twelve inexpert men should have the power to decide. I had the greatest respect for the Judge. I trusted only expert opinion. Experience of life has made me democratic. I began to see that many things sanctioned by expert opinion and denounced by popular opinion were wrong.''

"THE GREATEST LIFE INSURANCE WRONG," 1906

Brandeis's grasp of the public interest problems he investigated is typified by this article about the unfairness of the life insurance offered to workers by large companies and the reasons for his belief that savings bank living insurance [SBLI] would remedy them. He was effective in dealing with matters affecting the public because he could see and explain not only why the issue was of public importance and exactly how the current system worked but all the possible alternatives and their probable consequences. His understanding of the mechanics of different arenas of life enabled him, as here, to create truly innovative solutions. The great effort he put into having his proposals implemented became an example of the integration of the political and educational. He firmly believed that if he had found correct solutions and explained and publicized them sufficiently, they would garner public support. That is why he inundated potential supporters with letters, sent numerous letters to the editors of widely read newspapers, lectured to civic groups himself and urged others to emulate him. His "propaganda" would teach citizens where to throw their political weight. Education was the key to democracy; facts were the basis for understanding the problems faced by a democratic state at any given moment; citizen participation was the method by which the wisest possible pub-

lic policy would be attained. Brandeis himself was the strongest weapon in his democratic arsenal.

Nearly three-fourths of all level premium life insurance policies issued are of this character [workman's life insurance]. On December 31, 1905 . . . there were 16,872,583 industrial policies outstanding in the United States. In New York alone their number was then 3,898,810, and . . . an average of 67,200 such policies were being issued in that state every month.

Industrial insurance, the workingman's life insurance, is simply life insurance in small amounts, on which the premiums are collected weekly at the homes of the insured. It includes both adult and child insurance. The regular premium charge for such insurance is about double that charged by the Equitable, the New York Life, or the Mutual Life of New York, for ordinary life insurance. In the initial period of the industrial policy, the premium rate rises to eight times that paid for ordinary insurance, since, by a clause which will be found in most industrial policies, it is provided that, if death occurs within the first six months after the date of the policy, only one-fourth of the face of the policy will be paid, and if death occurs within the second six months, payment will be made of only one-half. So heavy are the burdens cast upon those least able to bear them.

The disastrous result to the policy-holder of this system of life insurance may be illustrated from the following data, drawn from Massachusetts official reports:

In the fifteen years ending December 31, 1905, the workingmen of Massachusetts paid to the so-called industrial life insurance companies an aggregate of $61,294,887 in premiums, and received back in death benefits, endowments, or surrender values an aggregate of only $21,819,606. The insurance reserve arising from these premiums still held by the insurance companies does not exceed $9,838,000. It thus appears that, in addition to interest on invested funds, about one-half of the amounts paid by the workingmen in premiums has been absorbed in the expense of conducting the business and in dividends to the stockholders of the insurance companies.

If this $61,294,887, instead of being paid to the insurance companies, had been deposited in Massachusetts savings banks, and the depositors had withdrawn from the banks an amount equal to the aggregate of $21,819,606 which they received from the insurance companies during the fifteen years, the balance remaining in the savings banks December 31, 1905, with the accumulated interest, would have amounted to $49,931,548.35—and this, although the savings banks would have been obliged to pay upon these increased deposits in taxes to the Commonwealth more than four times the amount which was actually paid by the insurance companies on account of the insurance.

Perhaps the appalling sacrifice of workingmen's savings through this system of insurance can be made more clear by the following illustration:

The average expectancy of life in the United States of a man 21 years old is, according to Meech's Table of Mortality, 40.25 years. In other words, take any large number of men who are 21 years old, and the average age which they will reach is 61 1/4 years.

If a man, beginning with his 21st birthday, pays throughout life 50 cents a week into Massachusetts savings banks and allows these deposits to accumulate for his family, the survivors will, in case of his death at this average age of 61 1/4 years, inherit $2,265.90 if an interest rate of 3 1/2 per cent a year is maintained.

If this same man should, beginning at the age of 21, pay throughout his life 50 cents a week to the Prudential Insurance Company as premiums on a so-called "industrial" life policy for the benefit of his family, the survivors would be legally entitled to receive, upon his death at the age of 61 1/4 years, only $820.

If this same man, having made his weekly deposit in a savings bank for 20 years, should then conclude to discontinue his weekly payments and withdraw the money for his own benefit, he would receive $746.20. If, on the other hand, having made for 20 years such weekly payments to the Prudential Insurance Company, he should then conclude to discontinue payments and surrender his policy, he would be legally entitled to receive only $165.

So widely different is the probable result to the workingman if he selects the one or the other of the two classes of savings investment which are open to him; and yet life insurance is but a method of saving. The savings banks manage the aggregate funds made up of many small deposits until such time as they shall be demanded by the depositor; the insurance company manages them ordinarily until the depositor's death. The savings bank pays back to the depositor his deposit with interest less the necessary expense of management. The insurance company in theory does the same, the difference being merely that the savings bank undertakes to repay to each individual depositor the whole of his deposit with interest; while the insurance company undertakes to pay to each member of a class the average amount (regarding the chances of life and death), so that those who do not reach the average age get more than they have deposited (including interest) and those who exceed the average age less than they have deposited (including interest).

It is obvious that the community should not and will not long tolerate such a sacrifice of the workingmen's savings as the present system of industrial insurance entails; for the causes of this sacrifice are easily determined and a remedy lies near.

The extraordinary wastefulness of the present system of industrial insurance is due in large part to the fact that the business, whether conducted by stock or by mutual companies, is carried on for the benefit of others than the policy-holders. The needs and financial inexperience of the wage-earner are exploited for the benefit of stockholders or officials. The Prudential (which was the first American company to engage in the business) pays annual dividends to its stockholders equivalent to more than 219 per cent upon the capital actually paid in; the Metropolitan dividends are equivalent to 28 per cent of such capital; and stock in the Columbian National Life Insurance Company, a corporation which commenced business but four years ago, has risen from par to $296.

But the excessive amounts paid in dividends or in salaries to the favored officials account directly for only a small part of the terrible shrinkage of the workingmen's savings. The main cause of waste lies in the huge expense of soliciting insurance, taken in connection with the large percentage of lapses, and in the heavy expenses incident to a weekly collection of premiums at the homes of the insured. The commission of the insurance solicitor is from ten to twenty times the amount of the first premium. The cost of collecting the premiums varies from one-fifth to one-sixth of the amount collected. And yet commissions for soliciting and collection are only a part of the expenses. The physician's fee, the cost of supervision, of accounting and of advertising, must all be added; with the result that no industrial policy "pays its way" until it has been in force about three years. In other words, if the policy lapses before it has been in force three years, not only does the policy-holder lose (except the temporary protection) all that he has paid in, but the company (that is the persisting policy-holders) bears a part—generally the larger part—of the cost of the lapsed policy.

And only a small percentage of industrial policies survive the third year. A majority of the policies lapse within the first year. In 1905, the average payments on a policy in the Metropolitan so lapsing continued little more than six weeks. The aggregate number of such lapses in a single year reaches huge figures. In 1905, 1,253,635 Metropolitan and 951,704 Prudential policies lapsed. The experience of their young and energetic rival, the Columbian National Life Insurance Company, is even more striking. On January 1, 1905, that company had outstanding 40,397 industrial policies. It wrote, during the year, 103,466. At the end of the year it had outstanding only 63,497; and yet, of the 143,863 policy-holders, only 699 had died, while 79,677 policies—that is, one hundred and fourteen times as many—had lapsed . . . It is obvious that a remedy cannot come from men holding such views—from men who refuse to recognize that the best method of increasing the demand for life insurance is not eloquent persistent persuasion, but to furnish a good article at a low price. A remedy can be provided only by some institution which will proceed upon the principle that its function is to supply insurance upon proper terms to those who want it and can carry it, and not to induce working people to take insurance regardless of their real interests. To attain satisfactory results the change of system must be radical.

The savings banks established on the plan prevailing in New York and generally through the New England states are managed upon principles and under conditions upon which alone a satisfactory system of life insurance for working men can be established. These savings banks have no stockholders, being operated solely for the benefit of the depositors. They are managed by trustees, usually men of large business experience and high character, who serve without pay, recognizing that the business of collecting and investing the savings of persons of small means is a quasi-public trust, which should be conducted as a beneficent, and not as a money-making institution. The trustees, the officers, and the employees of the savings banks have been trained in the administration of these savings to the practice of the strictest economy. While the expenses of managing the industrial departments of the Metropolitan, the Prudential and the John Hancock companies have, excluding taxes, exceeded 40 per cent of the year's premiums, the expense of management in 1905 (exclusive of taxes on surplus) of the 130 New York Savings banks, holding $1,292,358,866 of deposits, was only 0.28 of 1 per cent of the average assets, or 1 per cent of the year's deposits; and the $662,000,000 of deposits held in 1905 in the 189 Massachusetts savings banks were managed at an expense of 0.23 of 1 per cent of the average assets, or 1.36 per cent of the year's deposits.

Savings institutions so managed offer adequate means of providing insurance to the working man. With a slight enlargement of their powers, these savings banks can, at a minimum of expense, fill the great need of cheaper life insurance in small amounts. The only proper elements of the industrial insurance business not common to the savings bank business are simple, and can be supplied at a minimum of expense in connection with such existing savings banks. They are:

First—Fixing the terms on which insurance shall be given.
Second—The initial medical examination.
Third—Verifying the proof of death.

The first is the work of an insurance actuary; and the present cost of actuarial service can be greatly reduced both by limiting the forms of insurance policies to two or three standard forms of policy to be uniform throughout the state, and by providing for the appointment of a state actuary who, in connection with the insurance commissioner, shall serve all the savings insurance banks.

The initial medical examination and the verification of proof of death are services that may be readily performed for the savings banks at no greater pro rata expense than for the existing insurance companies.

The insurance department of the savings banks would, of course, be kept entirely distinct as a matter of accounting from the savings department; but it would be conducted with the same plant and the same officials, without any large increase of clerical force or incidental expense, except such as would be required if the deposits of the bank were increased. On the other hand, the insurance department of savings banks would open with an extensive and potent good-will, and under the most favorable conditions for teaching the value of life insurance— a lesson easily learned when insurance is offered at about half the premium exacted by the industrial companies. With an insurance clientele composed largely of thrifty savings banks depositors, the expensive house-to-house collection of premiums could be dispensed with, and more economical payments of premiums could probably be substituted for weekly payments. Indeed, it is probable that the following simple, convenient, and inexpensive method of paying premiums would, to a large extent, be adopted, namely, making deposits in the savings department from time to time, and giving, when the policy is issued, a standing order to draw on the savings fund in favor of the insurance fund to meet the premium payments as they accrue.

The safety of savings banks, would, of course, be in no way imperiled by extending their functions to life insurance. Life insurance rests upon substantial certainty, differing in this respect radically from fire, accident, and other kinds of insurance. Since practical experience has given to the world the mortality tables upon which life insurance premiums rest and the reserves for future needs are calculated, no life insurance company has ever failed which complied with the law governing the calculation, maintenance, and investment of the legal reserve. The causes of failure of life insurance companies have been excessive expense, unsound investment, or dishonest management. From these abuses our savings banks have been practically free, and that freedom affords strong reason for utilizing them as the urgent need arises to supply the kindred service of life insurance.

THE QUESTION OF LAND USE

Brandeis's representation of Collier's Weekly *during the Pinchot-Ballinger hearings before Congress (see chapter 1) led him to think about the policies that would best govern land use and prevent private exploitation of Alaska's natural resources. He read widely on the subject and became convinced that public ownership ought to be combined with private use. Public ownership would prevent private monopoly; private use would prevent the evils of public monopoly. Power would be distributed and thereby kept in balance. He wrote extensively on the subject to Robert M. La Follette, his ally in the hearings, in the hope that La Follette would be able to use his position in the Senate to get some of the ideas enacted into law. Brandeis's letter to Amos Pinchot, another ally, elaborated upon his thinking.*

Letter to Alice Brandeis, July 28, 1911

I have a book in & am sure there is only one solution for Alaska. A most comprehensive plan of Govt. ownership, Railroads, Utilities—with leasing only of most lands, & then a complete separation of the industrial property state from the political state. Control the property of the people of the U.S. from Washington & give the inhabitants of Alaska otherwise home rule.

Letter to Robert M. La Follette, July 29, 1911

This, very roughly, is my idea of the Alaska situation.

We know the territory is vastly rich. First it was fisheries; then gold; then copper began to promise even more than gold; and finally the value of the coal fields was recognized. Other wealth may be discovered at any time, for the possibilities are far vaster than thus far known . . .

The wealth of Alaska remains the property of the people of the United States with but slight exceptions . . . mainly on account of its inaccessibility and the difficulties and cost of the necessary development. The wealth is so great and the temptation so great to secure it that we are finding it impossible to protect it from depredations . . .

The people of the United States are entitled to begin to get the benefit and the comfort of a reduction in the cost of living which will come from the utilization of Alaska's treasures, and the few people who have gone to Alaska are entitled to exercise to the full the opportunities which their own courage and self sacrifice ought to open to them. All the wealth is of no good, without development, and the first step in the development is an adequate system of transportation. They need railroads, and they will need much else in the way of public utilities. The demand is so great for these facilities, and so well founded, that the people are becoming willing to pay for them . . . Development of transportation and other facilities by the capitalists would, in a way, seriously impair development, because to give them a return which would seem to them adequate would entail rates which would be oppressive to the people of Alaska, and would, in themselves, tend to retard development and the opening up of opportunities to the sturdy, courageous men who are willing to take up their residence in the territory. To preserve the territory it is essential that the capital required in order to furnish the facilities for development, that is capital to supply the public utilities, should be furnished by the people of the United States, whose property the territory is, and in whose interests its resources should be primarily conserved. The people of the United States can wait for their return. They do not require an immediate return by way of interest on their investment. The money raised by the people can be raised at less than three per cent interest. The charges entailed by such an investment of the people are small. Rates for transportation and for the sup-

plying of other public utilities may properly be low when the capital
cost is as small as the cost of the investment would be to the people
. . .

The control of the transportation system by the Morgan-Guggen-
heims, or any other capitalists, would be attended by conditions certain
to subject to the control of the owners of the transportation system a
large part of the property of Alaska dependent upon these transportation systems. We should have, in the most aggravated form, a control in
the same hands of the means of transportation and the commodities to
be transported. There would be a gradual tendency to crush out all of
the independent operators along the line of transportation, just as there
has been along the coal carrying roads in the states . . . The temptation
of the capitalistic ownership to secure the property would prove irresistible, and we would have in the most aggravated form the system of
discrimination and rebates and corruption which have characterized
the worst period of our railroad operation. No protection could be expected from local officials appointed for that purpose, because in their
positions they would prove helpless against the pressure and power of
the capitalists.

The essential thing, therefore, is to provide through the general government those facilities essential to the development of the country
. . . We must devise some system by which those who are willing to go
to Alaska, with a view to working there and developing its resources,
shall have not only the assurance of fair treatment, but the opportunity
of operating without undue oppression through monopolistically inclined competitors . . . In other words, the people of the United States
and the settlers of Alaska should get the increment in value which they
earn, through their investment and their own labor, and the sacrifices
attendant upon settling in a new country . . .

It seems to me that the government . . . should now acquire all of the
railroads in Alaska . . . that it should similarly provide for the development through the government of the other public utilities, as it has of
the telegraph and the telephone; and that it should adopt systems of
land tenure which should not only reserve in the government the title
to the coal lands, but also to the other mining properties . . . On the
other hand, the government should be extremely liberal in the terms
which it gives to those who use the property. Only an extremely small
return, at least for a long period in the future should be required . . .

As an incident of supplying facilities to the people of Alaska for their
operation, it may be necessary in the first instance for the government

to operate the coal mines. If it does so, operation should be merely for the purpose of quickly providing coal at reasonable prices, and in no sense with the idea of the government mining any appreciable part of the coal mines of Alaska. But government ownership of a mine there would always be valuable as a regulator, and particularly valuable as an experiment station to instruct the government as to the conditions and terms upon which the vast coal fields should be leased . . .

In such a development of Alaska, Alaskan interests would clearly divide themselves into two classes: First, the Alaskan resources which are the property of the people of the United States. These should be primarily administered for the benefit of the hundred million and countless more who will be the inhabitants of the United States, and not primarily for those who may chance to settle in Alaska . . . Our obligation to the Alaskans is to give them, and to all newcomers liberal and equal opportunities, to make what their brains and character entitle them to. Consequently, preserving the resources for the people of the United States to whom they belong, we should administer them through representatives of the general government . . . On the other hand, matters dealing with social and political conditions of the Alaskans ought to be determined by the Alaskans themselves. They should have in the highest degree, home rule . . . once we remove the temptations incident to the possibility of grabbing the Alaskan wealth, there is no reason why the officials of Alaska should not prove as loyal and honest as officials elsewhere.

Letter to Robert M. La Follette, July 31, 1911

How would this do for the Progressive slogan:

> "Alaska; the Land of Opportunity.
> Develop it by the People, for the people.
> Do not let it be exploited by the Capitalists,
>   for the Capitalists."

Letter to Amos Pinchot, August 2, 1911

(B.) As to Mineral Lands: I am confirmed in the belief that the plan of leasing ought not to be confined to coal, but to extend, with of course great variations, to all mineral lands.

(C.) Other Lands: Some plan should be worked out by which the fee simple title to practically all other lands is retained by the Government. There is no propriety in making the land a subject for speculation. The settler upon it, whether the land be town or country land, should be given the most favorable terms. We ought to be able to devise some system which will make profitable and encourage the use, and prevent the land itself becoming the subject of speculation . . .

(D.) Other public works: The development by the Government should include, I think, all public utilities. It is highly probable that such public utilities as are strictly local, like tramways or electric light and water ought to be matters for local as distinguished from general government.

3 / The Living Law

Louis Dembitz Brandeis was known to millions of Americans as the "People's Attorney." As such, he was the paradigm for today's public interest lawyers and groups: independent citizens who voluntarily assume responsibility for representing the people when they are confronted by large, wealthy, and sometimes capricious institutions, whether private or public. He is widely credited with helping formulate the fact-based sociological jurisprudence that has become the major methodology utilized by American courts and that is explained and evident in the judicial opinions included in this volume.

Brandeis was fortunate to attend Harvard when Christopher Columbus Langdell was dean and was beginning to revolutionize the way law was taught in the United States. Throughout much of the country's history, those who wished to "study" law read the few treatises available, talked with and listened to lawyers as much as possible, and spent a good deal of time in court watching the proceedings. Even law schools, still in their infancy when Brandeis was at Harvard, featured lectures by professors on the principles of evidence, contracts, torts, and such. Students were not encouraged to ask questions but were sent to specialized scholarly treatises. It was Langdell's radical belief that law was created as cases were decided rather than on the basis of abstract principles and that students should read the cases that grew out of particular historical moments and caused the law to develop as it had. He saw law as a "science" that reflected "the ever-tangled skein of human affairs," and considered classroom discussion of cases the best way to learn the doctrines law gradually had come to embody. Brandeis was sufficiently impressed to describe Langdell's innovation in "The Harvard Law School," an article he wrote for Harvard's *Green Bag* in 1889, and it underlay his own understanding of the origins and function of the law.

There were other ways in which Brandeis's conception of the attorney's role was untraditional. He resembled many lawyers in setting out to make money, and he proved to be a master at it. This is clear from the roughly $73,000 he earned each year and from his becoming a millionaire while in his forties. His emphasis on making money did not stem from a desire for material goods, however; he was well known for the frugality and modesty with which he and his wife lived. Even when he was just beginning practice in Boston, his desire for economic security was accompanied by a sense that law should provide room for creativity and self-fulfillment as well. He realized that independent wealth left him free to pick and choose his clients. "I would rather have clients," he said, "than be somebody's lawyer." By having clients he not only meant that he would pick his cases but that he, rather than his usually much older clients, would decide what their legal problems were and what would be the best way of handling them. Although he enjoyed litigation, he was pleased if his knowledge of his clients' affairs enabled them to minimize the need to go to court.

Brandeis insisted on knowing more than the specifics of a case both so that he could best represent his clients and because each case was a potential step in the development of law. He understood that law is society's way of dealing with the need for rules and for certainty. It reflects the values that a society considers so central that it puts behind them the coercive power of the state. As society and laws became more complex, the average citizen was less likely to know the law. Hence the demand arose for people who specialized in knowledge about the laws and the way they applied to specific situations—specialists called lawyers. He took his specialization seriously, learning constantly from his private and public practice, and used the lessons to develop what he eventually articulated as the role of the lawyer and the way law should be interpreted in a democratic society.

LETTER TO WILLIAM H. DUNBAR, FEBRUARY 2, 1893

Oliver Wendell Holmes, who served on the United States Supreme Court from 1902 to 1932, predicted in 1921 that the changed economy generated by rapid modernization and the growth of huge businesses would make "the man of statistics and the master of economics" the successful lawyer of his day. Brandeis agreed. Having learned from Dean Langdell that the law was a dynamic entity reflecting the society in which it developed, Brandeis emphasized the need lawyers had for facts: facts that clients might mistakenly think were irrelevant to the matter at hand. Thus lawyers had to investigate their clients' businesses for themselves. Brandeis added that the lawyer had to be well aware not only of the society from which the law had sprung but of the psychology of the clients who sought to turn it to their advantage. He put his advice into a letter to a young associate who was not doing as well as Brandeis thought he might. The advice, of course, reflects Brandeis's own approach to private practice. Dunbar eventually became a full partner and an influential Boston attorney.

For some time I have intended to lay before you my views in regard to your professional life—and what it is necessary for you to do in order to attain that degree of success to which your abilities and character clearly entitle you.

Cultivate the society of men—particularly men of affairs. This is essential to your professional success. Pursue that study as heretofore you have devoted yourself to books. Lose no opportunity of becoming acquainted with men, of learning to feel instinctively their inclinations, of familiarizing yourself with their personal and business habits, use your ability in making opportunities to do this. This is for you the indispensable study—as for another the study of law—or good habits of work are the missing desideratum.

The knowledge of men, the ability to handle, to impress them is needed by you—not only in order that clients may appreciate your advice and that you may be able to apply the law to human affairs—but also that you may more accurately and surely determine what the rules of law are, that is, what the courts will adopt. You are prone in legal investigation to be controlled by logic and to underestimate the logic of facts. Knowledge of the decided cases and of the rules of logic cannot alone make a great lawyer. He must know, must feel "in his bones" the facts to which they apply—must know, too, that if they do not stand the test of such application the logical result will somehow or other be avoided . . .

Knowledge of decisions and powers of logic are mere hand-maidens—they are servants not masters. The controlling force is the deep knowledge of human necessities . . . The man who does not know intimately human affairs is apt to make of the law a bed of Procrustes. No hermit can be a great lawyer, least of all a commercial lawyer. When from a knowledge of the law, you pass to its application the need of a full knowledge of men and of their affairs become even more apparent. The duty of a lawyer today is not that of a solver of legal conundrums; he is indeed a counsellor at law. Knowledge of the law is of course essential to his efficiency, but the law bears to his profession a relation very similar to that which medicine does to that of the physicians. The apothecary can prepare the dose; the more intelligent one even knows the specific for the most common diseases. It requires but a mediocre physician to administer the proper drug for the patient who correctly and fully describes his ailment. The great physicians are those who in addition to that knowledge of therapeutics which is opened to all, know not merely the human body but the human mind and emotions, so as to make themselves the proper diagnosis—to know the truth which their patients fail to disclose and who add to this an influence over the patients which is apt to spring from a real understanding of him [sic] . . .

Your duty is as much to know the fact as law—to apply from your own store of human experience the defects in the clients' statements and to probe the correctness of those statements in the light of your knowledge. That knowledge must also enable you to determine the practical working of the advice you are to give . . . Again acquaintance with men and knowledge of them is essential to the expedition of business, and impressing and satisfying the clients.

Your law may be perfect, your knowledge of human affairs may be such as to enable you to apply it with wisdom and skill, and yet without individual acquaintance with men, their haunts and habits, the pursuit of the profession becomes difficult, slow and expensive. A lawyer who does not know men is handicapped . . .

But perhaps most important of all is the impressing of clients and satisfying them. Your law may be perfect, your ability to apply it great and yet you cannot be a successful advisor unless your advice is followed; it will not be followed unless you can satisfy your clients, unless you impress them with your superior knowledge and that you cannot do unless you know their affairs better than they because you see them from a fullness of knowledge. The ability to impress them grows with your own success in advising others, with the confidence which you yourself feel in your powers. That confidence can never come from books; it is gained by human intercourse . . .

Clients want support—if they did not they would rarely be clients . . .

A man who practices law—who aspires to the higher places of his profession—must keep his mind fresh. It must be alert and he must be

capable of meeting emergencies—must be capable of the tour de force
. . . The bow must be strung and unstrung; work must be measured not
merely by time but also by its intensity; there must be time also for the
unconscious thinking which comes to the busy man in his play.

TWO SPEECHES TO LAWYERS

*There was virtually no tradition of lawyers taking cases in the public
interest, without fee, until Brandeis began doing so. As he points out in
"The Opportunity in the Law," many of the influential members of
government in the United States' early days were lawyers, and the assumption that lawyers and public matters were linked was taken for
granted. Alexis de Tocqueville noted in* Democracy in America *(1835),
"If I were asked where I place the American aristocracy, I should reply
without hesitation . . . that it occupies the judicial bench and the bar
. . ." This may be because, as de Tocqueville commented and Brandeis
repeated, the adoption of a written constitution as the basic instrument of government and law seemed to put a premium on the special
knowledge lawyers were assumed to have.*

*That had changed by the late nineteenth century. There were still
lawyers, working in their communities, who knew their clients by
their first names and who were turned to for advice in matters that
went beyond the law. The fastest-growing segment of the legal profession, however, and the wealthiest, was made up of lawyers using their
skills and knowledge for the benefit of the huge corporations that had
grown up with the end of the Civil War and the burgeoning of industrialization and urbanization in American life. Whole new areas of highly
specialized commercial and regulatory law developed. The lawyers
who mastered them found themselves in demand not for their ability
to litigate after corporations had made decisions but for the advice they
could give corporations about how legally to do the things that would
maximize their profits and keep them out of court. Attorneys became
hired economic advisers to big business, frequently ignoring ethical
considerations or any professional obligation to the public as their employers raced to increase profits. Such lawyers discussed not law but
techniques for protecting concentrations of private property. It was a
development that Brandeis, the "people's attorney," deplored. "What
the lawyer needs to redeem himself is not more ability or physical
courage," he told the* Harvard Law Review *Association in 1907, "but*

the moral courage in the face of financial loss and personal ill-will to stand for right and justice . . . We feel today that the lawyer belongs to another and is no longer a free man." That, to Brandeis, was a devastating indictment.

His speeches to lawyers emphasized a number of themes, including the need of a democratic state for the particular skills he found among them. He worried that the growing control of law by special interests was alienating the average person from the legal and political systems. His experiences advising his clients about business matters, his meetings with union leaders, his appearances before legislative bodies, and his wide reading enabled him to analyze the growing gap between the legal profession and the rest of society.

The cogency of his analysis did not endear him to many members of his profession, and it is doubtful that all the lawyers in his audiences took the words in his speeches on "The Living Law" and "The Opportunity in the Law" to heart. They were remembered, however. In 1912, when he was campaigning across the country for Woodrow Wilson, Brandeis wrote to his wife, "I am meeting here & there men who heard my lecture to the Law Students at Fogg Museum or at Brooks House years ago & say it wholly changed their point of view." One member of the audience upon whom the "The Opportunity in the Law" certainly made an impression was Felix Frankfurter, who was present as a Harvard Law School student.

"The Opportunity in the Law," 1905

I assume that in asking me to talk to you on the Ethics of the Legal Profession, you do not wish me to enter upon a discussion of the relation of law to morals, or to attempt to acquaint you with those detailed rules of ethics which lawyers have occasion to apply from day to day in their practice. What you want is this: Standing not far from the threshold of active life, feeling the generous impulse for service which the University fosters, you wish to know whether the legal profession would afford you special opportunities for usefulness to your fellowmen, and, if so, what the obligations and limitations are which it imposes. I say special opportunities, because every legitimate occupation, be it profession or business or trade, furnishes abundant opportunities for usefulness, if pursued in what Matthew Arnold called "the grand manner." It is, as a rule, far more important *how* men pursue their occupation than *what* the occupation is which they select.

But the legal profession does afford in America unusual opportunities for usefulness. That this has been so in the past, no one acquainted with the history of our institutions can for a moment doubt. The great achievement of the English-speaking people is the attainment of liberty through law. It is natural, therefore, that those who have been trained in the law should have borne an important part in that struggle for liberty and in the government which resulted. Accordingly, we find that in America the lawyer was in the earlier period almost omnipresent in the State. Nearly every great lawyer was then a statesman; and nearly every statesman, great or small, was a lawyer. DeTocqueville, the first important foreign observer of American political institutions, said of the United States seventy-five years ago:

"In America there are no nobles or literary men, and the people are apt to mistrust the wealthy; lawyers, consequently, form the highest political class . . . As the lawyers form the only enlightened class whom the people do not mistrust, they are naturally called upon to occupy most of the public stations. They fill the legislative assemblies and are at the head of the administration; they consequently exercise a powerful influence upon the formation of the law and upon its execution."

For centuries before the American Revolution the lawyer had played an important part in England. His importance in the State became much greater in America. One reason for this, as DeTocqueville indicated, was the fact that we possessed no class like the nobles, which took part in government through privilege. A more potent reason was that with the introduction of a written constitution the law became with us a far more important factor in the ordinary conduct of political life than it did in England. Legal questions were constantly arising and the lawyer was necessary to settle them. But I take it the paramount reason why the lawyer has played so large a part in our political life is that his training fits him especially to grapple with the questions which are presented in a democracy.

The whole training of the lawyer leads to the development of judgment. His early training—his work with books in the study of legal rules—teaches him patient research and develops both the memory and the reasoning faculties. He becomes practised in logic; and yet the use of the reasoning faculties in the study of law is very different from their use, say, in metaphysics. The lawyer's processes of reasoning, his logi-

One of the numerous articles about Brandeis in his role as "the People's Attorney." (University of Louisville Archives)

cal conclusions, are being constantly tested by experience. He is running up against facts at every point. Indeed it is a maxim of the law: Out of the facts grows the law; that is, propositions are not considered abstractly, but always with reference to facts.

Furthermore, in the investigation of the facts the lawyer differs very materially from the scientist or the scholar. The lawyer's investigations into the facts are limited by time and space. His investigations have reference always to some practical end. Unlike the scientist, he ordinarily cannot refuse to reach a conclusion on the ground that he lacks the facts sufficient to enable one to form an opinion. He must form an opinion from those facts which he has gathered; he must reason from the facts within his grasp.

If the lawyer's practice is a general one, his field of observation extends, in course of time, into almost every sphere of business and of life. The facts so gathered ripen his judgment. His memory is trained to retentiveness. His mind becomes practised in discrimination as well as in generalization. He is an observer of men even more than of things. He not only sees men of all kinds, but knows their deepest secrets; sees them in situations which "try men's souls." He is apt to become a good judge of men.

Then, contrary to what might seem to be the habit of the lawyer's mind, the practice of law tends to make the lawyer judicial in attitude and extremely tolerant. His profession rests upon the postulate that no contested question can be properly decided until both sides are heard. His experience teaches him that nearly every question has two sides; and very often he finds—after decision of judge or jury—that both he and his opponent were in the wrong. The practice of law creates thus a habit of mind, and leads to attainments which are distinctly different from those developed in most professions or outside of the professions. These are the reasons why the lawyer has acquired a position materially different from that of other men. It is the position of the adviser of men.

Your chairman said: "People have the impression to-day that the lawyer has become mercenary." It is true that the lawyer has become largely a part of the business world . . . The ordinary man thinks of the Bar as a body of men who are trying cases, perhaps even trying criminal cases. Of course there is an immense amount of litigation going on; and a great deal of the time of many lawyers is devoted to litigation. But by far the greater part of the work done by lawyers is done not in court, but in advising men on important matters, and mainly in business affairs. In guiding these affairs industrial and financial, lawyers are needed, not only because of the legal questions involved, but because the particular mental attributes and attainments which the legal profession develops are demanded in the proper handling of these large financial or industrial affairs. The magnitude and scope of these operations remove them almost wholly from the realm of "petty trafficking" which people formerly used to associate with trade. The questions which arise are more nearly questions of statesmanship. The relations created call in many instances for the exercise of the highest diplomacy. The magnitude, difficulty and importance of the problems involved are often as great as in the matters of state with which lawyers were formerly frequently associated. The questions appear in a different guise; but they are similar. The relations between rival railroad systems are like the relations between neighboring kingdoms. The relations of the great trusts to the consumers or to their employees is like that of feudal lords to commoners or dependents. The relations of public-service corporations to the people raise questions not unlike those presented by the monopolies of old.

So some of the ablest American lawyers of this generation, after acting as professional advisers of great corporations, have become finally their managers. The controlling intellect of the great Atchison Railroad System, its vice-president, Mr. Victor Morawetz, graduated at the Harvard Law School about twenty-five years ago, and shortly afterward attained distinction by writing an extraordinarily good book on the Law of Corporations. The head of the great Bell Telephone System of the United States, Mr. Frederick P. Fish, was at the time of his appointment to that office probably our leading patent lawyer. In the same way, and for the same reason, lawyers have entered into the world of finance. Mr. James J. Storrow, who was a law partner of Mr. Fish, has become a leading member of the old banking firm of Lee, Higginson & Co. A former law partner of Mr. Morawetz, Mr. Charles Steele, became a member of the firm of J. P. Morgan & Co. Their legal training was called for in the business world, because business has tended to become professionalized. And thus, although the lawyer is not playing in affairs of state the part he once did, his influence is, or at all events may be, quite as important as it ever was in the United States; and it is simply a question how that influence is to be exerted.

It is true that at the present time the lawyer does not hold as high a position with the people as he held seventy-five or indeed fifty years ago; but the reason is not lack of opportunity. It is this: Instead of holding a position of independence, between the wealthy and the people, prepared to curb the excesses of either, able lawyers have, to a large extent, allowed themselves to become adjuncts of great corporations and have neglected the obligation to use their powers for the protection of the people. We hear much of the "corporation lawyer," and far too little of the "people's lawyer." The great opportunity of the American Bar is and will be to stand again as it did in the past, ready to protect also the interests of the people.

The leading lawyers of the United States have been engaged mainly in supporting the claims of the corporations; often in endeavoring to evade or nullify the extremely crude laws by which legislators sought to regulate the power or curb the excesses of corporations.

Such questions as the regulation of trusts, the fixing of railway rates, the municipalization of public utilities, the relation between capital and labor, call for the exercise of legal ability of the highest order. Up to the present time the legal ability of a high order which has been expended on those questions has been almost wholly in opposition to the contentions of the people. The leaders of the Bar, without any preconceived intent on their part, and rather as an incident to their professional standing, have, with rare exceptions, been ranged on the side of the corporations, and the people have been represented, in the main, by men of very meagre legal ability.

If these problems are to be settled right, this condition cannot continue. Our country is, after all, not a country of dollars, but of ballots. The immense corporate wealth will necessarily develop a hostility from which much trouble will come to us unless the excesses of capital are curbed, through the respect for law, as the excesses of democracy were curbed seventy-five years ago. There will come a revolt of the people against the capitalists, unless the aspirations of the people are given some adequate legal expression; and to this end cooperation of the abler lawyers is essential.

For nearly a generation the leaders of the Bar have, with few exceptions, not only failed to take part in constructive legislation designed to solve in the public interest our great social, economic and industrial problems; but they have failed likewise to oppose legislation prompted by selfish interests. They have often gone further in disregard of common weal. They have often advocated, as lawyers, legislative measures which as citizens they could not approve, and have endeavored to justify themselves by a false analogy. They have erroneously assumed that the rule of ethics to be applied to a lawyer's advocacy is the same where he acts for private interests against the public, as it is in litigation between private individuals.

The ethical question which laymen most frequently ask about the legal profession is this: How can a lawyer take a case which he does not believe in? The profession is regarded as necessarily somewhat immoral, because its members are supposed to be habitually taking cases of that character. As a practical matter, the lawyer is not often harassed by this problem; partly because he is apt to believe, at the time, in most of the cases that he actually tries; and partly because he either abandons or settles a large number of those he does not believe in. But the lawyer recognizes that in trying a case his prime duty is to present his side to the tribunal fairly and as well as he can, relying upon his adversary to present the other side fairly and as well as he can. Since the lawyers on the two sides are usually reasonably well matched, the judge or jury may ordinarily be trusted to make such a decision as justice demands.

But when lawyers act upon the same principle in supporting the attempts of their private clients to secure or to oppose legislation, a very different condition is presented. In the first place, the counsel selected to represent important private interests possesses usually ability of a high order, while the public is often inadequately represented or wholly unrepresented. Great unfairness to the public is apt to result from this fact. Many bills pass in our legislatures which would not have become law, if the public interest had been fairly represented; and many good bills are defeated which if supported by able lawyers would have been enacted. Lawyers have, as a rule, failed to consider this distinction between practice in courts involving only private interests, and practice before the legislature or city council involving public interests. Some men of high professional standing have even endeavored to justify their course in advocating professionally legislation which in their character as citizens they would have voted against.

Furthermore, lawyers of high standing have often failed to apply in connection with professional work before the legislature or city council a rule of ethics which they would deem imperative in practice before the court. Lawyers who would indignantly retire from a court case in the justice of which they believed, if they had reason to think that a juror had been bribed or a witness had been suborned by their client, are content to serve their client by honest arguments before a legislative committee, although they have as great reason to believe that their client has bribed members of the legislature or corrupted public opinion. This confusion of ethical ideas is an important reason why the Bar does not now hold the position which it formerly did as a brake upon democracy, and which I believe it must take again if the serious questions now before us are to be properly solved.

Here, consequently, is the great opportunity in the law. The next generation must witness a continuing and ever-increasing contest between those who have and those who have not. The industrial world is in a state of ferment. The ferment is in the main peaceful, and, to a considerable extent, silent; but there is felt to-day very widely the inconsistency in this condition of political democracy and industrial absolutism. The people are beginning to doubt whether in the long run democracy and absolutism can co-exist in the same community; beginning to doubt whether there is a justification for the great inequalities in the distribution of wealth, for the rapid creation of fortunes, more mysterious than the deeds of Aladdin's lamp. The people have begun to think; and they show evidences on all sides of a tendency to act. Those of you who have not had an opportunity of talking much with laboring men can hardly form a conception of the amount of thinking that they are doing. With many these problems are all-absorbing. Many workingmen, otherwise uneducated, talk about the relation of employer and employee far more intelligently than most of the best educated men in the community. The labor question involves for them the whole of life, and they must in the course of a comparatively short time realize the power which lies in them. Often their leaders are men of signal ability, men who can hold their own in discussion or in action with the ablest and best-educated men in the community. The labor movement must necessarily progress. The people's thought will take shape in action; and it lies with us, with you to whom in part the future belongs, to say on what lines the action is to be expressed; whether it is to be expressed wisely and temperately, or wildly and intemperately; whether it is to be expressed on lines of evolution or on lines of revolution. Nothing can better fit you for taking part in the solution of these problems, than the study and preeminently the practice of law. Those of you who feel drawn to that profession may rest assured that you will find in it an opportunity for usefulness which is probably unequalled. There is a call upon the legal profession to do a great work for this country.

"The Living Law," 1916

The history of the United States, since the adoption of the Constitution, covers less than 128 years. Yet in that short period the American ideal of government has been greatly modified. At first our ideal was expressed as, "A government of laws and not of men." Then it became, "A government of the people, by the people, and for the people." Now it is, "Democracy and social justice."

In the last half century our democracy has deepened. Coincidentally there has been a shifting of our longing from legal justice to social justice, and—it must be admitted—also a waning respect for law. Is there any causal connection between the shifting of our longing from legal justice to social justice and waning respect for law? If so, was that result unavoidable?

Many different causes contributed to this waning respect for law. Some related specifically to the lawyer, some to the courts and some to the substantive law itself. The lessening of the lawyer's influence in the community came first. James Bryce called attention to this as a fact of great significance already a generation ago. Later criticism of the efficiency of our judicial machinery became widespread. Finally, the law as administered was challenged—a challenge which expressed itself vehemently a few years ago in the demand for recall of judges and of judicial decisions . . .

The challenge of existing law is not a manifestation peculiar to our country or to our time. Sporadic dissatisfaction has doubtless existed in every country at all times. Such dissatisfaction has usually been treated by those who govern as evidencing the unreasonableness of law-breakers. The lines, "No thief e'er felt the halter draw with good opinion of the law," express the traditional attitude of those who are apt to regard existing law as "the true embodiment of everything that's excellent." It required the joint forces of Sir Samuel Romilly and Jeremy Bentham to make clear to a humane, enlightened, and liberty-loving England that death was not the natural and proper punishment for theft. Still another century had to elapse before social science raised the doubt whether theft was not perhaps as much the fault of the community as of the individual.

In periods of rapid transformation, challenge of existing law, instead of being sporadic, becomes general. Such was the case in Athens, twenty-four centuries ago, when Euripides burst out in flaming words against "the trammelings of law which are not of the right" . . . Has not the recent dissatisfaction with our law as administered been due, in large measure, to the fact that it had not kept pace with the rapid development of our political, economic, and social ideals? In other words, is not the challenge of legal justice due to its failure to conform to contemporary conceptions of social justice?

Since the adoption of the Federal Constitution, and notably within the last fifty years, we have passed through an economic and social revolution which affected the life of the people more fundamentally than any political revolution known to history. Widespread substitution of machinery for hand labor (thus multiplying hundred-fold man's productivity), and the annihilation of space through steam and electricity, have wrought changes in the conditions of life which are in many respects greater than those which had occurred in civilized countries during thousands of years preceding. The end was put to legalized human slavery—an institution which had existed since the dawn of history. But of vastly greater influence upon the lives of the great majority of all civilized peoples was the possibility which invention and discovery created of emancipating women and of liberating men called free from the excessive toil theretofore required to securing food, clothing, and shelter. Yet while invention and discovery created the possibility of releasing men and women from the thraldom of drudgery, there actually came with the introduction of the factory system and the development of the business corporation, new dangers to liberty. Large publicly owned corporations replaced small privately owned concerns. Ownership of the instruments of production passed from the workman to the employer. Individual personal relations between the proprietor and his help ceased. The individual contract of service lost its character, because of the inequality in position between employer and employee. The group relation of employee to employer, with collective bargaining, became common; for it was essential to the workers' protection. Political as well as economic and social science noted these revolutionary changes. But legal science—the unwritten or judge-made laws as distinguished from legislation—was largely deaf and blind to them. Courts continued to ignore newly arisen social needs. They applied complacently eighteenth-century conceptions of the liberty of the individual and of the sacredness of private property. Early nineteenth-century scientific half-truths like "The survival of the fittest," which, translated into practice, meant "The devil take the hindmost," were erected by judicial sanction into a moral law. Where statutes giving expression to the new social spirit were clearly constitutional, judges, imbued with the relentless spirit of individualism, often construed them away. Where any doubt as to the constitutionality of such statutes could find lodgment, courts all too frequently declared the acts void. Also in other countries the strain upon the law has been great during the last generation; because there also the period has been one of rapid transformation; and the law has everywhere a tendency to lag behind the facts of life. But in America the strain became dangerous; because constitutional limitations were invoked to stop the natural vent of legislation. In the course of relatively few years hundreds of statutes which embodied attempts (often very crude) to adjust legal rights to the demands of social justice were nullified by the courts, on the grounds that the statutes violated the constitutional guaranties of liberty or property. Small wonder that there arose a clamor for the re-call of judges and of judicial decisions and that demand was made for amendment of the constitutions and even for their complete abolition. The assaults upon courts and constitutions culminated in 1912. They centered about two decisions: the Lochner case [*Lochner* v. *New York*, 1905], in which a majority of the judges of the Supreme Court of the United States had declared void a New York law limiting the hours of labor for bakers; and the Ives case [*Ives* v. *South Buffalo Ry. Co.*], in which the New York Court of Appeals had unanimously held void its accident compensation law.

Since 1912 the fury against the courts has abated. This change in the attitude of the public toward the courts is due not to any modification in judicial tenure, nor to amendments of the constitutions, but to the movement, begun some years prior to 1912, which has more recently re-sulted in a better appreciation by the courts of existing social needs.

In 1895 the Illinois court held [*Ritchie* v. *People*] that the eight-hour law for women engaged in manufacturing was unconstitutional. In 1908 the United States Supreme Court held in Muller v. Oregon that the Women's Ten-Hour Law was constitutional. In 1910 the Illinois court held the same [*Ritchie* v. *Wageman*]. The difference in decision in the two Ritchie cases was not due to the difference between a ten-hour day and a eight-hour day; for the Supreme Court of the United States has since held (as some state courts had held earlier) that an eight-hour law also was valid; and the Illinois court has since sustained a nine-hour law. In the two Ritchie cases the same broad principles of constitu-tional law were applied. In each the right of a legislature to limit (in the exercise of the police power) both liberty of contract and use of property was fully recognized. But in the first Ritchie case the court, reasoning from abstract conceptions, held a limitation of working hours to be ar-bitrary and unreasonable; while in the second Ritchie case, reasoning from life, it held the limitation of hours not to be arbitrary and unreasonable. In other words—in the second Ritchie case it took notice of those facts of general knowledge embraced in the world's experience with unrestricted working hours, which the court had in the earlier case ignored. It considered the evils which had flowed from unrestricted hours, and the social and industrial benefit which had attended curtailed working hours. It considered likewise the common belief in the advisability of so limiting working hours which the legislatures of many states and countries evidenced. In the light of this evidence as to the world's experience and beliefs it proved impossible for reasonable judges to say that the Legislature of Illinois had acted unreasonably and arbitrarily in limiting the hours of labor.

Decisions rendered by the Court of Appeals of New York show even more clearly than do those of Illinois the judicial awakening to the facts of life.

In 1907 . . . that court held that an act prohibiting night work for women was unconstitutional. In 1915 . . . it held that a similar night-work act was constitutional . . . the court holding valid the second compensation law (which was enacted after a constitutional amendment), expressly considered the facts of life, and said:

> "We should consider practical experience, as well as theory, in deciding whether a given plan in fact constitutes a taking of property in violation of the constitution. A compulsory scheme of insurance to secure injured workmen in hazardous employments and their dependents from becoming objects of charity certainly promotes the public welfare as directly as does an insurance of bank depositors from loss."

The court . . . realized that no law, written or unwritten, can be understood without a full knowledge of the facts out of which it arises, and to which it is to be applied. But the struggle for the living law has not been fully won. The Lochner case has not been expressly overruled. Within six weeks the Supreme Judicial Court of Massachusetts, in supposed obedience to its authority, held invalid a nine-hour law for certain railroad employees. The Supreme Court of the United States which, by many decisions, had made possible in other fields the harmonizing of legal rights with contemporary conceptions of social justice, showed by [a] recent decision . . . the potency of mental prepossessions. Long before, it has recognized that employers "and their operatives do not stand upon an equality"; that "the legislature being familiar with local conditions, is primarily the judge of the necessity of such enactments." And that unless a "prohibition is palpably unreasonable and arbitrary, we are not at liberty to say that it passes beyond the limitation of a state's protective authority." And in the application of these principles it has repeatedly upheld legislation limiting the right of free contract between employer and employee. But in the Adair case, and again in the Coppage case [*Adair* v. *U.S.*, 1908; *Coppage* v. *Kansas*, 1914], the Supreme Court declared unconstitutional a statute which prohibited an employer from requiring as a condition of his securing or retaining employment, that the workman should not be a member of a labor union, refusing to recognize that Congress or the Kansas Legislature might have had good cause to believe that such prohibition was essential to the maintenance of trade unionism, and that trade unionism was essential to securing equality between employer and employee. Our Supreme Court declared that the enactment of the anti-discrimination law which has been enacted in many states was an arbitrary and unreasonable interference with the right of contract.

The challenge of existing law does not, however, come only from the working classes. Criticism of the law is widespread among business men. The tone of their criticism is more courteous than that of the working classes; and the specific objections raised by business men are different. Business men do not demand recall of judges or of judicial decisions. Business men do not ordinarily seek constitutional amendments. They are more apt to desire repeal of statutes than enactment. But both business men and working-men insist that courts lack understanding of contemporary industrial conditions. Both insist that the law is not "up to date." Both insist that the lack of familiarity with the facts of business life results in erroneous decisions . . . What we need is not to displace the courts, but to make them efficient instruments of justice; not to displace the lawyer, but to fit him for his official or judicial task. And, indeed, the task of fitting the lawyer and the judge to perform adequately the functions of harmonizing law with life is a task far easier of accomplishment than that of endowing men, who lack legal training, with the necessary qualifications.

The training of the practicing lawyer is that best adapted to develop men not only for the exercise of strictly judicial functions, but also for the exercise of administrative functions, quasijudicial in character. It breeds a certain virile, compelling quality, which tends to make the possessor proof against the influence of either fear or favor. It is this quality to which the prevailing high standard of honesty among our judges is due. And it is certainly a noteworthy fact that in spite of the abundant criticism of our judicial system, the suggestion of dishonesty is rare; and instances of established dishonesty are extremely few.

The pursuit of the legal profession involves a happy combination of the intellectual with the practical life. The intellectual tends to breadth of view; the practical to that realization of limitations which are essential to the wise conduct of life. Formerly the lawyer secured breadth of view largely through wide professional experience. Being a general practitioner, he was brought into contact with all phases of contemporary life. His education was not legal only; because his diversified clientage brought him, by the mere practice of his profession, an economic and social education. The relative smallness of the communities tended to make his practice diversified not only in the character of matters dealt with, but also in the character or standing of his clients. For the same lawyer was apt to serve at one time or another both rich and poor, both employer and employee. Furthermore—nearly every lawyer of ability took some part in political life. Our greatest judges, Marshall, Kent, Story, Shaw, had secured this training. [Alexander] Hamilton was an apostle of the living law.

The last fifty years have wrought a great change in professional life . . . The term "corporation lawyer" is significant in this connection. The growing intensity of professional life tended also to discourage participation in public affairs, and thus the broadening of view which comes from political life was lost . . . The judge came to the bench unequipped with the necessary knowledge of economic and social science, and his judgment suffered likewise through lack of equipment in the lawyers who presented the cases to him. For a judge rarely performs his functions adequately unless the case before him is adequately presented. Thus were the blind led by the blind. It is not surprising that under such conditions the laws as administered failed to meet contemporary economic and social demands.

We are powerless to restore the general practitioner and general participation in public life. Intense specialization must continue. But we can correct its distorting effects by broader education—by study undertaken preparatory to practice—and continued by lawyer and judge throughout life: study of economics and sociology and politics which embody the facts and present the problems of today. "Every beneficent change in legislation," Professor Henderson said, "comes from a fresh study of social conditions and social ends, and from such rejection of obsolete laws to make room for a rule which fits the new facts. One can hardly escape from the conclusion that a lawyer who has not studied economics and sociology is very apt to become a public enemy.''

ORAL ARGUMENT IN *STETTLER V. O'HARA*, 1914

Muller v. Oregon (1908) was the occasion for the first ''Brandeis brief,'' a term that has come to denote legal arguments relying heavily on factual material to demonstrate that a law is or is not reasonable and that it therefore does or does not fit within the mandate given to governmental bodies by the Constitution. Traditionally, briefs had been compilations of legal citations and earlier decisions and had emphasized that courts should follow existing law. Brandeis, however, wanted to make the point that innovative laws also could be valid. The brief he and Josephine Goldmark put together gave short shrift to legal citations, confining them to a mere two pages. Instead, it included over 100 pages of factual information from the United States and European countries to demonstrate that it was not unreasonable to believe that excessive hours of labor were detrimental to the health of women and their families. All of Brandeis's exhortations in the speeches printed earlier in this chapter came together: his insistence that lawyers had to represent the public as well as the privileged, as he did here, without fee; his belief that law had to change along with and be based upon societal facts; and his analysis of the differences industrialization had made in life and should make in the law. The brief also reflected his conviction that the Constitution had to be interpreted so as to allow legislative experimentation in the light of new societal circumstances and that it was the lawyer's function to delineate those circumstances.

When the Court upheld the law, requests for copies of the brief poured in from all over the country. Illinois reenacted a women's maximum hours law that the Court had struck down in 1895, and Brandeis successfully defended it in court. He and Goldmark went on to assemble material for similar cases, and they were working on a brief defending Oregon's law setting maximum hours for men when Brandeis was named to the Supreme Court. At that point Felix Frankfurter joined Goldmark as the National Consumers' League team in the case.

The recitation of facts that made the briefs convincing makes them unwieldy reading, and so they are omitted in favor of Brandeis's oral argument in Stettler v. O'Hara, *defending the Oregon minimum wage statute for women. Although what follows is only part of Brandeis's presentation, it gives some feeling of his style and his emphasis on facts. The reaction of Chief Justice Edward Douglass White and, presumably, some of the other justices, is apparent from an account by historian Charles Warren. Writing to Felix Frankfurter, Warren, who was at the oral argument, reported, "each side had its time extended. Then the Court gave Brandeis an additional half hour, and when the time was up, Chief Justice White said: 'Mr. Brandeis, your time is up but we will consider that the clock has stopped and you may continue.' The Clerk of the Court told me later that he never recalled such a thing ever before being done by a Chief Justice."*

One more preliminary note should be added. Brandeis has been criticized for his brief in Muller v. Oregon *(and, by extension, in* Stettler*), which depicts women as weak, dependent, subordinate, and in special need of protection by the state. In fact, the depiction was a tactical move, and by the time of* Muller *he had actually become a suffragist. Brandeis deliberately held back some of the data that Goldmark, his sister-in-law and an official of the National Consumers' League, had unearthed during the brief's preparation. What it showed was that a worker's being adversely affected by excessive hours of labor had nothing to do with the worker's sex. That, however, was not a conclusion that would have helped Brandeis's argument before the Court. But he understood that the data could be used to encourage maximum hours laws for both men and women, and successfully urged the Russell Sage Foundation to publish all of her findings.*

By the time he argued Muller*, Brandeis had become aware of the equal value and responsibility of women as citizens. Speaking of them and of his goal of industrial democracy, he said, "I learned much from them in my work. So from having been of the opinion that we would advance best by leaving voting to the men, I became convinced that we needed all the forces of the community to bring about this advance." He had worked with strong women such as labor organizer Mary Kenney, Jane Addams, and his social activist sister-in-law Pauline Goldmark, in addition to Josephine Goldmark. By 1910 Brandeis had added his voice to those openly calling for women's suffrage, telling audiences at Boston's Tremont Temple and Fanueil Hall that watching the women with whom he worked had convinced him that women should be given the vote. His daughter Susan spent a year after graduation from Bryn Mawr campaigning for women's suffrage. When President Franklin Roosevelt named Frances Perkins as his Secretary of Labor,*

Brandeis wrote that she was "the best the U.S. affords" and that "it is a distinct advance to have selected a woman for the Cabinet."

For the first time, questions affecting minimum-wage laws are before this court. It may be helpful, therefore, if I discuss briefly the nature of these laws and state their origin and history. Counsel for the plaintiffs described the minimum-wage laws of Oregon, Wisconsin, Minnesota, Colorado, California, and Washington, as compulsory laws. It would be more accurate to call them prohibitory laws. They do not compel any employer to employ any person. They do not compel any employer to contribute to the needs of any person. They only prohibit him from employing women at a wage which is less than the living-wage. The laws would not prevent his employing a woman to whom no wage whatever was paid, and who was living wholly upon her independent income or was supported wholly by someone else. The Oregon minimum-wage law prevents his employing for wages a woman who receives less than a living-wage, in the same way that other laws would prevent a person from employing as an engineer someone who lacked the training necessary to entitle him to a certificate or license from the proper authorities, or as they would prevent him from employing as an elevator-tender someone under the age of eighteen or twenty-one . . .

The justification of that restriction may be read in the statute itself. It lies in three facts or conclusions drawn from facts. The first is, that wages which are not sufficient to support women in health, lead both to bad health and to immorality; hence they are detrimental to the interests of the state. The second proposition is, that women need protection against being led to work for inadequate wages. And the third proposition is, that adequate protection can be given to women only by way of prohibition; that is, by refusing to allow them to work for less than living-wages. Those are the three propositions which are, in substance, either expressly stated in recitals of the act, or necessarily deduced from its language and provisions.

On what do those propositions rest? They rest upon facts ascertained through an investigation into the conditions of women in industry actually existing in the state of Oregon. And the results reached in this Oregon investigation are confirmed by numerous investigations made in other states and countries by the United States Bureau of Labor. What these results are I have endeavored to set forth in my brief. In it you will find three hundred and sixty-nine extracts which present the facts from various publications bearing upon this subject . . .

Three important events contributed to the enactment of [minimum wage] legislation [in nine states]. One was the passage, by Great Britain, of its minimum-wage law in 1909.

The second event which called this subject specifically to the attention of Americans was the publication, in 1910 and 1911, by the Federal Bureau of Labor, of the results of its investigations into the labor of women and children in the United States, a monumental work, filling nineteen volumes and describing with great detail the wages and conditions of women in industry in the United States. The third event was the report of the Massachusetts Commission on the Minimum Wage of 1912, which was followed by the law enacted there in the same year . . .

Let us consider now the situation in the state of Oregon early in 1913, and see what induced its legislature to enact the law in question.

The first thing the people of Oregon did was to ascertain . . . that in the state of Oregon, whatever might be the case elsewhere, a majority of the women to whom the investigation extended, were working for a wage smaller than that required for decent living.

The next inquiry was what happened to women who worked for wages smaller than the minimum cost of decent living. It was found that in Oregon a large number of such women were ruining their health because they were not eating enough. That was the commonest result. They scrimped themselves on eating, in order to live decently in other respects or in order to dress and hold their jobs. Those that ate enough, roomed under conditions that were unwholesome, or they were insufficiently clothed. Besides those who lacked these ordinary necessaries of life, the investigators found another class of women whose wages were inadequate but who supplied themselves with the necessities by a sacrifice of morality. They found that in a large number of cases, the insufficient wage was supplemented by contributions from "gentlemen friends" . . .

The third subject of inquiry concerned the inference to be drawn . . . the legislature found that in Oregon, if women did not have wages sufficient to maintain them in health and in morals, detriment would result to the state in two ways. In the first place, degeneration would threaten the people of Oregon, because unhealthy women would not as a rule have healthy children. In the second place, unhealthy or immoral women would impose upon the community, directly or indirectly, heavy burdens by the development of ever-larger dependent classes which would have to be supported by taxpayers.

Such are the results which the legislature found would flow in Oregon from women working at less than living wages, results which affect vitally not only the present but also future generations . . .

It was not necessary to invent a new remedy because elsewhere in the world four different remedies had been tried for curing the prevalent social disease—wages insufficient to support working women in decency.

The first of these remedies was what might properly be called a voluntary remedy. The voluntary remedy for wages inadequate to sustain life in decency is education—education, economic and ethical . . . In course of time it might be possible so to extend the system of education as to make every employer in the State of Oregon recognize that he is doing something both economically and ethically wrong, when he employs women at less than living-wages. Employers might be convinced so thoroughly of these truths that the practice would be abolished. But the legislature of Oregon apparently decided that there was not time to await the fruits of this process of education; that meanwhile disaster would come to the state. For people have been as slow to recognize the wrongs of low wages as they have been slow in recognizing—or at least delinquent in acting upon—the great truth that "the wages of sin is death."

So the legislature of Oregon concluded that this voluntary remedy of education was not sufficient to meet these needs; and it turned to a consideration of compulsory remedies . . .

Then Oregon looked about the world and found the application of still another remedy, a remedy that seemed more promising. Her legislators considered the system which had been in force for eighteen years in Victoria, which had been gradually adopted by the other Australian colonies and by New Zealand, and which had been applied there with such extraordinary success that it was adopted in Great Britain in 1909. This legislation undertook to prohibit by law under threat of fine or imprisonment, the employment of persons at less than living-wages, instead of resorting merely to education or to trade unionism, or to publicity, as a means of eradicating the evil . . .

The legislators of Oregon recognized that they too must make an experiment. They rejected the three other remedies proposed and, in looking about for another, found this fourth remedy, compulsion by prohibition, instead of compulsion by publicity under law or the compulsion through trade-union organization under law, or mere educational processes; and they declared: "We will prohibit the employment of women at less than living-wages as we now prohibit their working more than ten hours; as other states prohibit their working at night, or without adequate opportunity for meals, or at certain industries which experience has shown are especially deleterious to health."

Thus Oregon concluded to follow the lead of a commonwealth of English-speaking free people who had made the experiment, entering upon it with much trepidation and with as much doubt as some now feel as to the wisdom of this experiment which is discussed today . . .

It was in the light of this wide experience, the experience of the old as well as of a new world, that the people of Oregon, outraged at the conditions which they found to exist in their midst, and stimulated by the reports of the Bureau of Labor of the United States describing the conditions that attended women's work elsewhere, concluded to try this remedy that had proved effective in Australia and Great Britain.

Oregon adopted this remedy for the same reason that the several Australian colonies adopted it and, later, England adopted it—because they found that the apprehensions of the wise men of business who had opposed it, were unfounded; that they had misjudged the human factors, and that, contrary to the prophecies of the opponents, important beneficent results were obtained.

If the three hundred and sixty-nine extracts from reports and other publications which appear in my brief, are examined, it will be found that few of those who describe the successes of this legislation, think it will bring the millennium. They say merely: "We have made advances; and the particular things which were apprehended from the enactment of these laws, did not come to pass" . . .

One hundred and twelve years ago, in 1802, the first factory-act was passed, limiting the employment of children in the textile mills. There is hardly an economic or social argument now urged against minimum-wage laws which you cannot find raised against that act in the parliamentary debates and in the contemporary literature of England. Yet the condition then was this: Children of five or six years, and in some instances even children of four, were at work in the textile mills from fifteen to sixteen hours a day. It took twenty-five years to raise the age limit for children to nine years. Today, in the State of Ohio, girls may not work in manufacturing establishments before they are sixteen, nor boys before they are fifteen; the permissible working-hours are reduced

to eight, and work after six or seven o'clock in the afternoon is prohibited . . .

Does that seem a revolutionary doctrine? Does it seem revolutionary
for the legislature of Oregon to pass a minimum-wage law when it
knows the conditions in Oregon to be such that degeneration of the
people, and heavy burdens upon the taxpayer and upon the industry of
the commonwealth, must necessarily result if women are permitted to
continue to be employed at less than living-wages? The Supreme Court
of Oregon, likewise knowing something of local conditions, held that it
was not.

Let me, at this point, discuss for a moment the question of constitutionality . . .

The test of constitutionality which this court has laid down was
this: whether this court can see that the legislature had reasonable
cause to believe that the act in question would produce the desired
result or had a reasonable relation to it; or whether this court could see
that the legislature of the State had no reasonable cause to believe that
the act would produce such a result and that it was an arbitrary exercise
of power. In only a very few instances has there been occasion to apply
the test with the result of annulling a State law. The burden of proof
must always be upon those who undertake to attack the law . . .

In answer to the question, whether this brief contains also all the
data opposed to minimum-wage law, I want to say this: I conceive it to
be absolutely immaterial what may be said against such laws. Each one
of these statements contained in the brief in support of the contention
that this is wise legislation, might upon further investigation be found
to be erroneous, each conclusion of fact may be found afterwards to be
unsound—and yet the constitutionality of the act would not be affected
thereby. This court is not burdened with the duty of passing upon the
disputed question whether the legislature of Oregon was wise or unwise, or probably wise or unwise, in enacting this law. The question is
merely whether, as has been stated, you can see that the legislators had
no ground on which they could, as reasonable men, deem this legislation appropriate to abolish or mitigate the evils believed to exist or apprehended. If you cannot find that, the law must stand . . .

The real test, as I conceive it, is, "Is there an evil?" If there is an evil,
is the remedy, this particular device introduced by the legislature, directed to remove that evil which threatens health, morals, and welfare?
Does it bear a reasonable relation to it? And in applying it, is there any-

thing discriminatory, which looks like a purpose to injure and not a purpose to aid? Has there been an arbitrary exercise of power?

Laws prescribing a minimum wage differ in no respect in principle from those other laws affecting wages just referred to. Indeed, they do not differ from still other acts held valid by this court, which declare void provisions in wage agreements designed to protect the employee; such as the acts preserving the right of recovery for accidents, although the employee has solemnly agreed to surrender that right in electing to take benefits from a railroad relief society.

No such distinction as that suggested exists in fact. Living-wages are most intimately connected with the occupation in which the wage-earner is engaged. The legislature interferes for the protection of women because it has found that the alleged law of supply and demand does not, in fact, operate—or if it does, it works destructively. The legislature interferes to protect health, safety, morals, and the general welfare in connection with this wage relation of employer and employee, just as it interferes with the conditions under which the employee may live, in prescribing how tenements must be constructed to insure health and safety . . .

In any or all this legislation there may be economic and social error. But our social and industrial welfare demands that ample scope should be given for social as well as mechanical invention. It is a condition not only of progress but of conserving that which we have. Nothing could be more revolutionary than to close the door to social experimentation. The whole subject of woman's entry into industry is an experiment. And surely the federal constitution—itself perhaps the greatest of human experiments—does not prohibit such modest attempts as the woman's minimum-wage act to reconcile the existing industrial system with our striving for social justice and the preservation of the race.

4 / Justice for the Workers

One of Brandeis's basic premises was that human beings had the right to govern themselves in the economic as well as the political sphere. When he discovered that was impossible for factory workers unless they were organized, he became an advocate of unionization. Power had to be balanced by power. Neither employers nor employees could be permitted to dominate, so that while Brandeis supported unionization, he deplored misuse of power by unions as well as employers. He opposed the closed union shop not only because it forced workers to join the union but because he thought the presence of nonunion workers would help balance the power of the union.

As he realized that unions were too weak to overcome the enormous concentrated power of the trusts, which had been enabled to grow by governmental policies designed to aid them, he began to call for governmental action to remedy the situation. He would have preferred nongovernmental solutions but recognized that only the government was sufficiently strong to create policies such as those limiting the maximum hours of laborers. Eventually he found himself willing to go further and defend minimum wage laws, in both cases to give workers the leisure time and access to the necessities of life that would enable them to fulfill themselves and participate fully in the political process. Recognizing that employers were becoming wealthy as the result of other people's labor, he started to talk about profit sharing. His experience with the governance agreement that had grown out of the 1910 New York garment workers' strike taught him that the mere creation of employee-employer committees within the framework of capitalist ownership was insufficient to overcome the differing goals of owners and workers. Eventually, as he read about workers' and consumers' cooperatives in England and Scandinavia, he became excited about the possibilities for worker-participation in American companies. At that point, however, he joined the Supreme Court, and whatever specific proposals he might have designed to achieve industrial democracy on an egalitarian basis were put aside because of the new demands on his time and the constraints on his activities.

Brandeis differed from many Progressives in concerning himself with the human fulfillment of the workers in addition to their material welfare. He told congressional committees and federal commissions that the development of the individual had to take place both in the factory and in the world outside of it and that people could not develop if they spent much of their day in a work situation over which they had no control. He disliked socialism for the big, concentrated bureaucracies he thought were implicit in it, and so the only possible solution was to bring Jeffersonianism into the industrial era: to make workers economically independent by making them their own employers. "In a democratic community," he said in 1915, "we naturally long for that condition where labor will hire capital, instead of capital hiring labor." That would be fair; it also would solve the problem of over concentration of power in the workplace.

There was no difference in his ideas after he joined the Court; the only novelty lay in the forum and manner in which he expressed them. Recognizing that there was no single acceptable answer to the problems of the workplace, he retained his support for unions as a balance to employer power and for experimentation by legislatures with statutes protective of workers and of labor techniques such as picketing and boycotts. Experimentation was the only intelligent way to proceed, and as long as a legislating body could produce facts to demonstrate that its solution to a social problem was not completely unreasonable, it was the obligation of the Court to interpret the Constitution so as to permit the experimental law to stand.

"THE INCORPORATION OF TRADES UNIONS,"
DEBATE WITH SAMUEL GOMPERS, 1902

Brandeis was convinced that unions were needed to ensure decent working conditions. He opposed irresponsibility by any person or institution, however, and recognized that labor leaders were as fallible as other human beings. Employers and the community had no way of punishing unions and union members that acted irresponsibly, short of jailing them or enjoining them from striking, because there was no formal legal entity to sue. He opposed injunctions against strikes, because injunctions frequently were employed to interfere with the legitimate

Workers during the New York garment workers' strike successfully mediated by Brandeis, 1920. (Library of Congress)

expression of grievances. As an alternative, he proposed incorporation of unions, which would make them legally liable when and if they acted irresponsibly. That approach was not unexpectedly opposed by labor leaders such as Samuel Gompers, president of the American Federation of Labor, who feared that lawsuits against unions would be misused in the same manner as injunctions. The public debate between these two champions of organized labor took place shortly after a sweeping injunction had been issued against striking anthracite coal miners.

Lest what I say on the advisability of incorporating trade unions be misunderstood, it seems wise to state at the outset my views of their value to the community.

They have been largely instrumental in securing reasonable hours of labor and proper conditions of work; in raising materially the scale of wages, and in protecting women and children from industrial oppression.

The trade unions have done this, not for the workingmen alone, but for all of us; since the conditions under which so large a part of our fellow citizens work and live will determine, in great measure, the future of our country for good or for evil.

This improvement in the condition of the workingmen has been almost a net profit to the community. Here and there individuals have been sacrificed to the movement; but the instances have been comparatively few, and the gain to the employees has not been attended by a corresponding loss to the employer. In many instances, the employer's interests have been directly advanced as an incident to improving the conditions of labor; and perhaps in no respect more than in that expressed by a very wise and able railroad president in a neighboring State, who said: "I need the labor union to protect me from my own arbitrariness."

It is true that the struggle to attain these great ends has often been attended by intolerable acts of violence, intimidation and oppression; but the spirit which underlies the labor movement has been essentially noble. The spirit which subordinates the interests of the individual to that of the class is the spirit of brotherhood—a near approach to altruism; it reaches pure altruism when it involves a sacrifice of present interests for the welfare of others in the distant future.

Modern civilization affords no instance of enlightened self-sacrifice on so large a scale as that presented when great bodies of men calmly and voluntarily give up steady work, at satisfactory wages and under proper conditions, for the sole reason that the employer refuses the recognition of their union, which they believe to be essential to the ultimate good of the workingmen. If you search for the heroes of peace, you will find many of them among those obscure and humble workmen who have braved idleness and poverty in devotion to the principle for which their union stands.

And because the trade unions have accomplished much, and because their fundamental principle is noble, it is our duty, where the unions misconduct themselves, not to attack the unions, not—ostrich-like—to refuse to recognize them, but to attack the abuses to which the unions, in common with other human institutions, are subject, and with which they are afflicted; to remember that a bad act is no worse, as it is no better, because it has been done by a labor union and not by a partnership or a business corporation. If unions are lawless, restrain and punish their lawlessness; if they are arbitrary, repress their arbitrariness; if their demands are unreasonable or unjust, resist them; but do not oppose the unions as such.

Now, the best friends of labor unions must and should admit that their action is frequently hasty and ill-considered, the result of emotion rather than of reason; that their action is frequently arbitrary, the natural result of the possession of great power by persons not accustomed to its use; and that the unions frequently ignore laws which seem to hamper them in their efforts, and which they therefore regard as unjust. For these defects, being but human, no complete remedy can be found; but the incorporation of labor unions would, among other things, tend in some measure to correct them.

The general experience in this country, in respect at least to the great strikes, has been that success or failure depended mainly upon whether public opinion was with or against the strikers. Nearly every American who is not prejudiced by his own peculiar interests recognizes the value of labor unions. Nearly every American who is not himself financially interested in a particular controversy sympathizes thoroughly with every struggle of the workingmen to better their own condition. But this sympathy for the working-men is quickly forfeited whenever the conduct of the strikers is unreasonable, arbitrary, lawless or unjust. The American people with their common sense, their desire for fair play and their respect for law, resent such conduct. The growth and success of labor unions, therefore, as well as their usefulness to the community at large, would be much advanced by any measures which tend to make them more deliberate, less arbitrary, and more patient with the trammels of a civilized community. They need, like the wise railroad president to whom I referred, something to protect them from their own arbitrariness.

TRUAX V. CORRIGAN, 1921

The Arizona legislature agreed with Brandeis that injunctions were used primarily as an anti-unionism measure, and it enacted a law restricting their use in labor disputes. The law was challenged by a restaurant owner whose premises were being picketed and who had applied unsuccessfully for an injunction. By then Brandeis had been on the Supreme Court for five years. Chief Justice Taft and the majority of the Court struck down the law. Brandeis's dissent contended, as he had argued in 1902, that limiting injunctions was a reasonable social experi-

ment. Here he added that it in no way violated the Constitution and that courts had to permit legislative experimentation if society was to progress.

MR. JUSTICE BRANDEIS, dissenting.

The first legislature of the State of Arizona adopted in 1913 a Civil Code. By Title 6, c. III, it sets forth conditions and circumstances under which the courts of the State may or may not grant injunctions. Paragraph 1464 contains, among other things, a prohibition against interfering by injunction between employers and employees, in any case growing out of a dispute concerning terms or conditions of employment, unless interposition by injunction is necessary to protect property from injury through violence. Its main purpose was doubtless to prohibit the courts from enjoining peaceful picketing and the boycott. With the wisdom of the statute we have no concern. Whether Arizona in enacting this statute transgressed limitations imposed upon the power of the States by the Fourteenth Amendment is the question presented for decision.

The employer has, of course, a legal right to carry on his business for profit; and incidentally the subsidiary rights to secure and retain customers, to fix such prices for his product as he deems proper, and to buy merchandise and labor at such prices as he chooses to pay. This right to carry on business, be it called liberty or property—has value; and, he who interferes with the right without cause renders himself liable. But for cause the right may be interfered with and even be destroyed. Such cause exists when, in the pursuit of an equal right to further their several interests, his competitors make inroads upon his trade, or when suppliers of merchandise or of labor make inroads upon his profits. What methods and means are permissible in this struggle of contending forces is determined in part by decisions of the courts, in part by acts of the legislatures. The rules governing the contest necessarily change from time to time. For conditions change; and, furthermore, the rules evolved, being merely experiments in government, must be discarded when they prove to be failures.

Practically every change in the law governing the relation of employer and employee must abridge, in some respect, the liberty or property of one of the parties—if liberty and property be measured by the standard of the law theretofore prevailing. If such changes are made by acts of the legislature, we call the modification an exercise of the police power. And, although the change may involve interference with existing liberty or property of individuals, the statute will not be declared a violation of the due process clause, unless the court finds that the interference is arbitrary or unreasonable or that, considered as a means, the measure has no real or substantial relation of cause to a permissible end . . .

Whether a law enacted in the exercise of the police power is justly subject to the charge of being unreasonable or arbitrary, can ordinarily be determined only by a consideration of the contemporary conditions, social, industrial and political, of the community to be affected thereby. Resort to such facts is necessary, among other things, in order to appreciate the evils sought to be remedied and the possible effects of the remedy proposed. Nearly all legislation involves a weighing of public needs as against private desires; and likewise a weighing of relative social values. Since government is not an exact science, prevailing public opinion concerning the evils and the remedy is among the important facts deserving consideration; particularly, when the pubic conviction is both deep-seated and widespread and has been reached after deliberation . . . Hence, in passing upon the validity of a law challenged as being unreasonable, aid may be derived from the experience of other countries and of the several States of our Union in which the common law and its conceptions of liberty and of property prevail . . . The divergence of opinion in this difficult field of governmental action should admonish us not to declare a rule arbitrary and unreasonable merely because we are convinced that it is fraught with danger to the public weal, and thus to close the door to experiment within the law.

[*The next paragraphs contain a summary of laws regarding unions, the right to strike, picketing, and boycotts in England, Australia, New Zealand, and Canada. They are followed by a similar survey of American laws and the changes in them.*]

The earliest reported American decision on peaceful picketing appears to have been rendered in 1888; the earliest on boycotting in 1886. By no great majority the prevailing judicial opinion in America declares the boycott as commonly practiced an illegal means, while it inclines towards the legality of peaceful picketing. But in some of the States, notably New York, both peaceful picketing and the boycott are declared permissible. Judges, being thus called upon to exercise a quasi-legislative function and weigh relative social values, naturally differed in their conclusions on such questions . . .

It was asserted that in these proceedings [applying for an injunction] an alleged danger to property, always incidental and at times insignificant, was often laid hold of to enable the penalties of the criminal law to be enforced expeditiously without that protection to the liberty of the individual which the Bill of Rights was designed to afford; that through such proceedings a single judge often usurped the functions not only of the jury but of the police department; that, in prescribing the conditions under which strikes were permissible and how they might be carried out he usurped also the powers of the legislature; and that incidentally he abridged the constitutional rights of individuals to free speech, to a free press and to peaceful assembly.

It was urged that the real motive in seeking the injunction was not ordinarily to prevent property from being injured nor to protect the owner in its use, but to endow property with active, militant power which would make it dominant over men. In other words, that, under the guise of protecting property rights, the employer was seeking sovereign power. And many disinterested men, solicitous only for the public welfare, believed that the law of property was not appropriate for dealing with the forces beneath social unrest; that in this vast struggle it was unwise to throw the power of the State on one side or the other according to principles deduced from that law; that the problem of the control and conduct of industry demanded a solution of its own; and that, pending the ascertainment of new principles to govern industry, it was wiser for the State not to interfere in industrial struggles by the issuance of an injunction.

Such was the diversity of view concerning peaceful picketing and the boycott expressed in judicial decisions and legislation in English-speaking countries when in 1913 the new State of Arizona, in establishing its judicial system, limited the use of the injunction and when in 1918 its Supreme Court was called upon to declare for the first time the law of Arizona on these subjects. In that case the Supreme Court [of Arizona], . . . rejecting the view held by the federal courts and the majority of the state courts on the illegality of the boycott, specifically accepted the law of New York, Montana and California, citing the decisions of those States . . . It rejected the law of New Jersey, Minnesota and Pennsylvania that it is illegal to circularize an employer's customers, and again adopted the rule declared in the decisions of the courts of New York, Montana, California and Connecticut. In deciding these three points the Supreme Court of Arizona made a choice between well-established precedents laid down on either side by some of the strongest courts in the country. Can this court say that thereby it deprived the plaintiff of his property without due process of law?

For these reasons . . . the judgment of the Supreme Court of Arizona should, in my opinion, be affirmed . . . because in permitting damage to be inflicted by means of boycott and peaceful picketing Arizona did not deprive the plaintiffs of property without due process of law or deny them equal protection of the laws.

"THE EMPLOYER AND TRADES UNIONS," 1904

In 1904, Brandeis represented the Typothetæ, an association of printing houses, in its fight with the Typographical Union. He did so because he considered the workers to be acting irresponsibly in this instance. The details are in the speech he gave at the Typothetæ's annual banquet, which is also a full statement of his thinking about unionism and the rational way to conduct business. In it, he urged his audience of employers to act more fairly toward their workers and emphasized his reasons for fearing the effects of concentration of power. He also reiterated a perhaps somewhat naive but deeply held view that labor conflicts could be settled if each party respected and truly listened to the other.

Let me review the facts:—

Prior to February 1, 1901, the minimum wage of compositors in Boston was $15 per week. A three years' agreement then entered into between your association and the Boston Typographical Union No. 13 fixed the minimum weekly wage at $16 for the first year, and $16.50 for the two succeeding years. Shortly before February 1, 1904, the Union demanded that the minimum wage be further increased to $18. You offered an increase to $17 for the first year, and $18 thereafter. The Union rejected your offer, and ordered a general strike. On February 1, 1904, the compositors went out.

No principle of trade unionism was involved, nor the question of increased wages for an indefinite period in the future. It was at most a matter of $1 a week for one year—the equivalent of what would be lost by each man in wages if the strike lasted just three weeks. To strike for such a stake was shockingly bad business. It was followed quickly by acts which also shocked the conscience.

The United Typothetæ had made a four years' contract with the International Printing Pressmen and Assistants' Union. This contract provided for arbitration of grievances, provided expressly against sympathetic strikes, and recognized expressly the open shop. In defiance of this agreement and in the face of the protest of Martin P. Higgins, the President of that Union, the Boston Typographical Union No. 13 undertook, by the promise of strike benefits, which in many cases exceeded the wages the men were receiving, to induce pressmen and feeders, who had no grievance whatever, to leave your employ. That was morally wrong. We believed it to be also illegal. You applied to the Supreme Judicial Court of Massachusetts for redress, and were accorded the protection of an injunction.

This was the beginning of the end; but the end itself came in a manner even more desirable. After the strike had continued five weeks, and the men had lost twice the paltry sum for which alone they struck, Mr. Lynch, the President of the International Typographical Union, and other members of its Executive Committee, came to Boston. They investigated the facts. They doubtless realized the hopelessness of the contest. They certainly realized the wrongfulness of inducing pressmen and feeders who had no grievance to go out in defiance of their contract. The strike was declared off—unconditionally. No promise of any kind was made to the compositors, pressmen and feeders who went out. The open shop was formally declared in every office. Many of the men who went out are still without work, and the strike benefits have ceased. The dynasty which for years has governed the Boston Typographical Union with unwisdom is tottering. The secretary has already resigned. The president, it is said, will not seek re-election.

So much for the past: what shall the future be? What should you do to make it an era of peace and prosperity? The answer involves a discussion of certain broad principles which, in my opinion, should govern the relations of employer and employee in all branches of industry, though in their application they would, like every rule, be subject to exceptions more or less temporary, dependent upon the peculiar facts of the individual case.

First. Prolonged peace and prosperity can rest only upon the foundation of industrial liberty. The peace which employers should seek is not the peace of fifty years ago, when the employers were absolute masters of the situation. The peace which the employees should seek is not the peace of medieval guilds, with their numberless restrictions. Industrial liberty must attend political liberty. The lead which America takes in the industrial world is no doubt due to our unbounded resources; but of these resources none are so great as the spirit and the ability incident to a free people. We lead the world industrially, not so much because the resources of nature are unbounded, as because the faculties and aspirations of men are comparatively unfettered. The prosperity of New England—this poor rich country—is ample evidence of this. We must have, therefore, for the development of our industries, as for the development of our citizens, the highest degree of liberty attainable. Industrial democracy should ultimately attend political democracy. Industrial absolutism is not merely impossible in this country at the present time, but is most undesirable. We must avoid industrial despotism, even though it be benevolent despotism. Our employers can no more afford to be absolute masters of their employees than they can afford to submit to the mastery of their employees, than the individual employees can afford to have their own abilities or aspirations hampered by the limitations of their fellows. Some way must be worked out by which employer and employee, each recognizing the proper sphere of the other, will each be free to work for his own and for the common good, and that the powers of the individual employee may be developed to the utmost. To attain that end, it is essential that neither should feel that he stands in the power—at the mercy—of the other. The sense of unrestricted power is just as demoralizing for the employer as it is for the employee. Neither our intelligence nor our characters can long stand the strain of unrestricted power. Every business requires for its continued health the *memento mori* of competition from without. It requires, likewise, a certain competition within, which can exist only where the ownership and management on one hand, and the employees on the other, shall each be alert, hopeful, self-respecting, and free to work out for themselves the best conceivable conditions.

Second. The right of labor to organize is recognized by law, and should be fully recognized by employers. There will be in most trades little probability of attaining the best conceivable conditions unless in some form a union of the employees exists. It is no answer to this proposition to point to instances of trade-union excesses and of the disasters which attended them. We believe in democracy despite the excesses of the French Revolution. Nor are claims of the trades unions disproved by pointing to the instances where the best results have been attained in businesses in which no trace of unionism existed. Wise, far-seeing employers act upon the spirit or the hint of union demands instead of waiting to have them enforced. ''A word to the wise is sufficient.'' The steps in advance have been taken often for the express purpose of preventing trades-unionism from finding a lodgment, often, unconsciously, as a result merely of the enlightenment which comes with the necessary thinking that trade-union agitation compels. Such successful businesses are, indeed, the greatest triumphs of unionism; and their marked success is due in large part to the fact that they have had all the advantages of unionism without having to bear the disadvantages which, in their imperfect state, attend the unions. We must not forget the merits of unionism in our righteous indignation against certain abuses of particular unionists.

Most people admit the immense service which the labor unions have rendered to the community during the last twenty-five years in raising of wages, shortening of the hours of labor, bettering of conditions under which labor is performed, and protecting women and children from excessive or ill-timed work; but the services which the labor unions can render in the future are even greater than they have rendered in the past. The employer needs the unions "to stay him from the fall of vanity"; the employees need them for their own protection; the community needs them to raise the level of the citizen.

Strong, stable trades unions can best serve these ends. The leaders of strong unions only will adequately feel the terrible responsibility resting upon them. The leaders of stable unions only can get the experience essential to an adequate performance of their duties; and experience almost invariably makes the leaders reasonable and conservative. Only long service as a labor leader can give that knowledge of the employer's side of the controversy which is essential to its just and proper settlement. Peace and prosperity, therefore, are not to be attained by any attempt to weaken trades unions. Our hope lies rather in their growing strength and stability.

At all events, the employer, whether he wills it or not, has in most trades to reckon with the union. What shall his attitude be?

Third. Employees are entitled to be represented by union officers. A short time ago it was common for an employer not to "recognize the union." That is, although he knew a large number of his employees were members of the union, he refused to negotiate in matters relating to the employees with its officers, on the theory that the employer should deal directly and only with his employees, and may not brook the interference of an outsider. This plausible but unsound theory has yielded generally to facts and to reason. One hears little now of employers arbitrarily refusing to deal with the chosen representatives of union employees. But, of course, recognizing that union officers are the proper representatives of the employees in any matter requiring consideration by the employer does not mean yielding to union demands, any more than recognizing a customer means conceding his demands.

How, then, shall the employer deal with the union's representative when a demand is made to which he feels he cannot accede, or when a controversy has already arisen? Many are ready with the answer: Arbitration; others again say: Conciliation. Arbitration and conciliation are each at times wise, but each involves the intercession of third parties. In arbitration it is the referee; in conciliation, the common friend. Ordinarily, neither is needed.

Fourth. Employers and employees should try to agree. A very able man, who taught the law of partnership at Harvard, once asked the class, "What shall be done if a controversy arises between partners?" The students suggested one legal remedy after another,—a receiver, an injunction, a dissolution. "No," said he, "they should try to agree." In the most important sense, employer and employee are also partners. They, too, should try to agree; and the attempt made in a properly conducted conference will generally be successful.

Nine-tenths of the serious controversies which arise in life result from misunderstanding, result from one man not knowing the facts which to the other man seem important, or otherwise failing to appreciate his point of view. A properly conducted conference involves a frank disclosure of such facts—patient, careful argument, willingness to listen and to consider. Bluff and bluster have no place there. The spirit must be, "Come, let us reason together." Such a conference is impossible where the employer clings to the archaic belief commonly expressed in the words, "This is my business, and I will run it as I please." It is impossible where the labor representative, swaggering in his power to inflict injury by strike and boycott, is seeking an unfair advantage of the employers, or would seek to maintain even a proper position by improper means. Such conferences will succeed only if employer and employee recognize that, even if there be no so-called system of profit-sharing, they are in a most important sense partners, and that each is entitled to a patient hearing, with a mind as open as the prejudice of self-interest permits.

The potent force of right reasoning in such conferences can hardly be overestimated. If applied with tact and in the aid of right action, it is almost irresistible. But it must be used only in the right spirit and in the aid of right action.

Fifth. It is necessary that the owners or the real managers of the business should themselves participate in the conferences, partly because the labor problem requires the best thought available and the most delicate treatment, and partly because the employees feel better satisfied and are apt to receive better treatment when they are dealing with the ultimate authority and not with an intermediary. Such conferences are necessarily time-consuming, but the time cannot be better spent. They are as instructive to the employer as to the employees. We must remember that there are no short cuts in evolution.

The greatest obstacle to the success of such conferences is the suspicion of the labor representatives—a suspicion due partly to ignorance of the employer's actual attitude, partly to knowledge of individual acts of unfairness of other employers, and partly also to a belief, which is frequently erroneous, that the employer will get some advantage through his supposed superior skill and ability. Suspicion yields only to experience; and for this reason, among others, the conferences are most successful when participated in by labor leaders of long standing. The more experienced the representative, the better.

But conferences, though wisely conducted and with the best of intentions on either side, do not always result in agreement. Men fail at times to see the right; and, indeed, what is right is often in doubt. For such cases arbitration affords frequently an appropriate remedy. This remedy deserves to take its place among the honorable means of settling those questions to which it properly applies. Questions arise however, which may not be arbitrated. Differences are sometimes fundamental. Demands may be made which the employer, after the fullest consideration, believes would, if yielded to, destroy the business. Such differences cannot be submitted to the decision of others. Again, the action of the union may appear to have been lawless or arbitrary, a substitution of force for law or for reason.

What, then, should be the attitude of the employer?

Sixth. Lawless or arbitrary claims of organized labor should be resisted at whatever cost. I have said that it is essential in dealing with these problems that the employer should strive only for the right. It is equally as important that he should suffer no wrong to be done unto him. The history of Anglo-Saxon and of American liberty rests upon that struggle to resist wrong—to resist it at any cost when first offered rather than to pay the penalty of ignominious surrender. It is the old story of the "ship money," of "the writs of assistance," and of "taxation without representation." The struggle for industrial liberty must follow the same lines.

If labor unions are arbitrary or lawless, it is largely because employers have ignominiously submitted to arbitrariness or lawlessness as a temporizing policy or under a mistaken belief as to their own immediate interests. You hear complaint, too, of lawless strikers in the legislature and in the city council; but, if lawlessness and corruption exist there, it is largely because the great corporations and moneyed interests have forgotten the good old maxim, "Not one cent for tribute, but millions for defence" . . .

You may compromise a matter of wages, you may compromise a matter of hours—if the margin of profit will permit. No man can say with certainty that his opinion is the right one on such a question. But you may not compromise on a question of morals, or where there is lawlessness or even arbitrariness. Industrial liberty, like civil liberty, must rest upon the solid foundation of law. Disregard the law in either, however good your motives, and you have anarchy. The plea of trades unions for immunity, be it from injunction or from liability for damages, is as fallacious as the plea of the lynchers. If lawless methods are pursued by trades unions, whether it be by violence, by intimidation, or by the more peaceful infringement of legal rights, that lawlessness must be put down at once and at any cost.

Likewise industrial liberty must rest upon reasonableness. We gain nothing by exchanging the tyranny of capital for the tyranny of labor. Arbitrary demands must be met by determined refusals, also at any cost.

In our international relations we are told that the best assurance of peace lies in preparedness for war. This is equally true in the industrial world. The union has its strike fund. The employer must also pay in some form the premium for insuring an honorable peace. He has adopted long since the guaranty fund for his credits, the depreciation fund for his machinery. He should now adopt another reserve fund to guard him against the losses attendant upon strikes, and, above all, should so organize his business as to be less vulnerable to them. Known weakness invites arbitrary attack, as opportunity makes the thief.

These are the principles by which alone the labor problem can be satisfactorily solved. They are broad, indeed; for they are the eternal principles of

LIBERTY, FRATERNITY, JUSTICE, HONOR.

DORCHY V. KANSAS, 1926

This opinion, which Brandeis wrote for the Supreme Court over twenty years after his speech to the Boston Typothetæ, shows that he had not changed his mind either about the basic legitimacy of unions or their obligation to act responsibly.

Mr. Justice Brandeis delivered the opinion of the Court.

Section 17 of the Court of Industrial Relations Act Laws of Kansas, 1920, while reserving to the individual employee the right to quit his employment at any time, makes it unlawful to conspire "to induce others to quit their employment for the purpose and with the intent to hinder, delay, limit or suspend the operation of" mining. Section 19 makes it a felony for an officer of a labor union willfully to use the power or influence incident to his office to induce another person to violate any provision of the Act. Dorchy was prosecuted criminally for violating 19 . . .

Some years prior to February 3, 1921, the George H. Mackie Fuel Company had operated a coal mine in Kansas. Its employees were members of District No. 14, United Mine Workers of America. On that day, Howat, as president, and Dorchy, as vice-president of the union, purporting to act under direction of its executive board, called a strike. So far as appears, there was no trade dispute. There had been no controversy between the company and the union over wages, hours or conditions of labor; over discipline or the discharge of an employee; concerning the observance of rules; or over the employment of non-union labor. Nor was the strike ordered as a sympathetic one in aid of others engaged in any such controversy. The order was made and the strike was called to compel the company to pay a claim of one Mishmash for $180. The men were told this; and they were instructed not to return to work until they should be duly advised that the claim had been paid. The strike order asserted that the claim had "been settled by the Joint Board of Miners and Operators but [that] the company refuses . . . to pay Brother Mishmash any part of the money that is due him." There was, however, no evidence that the claim had been submitted to arbitration, nor of any contract requiring that it should be. The claim was disputed. It had been pending nearly two years. So far as appears, Mishmash was not in the company's employ at the time of the strike order.

The men went out in obedience to the strike order; and they did not return to work until after the claim was paid, pursuant to an order of the Court of Industrial Relations. While the men were out on strike this criminal proceeding was begun . . .

Dorchy called this strike in violation of an injunction issued by the State court; and the particular controversy with Mishmash arose in this way. Under the contract between the company and the union, the rate of pay for employees under 19 was $3.65 a day and for those over 19 the rate was $5. Mishmash had been paid at the lower rate from August 31, 1917, to March 22, 1918, without protest. On that day he first demanded pay at the higher rate, and claimed back pay from August 31, 1917, at the higher rate. His contention was that he had been born August 31, 1898. The company paid him, currently, at the higher rate beginning April 1, 1918. It refused him the back pay, on the ground that he was in fact less than nineteen years old. One entry in the Mishmash family Bible gave August 31, 1898, as the date of his birth, another August 31, 1899. Hence the dispute. These additional facts were not put in evidence in the case at bar.

The right to carry on business—be it called liberty or property—has value. To interfere with this right without just cause is unlawful. The fact that the injury was inflicted by a strike is sometimes a justification. But a strike may be illegal because of its purpose, however orderly the manner in which it is conducted. To collect a stale claim due to a fellow member of the union who was formerly employed in the business is not a permissible purpose. In the absence of a valid agreement to the contrary, each party to a disputed claim may insist that it be determined only by a court. To enforce payment by a strike is clearly coercion. The legislature may make such action punishable criminally, as extortion or otherwise. And it may subject to punishment him who uses the power or influence incident to his office in a union to order the strike. Neither the common law, nor the Fourteenth Amendment, confers the absolute right to strike.

"HOURS OF LABOR," 1906

In this address to the first Annual meeting of the Civic Federation of New England, Brandeis expressed his beliefs about the needs of workers if they are to participate in democracy: a work day that is not overly long, regularity of employment, leisure, lifelong education, and development of mind and body.

Whether in a particular business at a particular time the hours of labor should be materially shortened presents usually a grave question. Such a change, owing to competition, direct or indirect, may seriously threaten the prosperity or even the life of the business; or the demand for the reduction of hours may be coupled with other terms or conditions clearly inadmissible. In such cases strenuous resistance becomes the duty of the employer. But, however commendable the resistance of the employer to a reduction of hours may be in a particular case, we should all recognize that a short working day is in general essential to the attainment of American economic, social and political ideals, and our efforts should be directed to that end.

Mr. Gompers quoted some time ago the saying of Heine that "Bread is Freedom." The ancient Greeks, recognizing that "Man cannot live by bread alone," declared that "Leisure is freedom." Undoubtedly "A full dinner pail" is a great achievement as compared with an empty one, but no people ever did or ever can attain a worthy civilization by the satisfaction merely of material needs, however high these needs are raised. The American standard of living demands not only a high minimum wage, but a high minimum of leisure, because we must meet also needs other than material ones.

The welfare of our country demands that leisure be provided for. This is not a plea for indolence. Leisure does not imply idleness. The provision for leisure does not contemplate working less hard. It means ability to work not less, but more—ability to work at something besides bread-winning—ability to work harder while working at bread-winning, and ability to work more years at bread winning. We need leisure, among other reasons, because with us every man is of the ruling class. Our education and condition of life must be such as become a ruler. Our great beneficent experiment in democracy will fail unless the people, our rulers, are developed in character and intelligence.

Now consider what, particularly in our large cities, the chance for such development is for men and women who are required regularly to work ten or even nine hours a day. A nine-hour work-day means, including the noon hour, ten hours at the factory or workshop. That means in Boston for most of those who live in the suburbs eleven or twelve hours devoted to the workshop and getting to and from it. When you add the time necessarily spent at breakfast and supper, dressing and undressing, house work, shopping and sleep, you find that at least twenty-one of the twenty-four hours are devoted to *subsistence* and a small fraction of the day is left for *living*, even if after the long work day one is in a condition mentally and physically to really live.

To attain proper development of character, mind and body, a short working day is essential, and the eight-hour day is in most occupations and for most people not too short. For the exceptional occupation and for the exceptional man in any occupation, no general rule is required; and right thinking on this subject cannot be aided by reference to such exceptional instances. Most professions, many positions in business, and some in trades fall within the class of excepted occupations. Good work in such occupations almost necessarily brings with it joy, because it implies development of faculties and, ordinarily, pecuniary advancement. In every occupation there are such possibilities for the exceptional man. But in most industrial occupations—in the unskilled trades and in many so-called skilled trades—the limits of development and of financial success for any individual are soon reached, and consequently there is little joy in such work except as compared with the hours of idleness, or such satisfaction as comes to the needy in securing the means of subsistence.

And what is necessary to living as distinguished from subsisting?

In the first place, bodily health is necessary; that is, not merely freedom from illness, but continued physical ability to work hard. For those engaged in the more favored occupations, like the professions, and the higher positions in business and some trades, such health, including the postponement of old age, has been measurably attained by better conditions of living, and notably by outdoor recreation. What has been found necessary for continued health and working capacity for those engaged in these favored occupations we should seek to make attainable for all our citizens. The burden and waste to the community and to the individual, and the suffering attendant upon sickness and premature superannuation, may be and should be lessened by a shortening of the hours of labor so as to permit of proper out-door recreation.

In the second place, mental development is necessary. Massachusetts, recognizing the education of her citizens to be an essential condition of a free and prosperous people, has made compulsory the schooling of her children to the age of fourteen, has prohibited their working in manufacturing or mercantile establishments under the age of fourteen, and has withheld the right to vote from illiterate adults as inexorably as from idiots. But the intellectual development of citizens may not be allowed to end at fourteen. With most people whose minds have really developed, the age of fourteen is rather the beginning than the end of the educational period. The educational standard required of a democracy is obviously high. The citizen should be able to comprehend among other things the many great and difficult problems of industry, commerce and finance, which with us necessarily become political questions. He must learn about men as well as things.

In this way only can the Commonwealth be saved from the pitfalls of financial schemers on the one hand or of ambitious demagogues on the other. But for the attainment of such an education, such mental development, it is essential that the education shall be continuous throughout life; and an essential condition of such continuous education is free time, that is, leisure—and leisure does not imply merely a time for rest, but free time when body and mind are sufficiently fresh to permit of mental effort. There is full justification for the common practice in trades of charging at the rate of fifty per cent additional for work in excess of the regular hours. Indeed, I doubt whether that rate of pay is not often grossly inadequate to compensate for what it takes out of the employee. An extra hour of labor may render useless those other hours which might have been devoted to development, or to the performance of other duties, or to pleasure. The excess load is wasteful with man as well as with horses or vehicles or machinery. Whether the needed education of the citizens is to be given in classes or from the political platform, in the discussion of the lodges or in the trades unions, or is to be gained from the reading of papers, periodicals, or books, freshness of mind is imperative; and to the preservation of freshness of mind a short work day is for most people essential.

Bodily and mental health and development will furthermore tend to promote innocent, rational pleasures and, in general, better habits of living. Such conditions will tend to lessen the great curse of drink, and with it some of the greatest burdens of the individual and of society.

It is, of course, no answer to the plea for a shorter work day to say that the leisure resulting from shorter hours may not be profitably employed. The art of using leisure time, like any other, must be learned; but it is certain that the proper use of leisure, as of liberty, can never be attained except by those who have the opportunity of leisure or of liberty.

Nor is it an answer to the plea for a shorter work day to say that most workingmen secure a certain amount of free time through the irregularity of their work. Such free time is literally time lost. Such irregular excessive free time presents an even greater evil than that of excessive work.

Although the reduction of the hours of labor is clearly desirable, it may, as already stated, be impossible, on account of competition or other cause, to grant the reduction at a particular time in a particular business. But in my opinion employers are apt to exaggerate the resulting loss of earnings, at least in the long run. Greater freshness, better health and mental development that go with shorter hours may be relied upon within reasonable limits to make up, in many businesses at least, in part, for a shortening of working time, where the employer receives, as he should, the full co-operation of the employees to secure the largest possible production.

Obviously no limitation should be imposed upon the output of the individual, nor any rule be insisted upon by the employees which would hamper the most efficient use of machinery. Such arbitrary restrictions are wasteful and uneconomic at all times, and necessarily act as a brake on the movement towards shorter hours. The natural gain in vigor and working efficiency on the part of the employee should be allowed to show itself in the shop results. If this gain in potential efficiency is nullified by artificial limitations on what and how much a man shall do, with the facilities placed at his disposal, the decrease in working time must inevitably mean increased cost, without either economic or moral justification, and under such circumstances the employer has no other course open to him than that of resistance to any attempt to reduce the working time.

If in any case we should find that, despite the fullest co-operation of employees, the reduced working time results in immediate economic loss, the welfare of our democratic community compels us to work nevertheless for a reasonably short work day as a condition essential to the making of good citizens.

"HOW FAR HAVE WE COME ON THE ROAD TO
INDUSTRIAL DEMOCRACY? — AN INTERVIEW," 1913

Brandeis's mediation in the garment workers' strike of 1910 resulted in a "protocol" that created, among other things, an elaborate conflict-solving mechanism. It also established the "preferential shop" in which union members were given preference in hiring but no one was forced to join the union, which Brandeis thought fairer than either a union shop or a completely open hiring system. The protocol eventually collapsed but while it existed Brandeis considered it a sound experiment in employer-employee relations.

As the interview suggests, Brandeis was optimistic about the eventual outcome of the labor struggle, but he anticipated a lengthy fight. The only possible resolution was industrial democracy.

Do you think the trade unionists are justified in their uncompromising demand that the right to strike shall under no circumstances be either abridged or suspended?

They are entirely justified. Labor cannot on any terms surrender the right to strike. In [the] last resort, it is its sole effective means of protest.

You are, then, opposed to compulsory arbitration, since it involves penalizing the striker?

Absolutely.

What, now, of voluntary arbitration?

No, except in a few cases . . . The burden of the task of adjustment is shifted onto the shoulders of some alien tribunal. The result is that employer and workmen fail to get the discipline they ought to have, and they are prevented from obtaining that intimate insight into one another's needs and difficulties without which essential justice is likely to be missed.

But beyond that, the arbitrators are rather likely, from the very nature of their task, to hand down a wrong award. They may easily miss the heart of the difficulty, because they are not in the midst of the actual struggle.

What, then, have you left?

The best of all is left—strong unions and direct adjustment between employer and workmen. This is the source of the strength of the elements combined in the cloakmakers' protocol of 1910. By the terms of that agreement the employers and workmen in the garment industry have simply been forced—not by law, but by their mutual bargain—to work together. They are brought together on the boards of grievances every week, where they sit face to face with their common problems and learn to know one another. Each comes to see the other's side, to make allowances, to accommodate and compromise. Mutual understanding and forbearance, self-knowledge and discipline, tend to become realized more and more.

If, in the absence of any such voluntary working agreement . . . strikes should continue to occur . . . and the public would still be exposed to whatever inconvenience, cost, and danger might ensue? Industrial wars must still be fought, let the consequences be what they may?

We cannot hope to get on without struggle . . . In the last resort, labor will fight for its rights. It is a law of life. Must we not fight, all of us, even for the peace that we most crave?

I believe that the possibilities of human advancement are unlimited. I believe that the resources of productive enterprise are almost untouched, and that the world will see a vastly increased supply of comforts, a tremendous social surplus out of which the great masses will be apportioned a degree of well-being that is now hardly dreamed of.

But precisely because I believe in this future . . . I also believe that the race must steadily insist upon preserving its moral vigor unweakened . . . There is something better than peace, and that is the peace won by struggle.

What of the future, Mr. Brandeis? What, as you see it, is to be the outcome of the industrial struggle?

In my judgment, we are going through the following stages: We already have had industrial despotism. With the recognition of the unions, this is changing into a constitutional monarchy, with well-defined limitations placed about the employers' formerly autocratic power. Next comes profit-sharing. This, however, is to be only a transitional, half-way stage. The eventual outcome promises to be full-grown industrial democracy.

TESTIMONY BEFORE THE UNITED STATES
COMMISSION ON INDUSTRIAL RELATIONS,
JANUARY 23, 1915

This is as complete and coherent a statement as exists of Brandeis's progression from labor union supporter to believer in profit sharing and to advocate of worker-participation, although it does not represent the end of his thinking about the subject and must be read in conjunction with the interview that follows.

Chairman Walsh. What is your profession, Mr. Brandeis?

Mr. Brandeis. Lawyer.

Chairman Walsh. You have also been engaged in public work, Mr. Brandeis?

Mr. Brandeis. Yes; but not in office.

Chairman Walsh. I wish you would please state the general character of the work which you have been doing, so far as it might affect industry.

Mr. Brandeis. I have, for quite a number of years, devoted myself, among other things, to a consideration of the social industrial problems, and especially the relations between employer and employee.

Chairman Walsh. Would you kindly state what your observation has been, with respect to the question as to whether or not the high concentration and the growth of [large] corporations have improved the physical conditions under which workmen are employed, or otherwise . . . Have you observed the extent to which potential control over labor conditions is concentrated in the hands of financial directors of large corporations?

Mr. Brandeis. To a certain extent . . . There has been undoubtedly great financial concentration . . . and tat influence which came from the concentration in comparatively few hands of a deciding voice in important financial and industrial questions almost necessarily affects the labor problems . . . what is perhaps more important or fully as important is the fact that neither these same men nor anybody else can properly deal with these problems without a far more intimate knowledge of the facts than it is possible for men to get who undertake to have a voice in so many different businesses. They are prevented from obtaining an understanding not so much because of their point of view or motive, but because of human limitations. These men have endeavored to cover far more ground than it is possible for men to cover properly and without an intimate knowledge of the facts that they can not possibly deal with the problems involved.

Perhaps I would have to go a little further into my general feeling in this respect as to the causes of the difficulty and of the unrest.

Chairman Walsh. I wish you would please do so.

Mr. Brandeis. My observation leads me to believe that while there are many contributing causes to unrest, that there is one cause which is fundamental. That is the necessary conflict—the contrast between our political liberty and our industrial absolutism. We are as free politically, perhaps, as free as it is possible for us to be. Every male has his voice and vote; the law has endeavored to enable, and succeeded practically, in enabling him to exercise his political franchise without fear. He therefore has his part; and certainly can secure an adequate part in the Government of the country in all of its political relations; that is, in all relations which are determined directly by legislation or governmental administration.

On the other hand, in dealing with industrial problems the position of the ordinary worker is exactly the reverse. The individual employee has no effective voice or vote. And the main objection, as I see it, to the very large corporation is, that it makes possible—and in many cases makes inevitable—the exercise of industrial absolutism . . . we have the situation of an employer so potent, so well-organized, with such concentrated forces and with such extraordinary powers of reserve and the ability to endure against strikes and other efforts of a union, that the relatively loosely organized masses of even strong unions are unable to cope with the situation . . . when a great financial power has developed . . . you have necessarily a condition of inequality between the two contending forces. Such contests, though undertaken with the best motives and with strong conviction on the part of the corporate managers that they are seeking what is for the best interests not only of the company but of the community, lead to absolutism . . . There develops within the State a state so powerful that the ordinary social and industrial forces existing are insufficient to cope with it.

I noted, Mr. Chairman, that the question you put to me concerning the employees of these large corporations related to their physical condition. Their mental condition is certainly equally important. Unrest, to my mind, never can be removed—and fortunately never can be removed—by mere improvement of the physical and material condition of the workingman. If it were possible we should run great risk of improving their material condition and reducing their manhood. We must bear in mind all the time that however much we may desire material improvement and must desire it for the comfort of the individual, that the United States is a democracy, and that we must have, above all things, men. It is the development of manhood to which any industrial and social system should be directed. We Americans are committed . . . primarily to democracy. The social justice for which we are striving is an incident of our democracy, not the main end. It is rather the result of democracy—perhaps its finest expression—but it rests upon democracy, which implies the rule by the people. And therefore the end for which we must strive is the attainment of rule by the people, and that involves industrial democracy as well as political democracy. That means that the problem of a trade should be no longer the problems of the employer alone. The problems of his business, and it is not the employer's business alone, are the problems of all in it. The union can not shift upon the employer the responsibility for conditions, nor can the employer insist upon determining, according to his will, the conditions which shall exist. The problems which exist are the problems of the trade; they are the problems of employer and employee. Profit sharing, however liberal, can not meet the situation. That would mean merely dividing the profits of business . . .

There must be a division not only of profits, but a division also of responsibilities. The employees must have the opportunity of participating in the decisions as to what shall be their condition and how the business shall be run. They must learn also in sharing that responsibility that they, too, must bear the suffering arising from grave mistakes, just as the employer must. But the right to assist in making the decisions, the right of making their own mistakes, if mistakes there must be, is a privilege which should not be denied to labor. We must insist upon labor sharing the responsibilities for the result of the business.

Chairman Walsh. You have probably noticed . . . the very general and broad statements that are made by directors in these corporations . . . to the effect that they feel that they discharge their duties when labor policies are left to their local officials or to their executive officers here.

Mr. Brandeis. That position, so far as it may have been taken, seems to be absolutely unsound . . . Nobody can form a judgment that is worth having without a fairly detailed and intimate knowledge of the facts, and the circumstances of these gentlemen, largely bankers of importance, with a multitude of different associations and occupations— the fact that those men can not know the facts is conclusive to my mind against a system by which the same men are directors in many different companies. I doubt whether anybody who is himself engaged in any important business has time to be a director in more than one large corporation . . .

Chairman Walsh. For the purposes of illustration, take a corporation such as the Steel Corporation and explain what you mean by the democratization of industry.

Mr. Brandeis. The unit is so large that it is almost inconceivable that the men in control can be made to realize the necessity of yielding a part of their power to the employee.

Now, when they resist . . . the unionization of shops, and they do resist it violently, most of the officials do so in absolute good faith, convinced that they are doing what they ought to do . . . The possession of almost absolute power makes them believe this. It is exactly the same condition that presents itself often in the political world . . .

It is almost inconceivable to my mind that a corporation with powers so concentrated as the Steel Corporation could get to a point where it would be willing to treat with the employees on equal terms. And unless they treat on equal terms then there is no such thing as democratization. The treatment on equal terms with them involves not merely the making of a contract; it must develop into a continuing relation . . . In order that collective bargaining should result in industrial democracy it must go further and create practically an industrial government—a relation between employer and employee where the problems as they arise from day to day, or from month to month, or from year to year, may come up for consideration and solution as they come up in our political government.

Chairman Walsh. Past experience indicates that large corporations can be trusted to bring about these reforms themselves?

Mr. Brandeis. I think all of our human experience shows that no one with absolute power can be trusted to give it up even in part . . . Industrial democracy will not come by gift. It has got to be won by those who desire it. And if the situation is such that a voluntary organization like a labor union is powerless to bring about the democratization of a business, I think we have in this fact some proof that the employing organization is larger than is consistent with the public interest. I mean by larger, is more powerful, has a financial influence too great to be useful to the State; and the State must in some way come to the aid of the workingmen if democratization is to be secured.

Chairman Walsh. Do you believe that the existing State and Federal legislation is adequately and properly drawn to provide against abuses in industry, as far as the employees are concerned?

Mr. Brandeis. I have grave doubt as to how much can be accomplished by legislation, unless it be to set a limit upon the size of corporate units . . . As long as there is such concentration of power no effort of the workingmen to secure democratization will be effective . . . size may become such a danger in its results to the community that the community may have to set limits. A large part of our protective legislation consists of prohibiting things which we find are dangerous, according to common experience. Concentration of power has been shown to be dangerous in a democracy, even though that power may be used beneficently. For instance, on our public highways we put a limit on the size of an autotruck, no matter how well it is run. It may have the most skillful and considerate driver, but its mere size may make it something which the community can not tolerate, in view of the other uses of the highway and the danger inherent in its occupation to so large an extent by a single vehicle.

Commissioner Lennon. Mr. Brandeis, in speaking with regard to the physical betterment that has come about in some instances in these great industries, did you mean to indicate that these physical betterments were not something of an element toward progress, toward democratic manhood?

Mr. Brandeis. They are all gains for manhood; and we recognize that manhood is what we are striving for in America. We are striving for democracy; we are striving for the development of men. It is absolutely essential in order that men may develop that they be properly fed and properly housed, and that they have proper opportunities of education and recreation. We can not reach our goal without those things. But we may have all those things and have a nation of slaves.

Commissioner Weinstock. I take it your prime remedy for industrial unrest . . . is a condition of industrial democracy? . . . I understand by industrial democracy a condition whereby the worker has a voice in the management of the industry—a voice in its affairs. Do we agree on that?

Mr. Brandeis. Yes, sir; and not only a voice but a vote; not merely a right to be heard, but a position through which labor may participate in management . . .

Commissioner Weinstock. On the other hand, Mr. Brandeis, what are the mistakes of organized labor, as you see them?

Mr. Brandeis. I think in the first place the commonest mistake is a belief that the employer is earning a tremendous amount of money at the expense of labor . . . The workingmen are mostly unfamiliar with large figures and are misled by them . . .

Now, what the employer needs most is to have proper representatives of labor understand the problems of his business . . . Put a competent representative of labor on your board of directors; make him grapple with the problems whether to do or not to do a specific thing, and undertake to balance the advantages and disadvantages presented, and he will get a realizing sense of how difficult it is to operate a business successfully . . . A few years ago, when union leaders were demanding from my client an increase in wages, and I asked them: "How much do you think the employer ought to earn before he increases your wages?" they named a figure which was far above his actual earnings, and I said to them, "Gentlemen, the books are open. If you can find either that more is being earned, or can show any way in which the employer can earn more than he is earning, the balance shall go to you." That put the responsibilities upon the labor leaders . . . The second cause of discord is the natural distrust felt by labor due largely to their lack of knowledge and of opportunities for knowledge.

The third cause is the sense of being subject to the power of the employer. That feeling of subjection can not be removed without changing the conditions under which industry is being carried on . . .

Commissioner Weinstock. If you were an employer, on the other hand, Mr. Brandeis, and had to deal with an unreasonable union . . . what would you do?

Mr. Brandeis. If it was clear that they were unfair and unreasonable, I think the only thing to do is to resist . . . But if you have a continuing government in which these questions are being taken up from day to day and grievances are averted rather than settled, the representatives of employer and employee learn to respect each other's intelligence as well as each other's motives. There are very few difficulties which can not be adjusted by a careful discussion of the facts . . .

Commissioner Ballard. I think it would not be out of place if, perhaps, you could tell your view of the minimum wage.

Mr. Brandeis. Whether or not the minimum wage should be adopted or not would depend upon the conditions in the particular community and trade to which it applies . . . The principle is perfectly clear that you ought not to interfere with the right of contract unless society demands that you should. But the principle is equally clear that we should interfere with the right of contract so far as the conditions make it necessary in order to protect the community—present and future generations.

The condition is such in many of our industrial communities that this necessity exists. The women in industry are largely unorganized; they are largely untrained, being to a great extent in business only for a short time; the percentage of the young and inexperienced is large. In all those respects their condition differs from that of men, and the consequence of their receiving less than a decent wage is far more serious than in the case of men. It is necessary, therefore, for the protection of society that we should fix or rather create boards which can upon investigation fix a minimum wage, having due regard to the position of employers as well as of the employee. And in fixing a minimum wage, it merely sets up a prohibition designed to protect the community from social danger.

"LABORERS AS DIRECTORS WITH BOSS POSSIBLE,
SAYS LOUIS D. BRANDEIS," INTERVIEW, 1915

Brandeis became convinced that the solution to the problem of indus-
trial democracy lay in cooperatives that would negate the distinction
between worker and employer. By 1915, when he gave this interview to
the Boston Post, *he had read Beatrice Potter's* Cooperative Movement
in Great Britain. *He drew heavily upon it for the description of the*
British Co-operative Wholesale Society. In the years following, he read
The Consumer's Cooperative Movement *and* The Decay of Capitalist
Civilization *by Potter and her husband, Sidney Webb, and recom-*
mended them and their ideas to his economist daughter Elizabeth
Raushenbush and to Felix Frankfurter. Brandeis became an admirer of
the consumers' cooperatives of Sweden, Denmark, and Switzerland as
well and an advocate of producers' cooperatives, cooperative banks, and
credit unions. Producers' cooperatives would tend to merge into con-
sumers' cooperatives, he thought, and the creation of such institutions
would distribute responsibility and thereby serve as a force for democ-
racy and individual development. His interest in Denmark's coopera-
tive factories and consumers' cooperatives led him to encourage his
wife and one of her sisters to publish a volume entitled Democracy in
Denmark. *What is today called worker management became Bran-*
deis's hope for the future of industry.

The question of introducing workers into the boards of directors of
big corporations . . . is one that must, at present, be treated broadly.

It cannot be effected merely by introducing a certain number of
workingmen into the board of directors. It must come through creating
a joint management of business; that is, giving to its workers a substantial share in the responsibility of management . . .

In other words, we must have industrial democracy . . . It is, of
course, difficult to effect the transition from an absolutist capitalistic
system to a system of industrial democracy, but it must be worked out,
and it is being worked out.

One marked example of what has been and can be done is presented
by the co-operative societies, which have attained such extraordinary
success in England and Scotland and many parts of Europe, and which
are now developing in America.

In a democratic community we naturally long for that condition where labor will hire capital, instead of capital hiring labor. The community should be served either by laborers who hire capital or through those co-operative enterprises, private or public, by which the community undertakes to provide itself with necessaries . . .

Fifty years of growing success of the co-operative movement in England shows what can be accomplished on these lines. It shows also to what extent the ordinary working man may develop under democratic conditions to be manager of 'Big Business.'

England's 'Big Business' is her co-operative Wholesale Society. Its annual turnover is now about $150,000,000, an amount exceeded by the sales of only a few American industries; an amount larger than the gross receipts of any American railroad except the Pennsylvania and the New York Central.

Its business is very diversified. It includes that of wholesale dealer, of manufacturer, or grower, of miner, of banker, of insurer and of carrier. It operates the biggest flour mills and the biggest shoe factory in all Great Britain. It manufactures woolen clothes, all kinds of men's, women's and children's clothing, a dozen kinds of prepared foods and as many household articles. It operate creameries. It carries on every branch of the printing business. It is now buying coal lands. It has a bacon factory in Denmark and a tallow and oil factory in Australia. It grows tea in Ceylon.

And through all the purchasing done by the society runs this general principle: Go direct to the source of production whether at home or abroad . . .

Accordingly, it has buyers and warehouses in the United States, Canada, Australia, Spain, Denmark and Sweden. It owns steamers plying between continental and English ports; it has an important banking department; it insures the property and person of its members . . .

The Co-operative Wholesale Society makes it purchases and manufactures its products in order to supply 1309 local distribute co-operative societies scattered over all England . . . and it is able besides to return to the local a fair dividend on its purchase.

Now, how are the directors of this great business chosen? Not by England's leading bankers or other notables supposed to possess unusual wisdom, but democratically, by all the people interested in the operations of the society, and the number of such persons who have directly or indirectly a voice in the selection of the directors of the English Co-operative Wholesale Society is 2,750,000, for the directors of the wholesale society are elected by vote of the delegates of the 1,899 retail soci-

" 'THAT BRANDEIS APPOINTMENT.' CHORUS OF GRIEF-STRICKEN CONSERVA-
TIVES: Oh, what an associate for such a pure and innocent girl! And we have
tried to bring her up so carefully, too!" This cartoon was published in Puck on
February 19, 1916, shortly after Brandeis's nomination to the Court was announced. (Nelson Greene in Puck, courtesy of the Library of Congress)

eties, and the delegates of the retail societies are in turn selected by the members of the local societies, that is, by the consumers, on the principle of one man, one vote, regardless of the amount of capital contributed.

Note what kind of men these industrial democrats selected to exercise executive control of their vast organizations—not all wise bankers, or their dummies, but men who have risen from the ranks of co-operation, men who by conspicuous service in the local societies have won the respect and confidence of their fellows . . .

Thirty-two directors are selected in this manner; each gives to the business his whole time and attention, and the aggregate salaries of the 32 is less than that of many a single executive in American corporations, for these directors of England's big business serve each for a salary of about $1500 a year. That shows what industrial democracy can do.

We in America must come to the co-operative idea . . . Management and labor should be one; because the principles of efficient management ought to penetrate every part of the field of labor.

HITCHMAN COAL & COKE CO. V. MITCHELL, 1917

Two years after he testified before the Commission on Industrial Relations, Brandeis was on the Supreme Court, expressing his support for the legal right of unions to organize. The case was one of many that represented attempts to destroy such successful unions as the United Mine Workers of America. Read in conjunction with the opinions that follow, this dissent that he wrote when the Court upheld an injunction against efforts at unionization shows the way he combined his support for unions with diatribes against bigness and with his opposition to courts' substituting their judgment for that of the legislatures elected by the people and presumably more familiar with their problems.

MR. JUSTICE BRANDEIS, dissenting.

The Hitchman Coal & Coke Company, plaintiff below, is the owner of a coal mine in West Virginia. John Mitchell and nine others, defendants below, were then the chief executive officers of the United Mine Workers of America and of its district and sub-district organizations having ''jurisdiction'' over the territory in which plaintiff's mine is sit-

Brandeis and the Supreme Court in 1916, his first year as a justice. Standing, left to right: Brandeis, Willis Van Devanter, James McReynolds, John H. Clarke. Seated: William Rufus Day, Joseph McKenna, Chief Justice Edward Douglass White, Oliver Wendell Holmes, Mahlon Pitney. (Harris and Ewing, Collection of the Supreme Court of the United States)

uated; and were sued both individually and as such officers. The mine had been "unionized" about three years prior to April 16th, 1906; and until about that date was operated as a "union" mine, under a collective agreement with a local union of the United Mine Workers of America. Then a strike was declared by the union; and a short shut-down followed. While the strike so declared was still in force, as the bill alleges, the company re-opened the mine as a closed non-union mine. Thereafter persons applying for work were required as condition of obtaining employment to agree that they would not, while in the service of the company, be a member of the union, and if they joined the union would withdraw from the company's employ.

Alleging that efforts were being made illegally to unionize its mine "without its consent," the company brought in the United States Circuit (now District) Court for the Northern District of West Virginia this suit to enjoin such efforts . . .

The fundamental prohibition of the injunction is against acts done "for the purpose of unionizing plaintiff's mine without plaintiff's consent." Unionizing a shop does not mean inducing the employees to become members of the union. It means inducing the employer to enter into a collective agreement with the union governing the relations of the employer to the employees. Unionizing implies, therefore, at least *formal* consent of the employer. Both plaintiff and defendants insisted upon exercising the right to secure contracts for a closed shop. The plaintiff sought to seclude the *closed non-union shop* through individual agreements with employees. The defendants sought to secure the *closed union shop* through a collective agreement with the union. Since collective bargaining is legal, the fact that the workingmen's agreement is made not by individuals directly with the employer, but by the employees with the union and by it, on their behalf, with the employer, is of no significance in this connection. The end being lawful, defendant's efforts to unionize the mine can be illegal only if the methods or means pursued were unlawful unless indeed there is some special significance in the expression "unionizing without plaintiff's consent."

It is urged that a union agreement curtails the liberty of the operator. Every agreement curtails the liberty of those who enter into it. The test of legality is not whether an agreement curtails liberty, but whether the parties have agreed upon some thing which the law prohibits or declares otherwise to be inconsistent with the public welfare. The operator by the union agreement binds himself: (1) to employ only members of the union; (2) to negotiate with union officers instead of with employees individually the scale of wages and the hours of work; (3) to treat with the duly constituted representatives of the union to settle disputes concerning the discharge of men and other controversies arising out of the employment. These are the chief features of a "unionizing" by which the employer's liberty is curtailed. Each of them is legal. To obtain any of them or all of them men may lawfully strive and even strike. And, if the union may legally strike to obtain each of the things for which the agreement provides, why may it not strike or use equivalent economic pressure to secure an agreement to provide them?

It is also urged that defendants are seeking to "coerce" plaintiff to "unionize" its mine. But coercion, in a legal sense, is not exerted when a union merely endeavors to induce employees to join a union with the intention thereafter to order a strike unless the employer consents to unionize his shop. Such pressure is not coercion in a legal sense. The employer is free either to accept the agreement or the disadvantage. Indeed, the plaintiff's whole case is rested upon agreements secured under similar pressure of economic necessity or disadvantage. If it is coercion to threaten to strike unless plaintiff consents to a closed union shop, it is coercion also to threaten not to give one employment unless the applicant will consent to a closed non-union shop. The employer may sign the union agreement for fear that *labor* may not be otherwise obtainable; the workman may sign the individual agreement for fear that *employment* may not be otherwise obtainable. But such fear does not imply coercion in a legal sense.

In other words an employer, in order to effectuate the closing of his shop to *union* labor, may exact an agreement to that effect from his employees. The agreement itself being a lawful one, the employer may withhold from the men an economic need—employment—until they assent to make it. Likewise an agreement closing a shop to *non-union* labor being lawful, the union may withhold from an employer an economic need—labor—until he assents to make it. In a legal sense an agreement entered into, under such circumstances, is voluntarily entered into; and as the agreement is in itself legal, no reason appears why the general rule that a legal end may be pursued by legal means should not be applied. Or, putting it in other words, there is nothing in the character of the agreement which should make *unlawful* means used to attain it, which in other connections are recognized as *lawful* . . .

Sixth: Merely persuading employees to leave plaintiff's employ or others not to enter it was not unlawful . . .

As persuasion, considered merely as a means, is clearly legal, defendants were within their rights if, and only if, their interference with the relation of plaintiff to its employees was for justifiable cause. The purpose of interfering was confessedly in order to strengthen the union, in the belief that thereby the condition of workmen engaged in mining would be improved; the bargaining power of the individual workingman was to be strengthened by collective bargaining; and collective bargaining was to be ensured by obtaining the union agreement. It should not, at this day, be doubted that to induce workingmen to leave or not to enter an employment in order to advance such a purpose is justifiable when the workmen are not bound by contract to remain in such employment.

Seventh: There was no "threat, violence or intimidation."

The decree enjoined "threats, violence or intimidation." Such action would, of course, be unlawful though employed in a justifiable cause. But there is no evidence that any of the defendants have resorted to such means. The propaganda among plaintiff's employees was conducted almost entirely by one man, the defendant Hughes, a District No. 6 organizer. His actions were orderly and peaceable, consisting of informal talks with the men, and a few quietly conducted public meetings, in which he argued the benefits of organization and pointed out to the men that, although the company was then paying them according to union scale, there would be nothing to prevent a later reduction of wages unless the men united. He also urged upon the men that if they lost their present jobs, membership in the union was requisite to obtaining employment in the union mines of the neighboring States. But there is no suggestion that he exceeded the moderate bounds of peaceful persuasion, and indeed, if plaintiff's witnesses are to be believed, men with whom Hughes had talked, his argument made no impression on them, and they expressed to him their satisfaction with existing conditions at the mine.

When this suit was filed no right of the plaintiff had been infringed and there was no reasonable ground to believe that any of its rights would be interfered with.

DUPLEX COMPANY V. DEERING, 1920

Brandeis's role as a spokesperson on the Supreme Court for unions is exemplified by this and the following opinion. He recognized that unions could not merely be supported in principle; they also had to be allowed to use the legal weapons available to them in order to combat unfair practices by employers.

MR. JUSTICE BRANDEIS, dissenting, with whom MR. JUSTICE HOLMES and MR. JUSTICE CLARKE concur.

The Duplex Company, a manufacturer of newspaper printing presses, seeks to enjoin officials of the machinists' and affiliated unions from interfering with its business by inducing their members not to work for plaintiff or its customers in connection with the setting up of presses made by it. Unlike *Hitchman Coal & Coke Co. v. Mitchell*, there is here no charge that defendants are inducing employees to break their contracts. Nor is it now urged that defendants threaten acts of violence. But plaintiff insists that the acts complained of violate both the common law of New York and the Sherman Act and that, accordingly, it is entitled to relief by injunction under the state law and under §16 of the Clayton Act, October 15, 1914.

The defendants admit interference with plaintiff's business but justify on the following ground: There are in the United States only four manufacturers of such presses; and they are in active competition. Between 1909 and 1913 the machinists' union induced three of them to recognize and deal with the union, to grant the eight-hour day, to establish a minimum wage scale and to comply with other union requirements. The fourth, the Duplex Company, refused to recognize the union; insisted upon conducting its factory on the open shop principle; refused to introduce the eight-hour day and operated for the most part, ten hours a day; refused to establish a minimum wage scale; and disregarded other union standards. Thereupon two of the three manufacturers who had assented to union conditions, notified the union that they should be obliged to terminate their agreements with it unless their competitor, the Duplex Company, also entered into the agreement with the union, which, in giving more favorable terms to labor, imposed correspondingly greater burdens upon the employer. Because the Duplex Company refused to enter into such an agreement and in order to induce it to do so, the machinists' union declared a strike at its factory, and in aid of that strike instructed its members and the members of affiliated unions not to work on the installation of presses which plaintiff had delivered in New York . . .

First . . . Defendants' justification is that of self-interest. They have supported the strike at the employer's factory by a strike elsewhere against its product. They have injured the plaintiff, not maliciously, but in self-defense. They contend that the Duplex Company's refusal to deal with the machinists' union and to observe its standards threatened the interest not only of such union members as were its factory employees, but even more of all members of the several affiliated unions employed by plaintiff's competitors and by others whose more advanced standards the plaintiff was, in reality, attacking; and that none of the defendants and no person whom they are endeavoring to induce to refrain from working in connection with the setting up of presses made by plaintiff is an outsider, an interloper. In other words, that the contest between the company and the machinists' union involves vitally the interest of every person whose cooperation is sought. May not all with a common interest join in refusing to expend their labor upon articles whose very production constitutes an attack upon their standard of living and the institution which they are convinced supports it? Applying common-law principles the answer should, in my opinion, be: Yes, if as matter of fact those who so cooperate have a common interest.

The change in the law by which strikes once illegal and even criminal are now recognized as lawful was effected in America largely without the intervention of legislation. This reversal of a common-law rule was not due to the rejection by the courts of one principle and the adoption in its stead of another, but to a better realization of the facts of industrial life. It is conceded that, although the strike of the workmen in plaintiff's factory injured its business, the strike was not an actionable wrong; because the obvious self-interest of the strikers constituted a justification. Formerly courts held that self-interest could not be so served. But even after strikes to raise wages or reduce hours were held to be legal because of the self-interest, some courts held that there was not sufficient causal relationship between a strike to unionize a shop and the self-interest of the strikers to justify injuries inflicted. But other courts, repeating the same legal formula, found that there was justification, because they viewed the facts differently. When centralization in the control of business brought its corresponding centralization in the organization of workingmen, new facts had to be appraised. A single employer might, as in this case, threaten the standing of the whole organization and the standards of all its members; and when he did so the union, in order to protect itself, would naturally refuse to work on his materials wherever found. When such a situation was first presented to the courts, judges concluded that the intervention of the purchaser of the materials established an insulation through which the direct relationship of the employer and the workingmen did not penetrate; and the strike against the material was considered a strike against the purchaser by unaffected third parties. But other courts, with better appreciation of the facts of industry, recognized the unity of interest throughout the union, and that, in refusing to work on materials which threatened it, the union was only refusing to aid in destroying itself.

Second. As to the anti-trust laws of the United States: [the Clayton Anti-trust Act] was the fruit of unceasing agitation, which extended over more than twenty years and was designed to equalize before the law the position of workingmen and employer as industrial combatants . . .

By 1914 the ideas of the advocates of legislation had fairly crystallized upon the manner in which the inequality and uncertainty of the law should be removed. It was to be done by expressly legalizing certain acts regardless of the effects produced by them upon other persons . . . In other words the Clayton Act . . . declared that the relations between employers of labor and workingmen were competitive relations, that organized competition was not harmful and that it justified injuries necessarily inflicted in its course.

Because I have come to the conclusion that both the common law of a State and a statute of the United States declare the right of industrial combatants to push their struggle to the limits of the justification of self-interest, I do not wish to be understood as attaching any constitutional or moral sanction to that right. All rights are derived from the purposes of the society in which they exist; above all rights rises duty to the community. The conditions developed in industry may be such that those engaged in it cannot continue their struggle without danger to the community. But it is not for judges to determine whether such conditions exist, nor is it their function to set the limits of permissible contest and to declare the duties which the new situation demands. This is the function of the legislature which, while limiting individual and group rights of aggression and defense, may substitute processes of justice for the more primitive method of trial by combat.

BEDFORD CUT STONE V. JOURNEYMEN
STONE CUTTERS' ASSOCIATION, 1926

Brandeis's dissent in this case is in keeping with his opinion in Duplex *v.* Deering *(above). The Supreme Court held that it was an unreasonable interference with interstate commerce for the stone cutters' union, spread across the country, to tell its members not to work on stone that had been cut by stone cutters who did not belong to the union. The union's act came in the context of an attempt to unionize the Bedford Cut Stone Company and twenty-three other producers of Indiana limestone. Brandeis compared the relative weakness of small journeymen's locals with the wealth and organized strength of the plaintiffs. The Sherman and Clayton Anti-trust Acts prohibited only "unreasonable" restraints of trade, and to Brandeis, if joining in a union was reasonable and legal, so was a call for union solidarity. Justices Edward T. Sanford and Harlan Fiske Stone announced themselves bound by the rule enunciated in* Duplex. *The other justices in the majority, however, clearly*

*differed with Brandeis and Holmes in their assessment—and fear—of
the relative strength of laborers and employers.*

MR. JUSTICE BRANDEIS, dissenting.

The constitution of the Journeymen Stone Cutters' Association provides: "No member of this Association shall cut, carve or fit any material that has been cut by men working in opposition to this Association." For many years, the plaintiffs had contracts with the Association under which its members were employed at their several quarries and works. In 1921, the plaintiffs refused to renew the contracts because certain rules or conditions proposed by the Journeymen were unacceptable.

Then came a strike. It was followed by a lockout, the organization by the plaintiffs of a so-called independent union, and the establishment of it at their plants. Repeated efforts to adjust the controversy proved futile. Finally, the Association urged its members working on buildings in other States to observe the above provision of its constitution. Its position was "that if employers will not employ our members in one place, we will decline to work for them in another, or to finish any work that has been started or partly completed by men these employers are using to combat our organization."

If, in the struggle for existence, individual workingmen may, under any circumstances, co-operate in this way for self-protection even though the interstate trade of another is thereby restrained, the lower courts were clearly right in denying the injunction sought by plaintiffs. I have no occasion to consider whether the restraint, which was applied wholly intrastate, became in its operation a direct restraint upon interstate commerce. For it has long been settled that only unreasonable restraints are prohibited by the Sherman Law. And the restraint imposed was, in my opinion, a reasonable one. The Act does not establish the standard of reasonableness. What is reasonable must be determined by the application of principles of the common law, as administered in federal courts unaffected by state legislation or decisions. Compare *Duplex Printing Co. v. Deering*. Tested by these principles, the propriety of the unions' conduct can hardly be doubted by one who believes in the organization of labor.

Neither the individual stonecutters nor the unions had any contract with any of the plaintiffs or with any of their customers. So far as concerned the plaintiffs and their customers, the individual stonecutters were free either to work or to abstain from working on stone which had been cut at the quarries by members of the employers' union. So far as concerned the Association, the individual stonecutter was not free. He had agreed, when he became a member, that he would not work on stone "cut by men working in opposition to" the Association. It was in duty bound to urge upon its members observance of the obligation assumed. These cut stone companies, who alone are seeking relief, were its declared enemies. They were seeking to destroy it. And the danger was great.

The plaintiffs are not weak employers opposed by a mighty union. They have large financial resources. Together, they ship 70 per cent. of all the cut stone in the country. They are not isolated concerns. They had combined in a local employers' organization. And their organization is affiliated with the national employers' organization, called "International Cut Stone & Quarrymen's Association." Standing alone, each of the 150 Journeymen's locals is weak. The average number of members in a local union is only 33. The locals are widely scattered throughout the country. Strong employers could destroy a local "by importing scabs" from other cities. And many of the builders by whom the stonecutters were employed in different cities, are strong. It is only through combining the 5,000 organized stonecutters in a national union, and developing loyalty to it, that the individual stonecutter anywhere can protect his own job.

The manner in which these individual stonecutters exercised their asserted right to perform their union duty by refusing to finish stone "cut by men working in opposition to" the Association was confessedly legal. They were innocent alike of trespass and of breach of contract. They did not picket. They refrained from violence, intimidation, fraud and threats. They refrained from obstructing otherwise either the plaintiffs or their customers in attempts to secure other help. They did not plan a boycott against any of the plaintiffs or against builders who used the plaintiffs' product. On the contrary, they expressed entire willingness to cut and finish anywhere any stone quarried by any of the plaintiffs, except such stone as had been partially "cut by men working in opposition to" the Association. A large part of the plaintiffs' product consisting of blocks, slabs and sawed work was not affected by the order of the union officials. The individual stonecutter was thus clearly innocent of wrongdoing, unless it was illegal for him to agree with his fellow craftsmen to refrain from working on the "scab"-cut stone because it was an article of interstate commerce.

The manner in which the Journeymens' unions acted was also clearly legal. The combination complained of is the co-operation of persons wholly of the same craft, united in a national union, solely for self-protection. No outsider—be he quarrier, dealer, builder or laborer—was a party to the combination. No purpose was to be subserved except to promote the trade interests of members of the Journeymens' Association. There was no attempt by the unions to boycott the plaintiffs. There was no attempt to seek the aid of members of any other craft, by a sympathetic strike or otherwise. The contest was not a class struggle. It was a struggle between particular employers and their employees. But the controversy out of which it arose, related, not to specific grievances, but to fundamental matters of union policy of general application throughout the country. The national Association had the duty to determine, so far as its members were concerned, what that policy should be. It deemed the maintenance of that policy a matter of vital interest to each member of the union. The duty rested upon it to enforce its policy by all legitimate means. The Association, its locals and officers were clearly innocent of wrongdoing, unless Congress has declared that for union officials to urge members to refrain from working on stone "cut by men working in opposition" to it is necessarily illegal if thereby the interstate trade of another is restrained . . .

Members of the Journeymen Stone Cutters' Association could not work anywhere on stone which had been cut at the quarries by "men working in opposition" to it, without aiding and abetting the enemy. Observance by each member of the provision of their constitution which forbids such action was essential to his own self-protection. It was demanded of each by loyalty to the organization and to his fellows. If, on the undisputed facts of this case, refusal to work can be enjoined, Congress created by the Sherman Law and the Clayton Act an instrument for imposing restraints upon labor which reminds of involuntary servitude. The Sherman Law was held in *United States v. United States Steel Corporation*, to permit capitalists to combine in a single corporation 50 per cent. of the steel industry of the United States dominating the trade through its vast resources. The Sherman Law was held in *United States v. United Shoe Machinery Co.*, to permit capitalists to combine in another corporation practically the whole shoe machinery industry of the country, necessarily giving it a position of dominance over shoe-manufacturing in America. It would, indeed, be strange if Congress had by the same Act willed to deny to members of a small craft of workingmen the right to cooperate in simply refraining from work, when that course was the only means of self-protection against a combination of militant and powerful employers. I cannot believe that Congress did so.

MR. JUSTICE HOLMES concurs in this opinion.

5 / Business and "The Curse of Bigness"

Brandeis, the son of a successful merchant, was pleased to see the emergence of business as a profession rather than a trade. As he pointed out in "Business—A Profession," reprinted below, universities had begun establishing business schools. This implied that intellectual training was as necessary to the practice of business as to the profession of medicine or law. He spoke of business as "an applied science" in which the notion of "a good contract" had changed from "a transaction in which one man got the better of another" to one "which is good for both parties to it." It had become "an occupation which is pursued largely for others and not merely for one's self."

This, of course, was a statement that reflected Brandeis's view of what business ought to be rather than what it was in reality. He undertook his long fight with the New Haven Railroad because he believed that the railroad had violated the precepts of business as a profession. Not only was it being run for individual profit and against the best interests of workers and consumers; it was unforgivably inefficient as well. Quite aside from the malice he attributed to J. P. Morgan and his associates, Brandeis thought the New Haven had ignored the fact that excessive bigness was incompatible with the profession of business.

Bigness became excessive when an organization grew so large that its managers could not know the details of its operations. The result was that no one was in charge; waste, inefficiency, and exorbitant costs inevitably followed. That, along with a fear of concentrated and unaccountable power, was the reason for Brandeis's campaign against trusts. Brandeis eventually persuaded presidential candidate Woodrow Wilson to campaign on a platform of destroying the trusts. He did not see Theodore Roosevelt as a "trust-buster"; on the contrary, Roosevelt advocated letting the trusts exist but regulating them. Brandeis thought that impossible, given the enormous size of trusts and the power it gave them. His opposition to them was both moral and pragmatic: concentrated power made for irresponsibility; excessive size negated creativity and resulted in unnecessary expense.

"BUSINESS — A PROFESSION," 1912

The experiences that Brandeis had with the McElwain factory and the Filene clothing store in Boston are recounted in this commencement speech, delivered at Brown University, which hammers away at the ills wrought by irregularity of employment and the creativity business ought to exercise in redefining its relationship with labor. Elsewhere, in describing the way his ideas were altered by experience, he told an interviewer, "I first saw unemployment in its true features in the case of a New England shoe manufacturer whose men were going on strike. I had been called in. The more I studied it the more it seemed to me absurd that men willing to work should have to be idle during ten or fifteen weeks of each year. I said: 'This is unnecessary. It is an outrage that in an intelligent society a great industry should be so managed.' They talked to me of seasonal conditions and of averages. I abhor averages. I like the individual case. A man may have six meals one day and none the next, making an average of three per day, but that is not a good way to live. Unemployment in this industry was all the less excusable because of the fact that neither the raw material nor the finished product was perishable. My client was a man of unusual ability. He began to see it as I did. He inclined his thoughts to solve the problem, and it was solved. The disgrace of unemployment in his share of that industry was eliminated."

"Is that generally feasible, you think?"

"Unemployment is as unnecessary as disease epidemics. One who says in this intelligent age that unemployment is necessary or unavoidable is like one a generation ago who would have continued to insist that epidemics were, if not necessary and divinely imposed, at least inevitable."

Each commencement season we are told by the college reports the number of graduates who have selected the professions as their occupations and the number of those who will enter business. The time has come for abandoning such a classification. Business should be, and to some extent already is, one of the professions. The once meagre list of the learned professions is being constantly enlarged. Engineering in its many branches already takes rank beside law, medicine and theology. Forestry and scientific agriculture are securing places of honor. The new professions of manufacturing, of merchandising, of transportation and of finance must soon gain recognition. The establishment of business schools in our universities is a manifestation of the modern conception of business.

The peculiar characteristics of a profession as distinguished from other occupations, I take to be these:

First. A profession is an occupation for which the necessary preliminary training is intellectual in character, involving knowledge and to some extent learning, as distinguished from mere skill.

Second. It is an occupation which is pursued largely for others and not merely for one's self.

Third. It is an occupation in which the amount of financial return is not the accepted measure of success.

Is not each of these characteristics found today in business worthily pursued?

The field of knowledge requisite to the more successful conduct of business has been greatly widened by the application to industry not only of chemical, mechanical and electrical science, but also the new science of management; by the increasing difficulties involved in adjusting the relations of labor to capital; by the necessary intertwining of social with industrial problems; by the ever extending scope of state and federal regulation of business. Indeed, mere size and territorial expansion have compelled the business man to enter upon new and broader fields of knowledge in order to match his achievements with his opportunities.

This new development is tending to make business an applied science. Through this development the relative value in business of the trading instinct and of mere shrewdness have, as compared with other faculties, largely diminished. The conception of trade itself has changed. The old idea of a good bargain was a transaction in which one man got the better of another. The new idea of a good contract is a transaction which is good for both parties to it.

Under these new conditions, success in business must mean something very different from mere money-making. In business the able man ordinarily earns a larger income than one less able. So does the able man in the recognized professions—in law, medicine or engineering; and even in those professions more remote from money-making, like the ministry, teaching or social work. The world's demand for efficiency is so great and the supply so small, that the price of efficiency is high in every field of human activity.

The recognized professions, however, definitely reject the size of the financial return as the measure of success. They select as their test, excellence of performance in the broadest sense—and include, among other things, advance in the particular occupation and service to the community. These are the basis of all worthy reputations in the recognized professions. In them a large income is the ordinary incident of success; but he who exaggerates the value of the incident is apt to fail of real success.

To the business of to-day a similar test must be applied. True, in business the earning of profit is something more than an incident of success. It is an essential condition of success; because the continued absence of profit itself spells failure. But while loss spells failure, large profits do not connote success. Success must be sought in business also in excellence of performance; and in business, excellence of performance manifests itself, among other things, in the advancing of methods and processes; in the improvement of products; in more perfect organization, eliminating friction as well as waste; in bettering the condition of the workingmen, developing their faculties and promoting their happiness; and in the establishment of right relations with customers and with the community.

In the field of modern business, so rich in opportunity for the exercise of man's finest and most varied mental faculties and moral qualities, mere money-making cannot be regarded as the legitimate end. Neither can mere growth in bulk or power be admitted as a worthy ambition. Nor can a man nobly mindful of his serious responsibilities to society, view business as a game; since with the conduct of business human happiness or misery is inextricably interwoven.

Real success in business is to be found in achievements comparable rather with those of the artist or the scientist, of the inventor or the statesman. And the joys sought in the profession of business must be like their joys and not the mere vulgar satisfaction which is experienced in the acquisition of money, in the exercise of power or in the frivolous pleasure of mere winning.

It was such real success, comparable with the scientist's, the inventor's, the statesman's, which marked the career of William H. McElwain of Boston, who died in 1908 at the age of forty-one. He had been in business on his own account but thirteen years. Starting without means, he left a fortune, all of which had been earned in the competitive business of shoe manufacturing, without the aid of either patent or trademark. That shows McElwain did not lack the money-making faculty. His company's sales grew from $75,957 in 1895 to $8,691,274 in 1908. He became thus one of the largest shoe manufacturers in the world. That shows he did not lack either ambition or organizing ability. The working capital required for this rapidly growing business was obtained by him without surrendering to outside investors or to bankers any share in the profits of business: all the stock in his company being owned either by himself or his active associates. That shows he did not lack financial skill.

But this money-making faculty, organizing ability and financial skill were with him servants, not masters. He worked for nobler ends than mere accumulation or lust of power. In those thirteen years McElwain made so many advances in the methods and practices of the long-established and prosperous branch of industry in which he was engaged, that he may be said to have revolutionized shoe manufacturing. He found it a trade; he left it an applied science.

This is the kind of thing he did: In 1902 the irregularity in the employment of the shoe worker was brought to his attention. He became greatly impressed with its economic waste, with the misery to the workers and the demoralization which attended it. Irregularity of employment is the worst and most extended of industrial evils. Even in fairly prosperous times the workingmen of America are subjected to enforced idleness and loss of earnings, on the average, probably ten to twenty per cent of their working time. The irregularity of employment was no greater in the McElwain factories than in other shoe factories. The condition was not so bad in shoe manufacturing as in many other branches of industry. But it was bad enough; for shoe manufacturing was a seasonal industry. Most manufacturers closed their factories twice a year. Some manufacturers had two additional slack periods.

This irregularity had been accepted by the trade—by manufacturers and workingmen alike—as inevitable. It had been bowed to as if it were a law of nature—a cross to be borne with resignation. But with McElwain an evil recognized was a condition to be remedied; and he set his great mind to solving the problem of irregularity of employment in his own factories; just as Wilbur Wright applied his mind to the aeroplane, as Bell, his mind to the telephone, and as Edison, his mind to the problems of electric light. Within a few years irregularity of employment had ceased in the McElwain factories; and before his death every one of his many thousand employees could find work three hundred and five days in the year.

Closely allied with the establishment of regularity of employment was the advance made by McElwain in introducing punctual delivery of goods manufactured by his company. Shoes are manufactured mainly upon orders; and the orders are taken on samples submitted. The samples are made nearly a year before the goods are sold to the consumer. Samples for the shoes which will be bought in the spring and summer of 1913 were made in the early summer of 1912. The solicitation of orders on these samples began in the late summer. The manufacture of the shoes commences in November; and the order is filled before July.

Dates of delivery are fixed, of course, when orders are taken; but the dates fixed had not been taken very seriously by the manufacturers; and the trade was greatly annoyed by irregularities in delivery. McElwain recognized the business waste and inconvenience attendant upon such unfulfilled promises. He insisted that an agreement to deliver on a certain day was as binding as an agreement to pay a note on a certain day.

He knew that to make punctual delivery possible, careful study and changes in the methods of manufacture and of distribution were necessary. He made the study; he introduced the radical changes found necessary; and he so perfected his organization that customers could rely absolutely upon delivery on the day fixed. Scientific management practically eliminated the recurring obstacles of the unexpected. To attain this result business invention of a high order was of course necessary—invention directed to the departments both of production and of distribution.

The career of the Filenes of Boston affords another example of success in professionalized business. In 1891 the Filenes occupied two tiny retail stores in Boston. The floor space of each was only twenty feet square. One was a glove stand, the other a women's specialty store. Twenty years later their sales were nearly $5,000,000 a year. In September, 1912 they moved into a new building with more than nine acres of floor space. But the significant thing about their success is not their growth in size or in profits. The trade offers many other examples of similar growth. The pre-eminence of the Filenes lies in the advance which has been made in the nature, the aims and the ideals of retailing, due to their courage, initiative, persistence and fine spirit. They have applied minds of a high order and a fine ethical sense to the prosaic and seemingly uninteresting business of selling women's garments. Instead of remaining petty tradesmen, they have become, in every sense of the word, great merchants.

The Filenes recognized that the function of retail distribution should be undertaken as a social service, equal in dignity and responsibility to the function of production; and that it should be studied with equal intensity in order that the service may be performed with high efficiency, with great economy and with nothing more than a fair profit to the retailer. They recognized that to serve their own customers properly, the relations of the retailer to the producer must be fairly and scientifically adjusted; and, among other things, that it was the concern of the retailer to know whether the goods which he sold were manufactured under conditions which were fair to the workers—fair as to wages, hours of work and sanitary conditions.

But the Filenes recognized particularly their obligations to their own employees. They found as the common and accepted conditions in large retail stores, that the employees had no voice as to the conditions or rules under which they were to work; that the employees had no appeal from policies prescribed by the management; and that in the main they were paid the lowest rate of wages possible under competitive conditions.

In order to insure a more just arrangement for those working in their establishment, the Filenes provided three devices:

First. A system of self-government for employees, administered by the store co-operative association. Working through this association, the employees have the right to appeal from and to veto policies laid down by the management. They may adjust the conditions under which employees are to work, and, in effect, prescribe conditions for themselves.

Second. A system of arbitration, through the operation of which individual employees can call for an adjustment of differences that may exist between themselves and the management as to the permanence of employment, wages, promotion or conditions of work.

Third. A minimum wage scale, which provides that no woman or girl shall work in their store at a wage less than eight dollars a week, no matter what her age may be or what grade of position she may fill.

The Filenes have thus accepted and applied the principles of industrial democracy and of social justice. But they have done more—they have demonstrated that the introduction of industrial democracy and of social justice is at least consistent with marked financial success. They assert that the greater efficiency of their employees shows industrial democracy and social justice to be money-makers. The so-called "practical business man," the narrow money-maker without either vision or ideals, who hurled against the Filenes, as against McElwain, the silly charge of being "theorists," has been answered even on his own low plane of material success.

McElwain and the Filenes are of course exceptional men; but there are in America to-day many with like perception and like spirit. The paths broken by such pioneers will become the peopled highways. Their exceptional methods will become accepted methods. Then the term "Big business" will lose its sinister meaning, and will take on a new significance. "Big business" will then mean business big not in bulk or power, but great in service and grand in manner. "Big business" will mean professionalized business, as distinguished from the occupation of petty trafficking or mere money-making. And as the profession of business develops, the great industrial and social problems expressed in the present social unrest will one by one find solution.

"BIG BUSINESS AND INDUSTRIAL
LIBERTY," FEBRUARY 10, 1912

Business was not an evil to Brandeis, but there was definite evil inherent in businesses so large that they could treat their laborers exactly as they liked and were ungovernable and inefficient. He thought the Steel Trust all too good an example of these phenomena. Like other trusts, it also destroyed the competition that led to creativity, opened new opportunities for each generation, and protected the interests of consumers. He viewed the kind of bigness favored by captains of industry as incompatible with industrial liberty and with democracy and felt it his obligation as a citizen to speak out against it.

In ten years [the Steel Trust] has reaped above a very generous return on its actual capital, $650,000,000. Two-thirds of that still remains as an accumulation held by the corporation for its employees; the other third was distributed in dividends on common stock, originally representing water [i.e., worthless].

The Associated Charities of Pittsburgh recently determined by actual investigation what it costs for a family consisting of husband, wife, and three children, not to live, but barely to subsist. If the common laborers in the steel industry were to work 12 hours a day for 365 days a year they would be unable to earn even that minimum amount; they would fall just $1.50 short of that bare subsistence wage. Of course, it is physically impossible for any man to work 12 hours a day for 365 days. Moreover, there are only two holidays in the steel industry—Christmas and the Fourth of July—and in the shriveling heat of blast furnaces even these holidays are denied. Think of that situation side by side with the enormous profits taken from the American people to be distributed among stockholders of the Steel Trust.

It is a life so inhuman as to make our former Negro slavery infinitely preferable, for the master owned the slave, and tried to keep his property in working order for his own interest. The Steel Trust, on the other hand, looks on its slaves as something to be worked out and thrown aside. The result is physical and moral degeneracy—work, work, work, without recreation or any possibility of relief save that which dissipation brings. The men coming out of these steel mills move on pay day straight to the barroom. Think what such men transmit as a physical and moral heritage to their children and think of our American citizenship for men who live under such conditions.

There is only one explanation. This great corporation, which exemplifies the power of combination, and in connection with which combination has been justified, has made it its first business to prevent combination among its employees when they sought to procure decent working conditions and living conditions. It stamped out, through its immense powers of endurance, one strike after another. It developed a secret service, a system of espionage among its workmen, singling out individuals who favor unionism; and anyone fomenting dissatisfaction with existing conditions, as it was called, was quietly discharged. The trust is buttressed on one hand by the powers of the railroads and on the other by great financial interests; against it stands the poor miserable individual working man.

It has instanced as one of its benefits to its employees, its pension system, but this is only another system by which it deprives the worker of his just due. Nothing is so ever-present in the worker's mind as the fear of old age and his elimination from business thereby. Under the pension system everyone who remains with the corporation may look forward to getting a pension, but he has no right to it. It is absolutely in the discretion of the directors whether or not he shall get it or if it shall be withdrawn even after it has been granted. Anything that may in their opinion indicate that the worker is not loyal or working for the interests of the corporation, as they interpret them, will result in loss of pension.

Here you have a corporation that has made it its cardinal principle of action that its employees must be absolutely subject to its will. It is treason for an employee to participate with other employees for combination. In this corporation, and in other corporations, there is growing up under the guise of welfare work and efforts for more humane conditions for labor, a system which robs the laborer of what little liberty he should have. It is a condition which explains with peculiar force the term "iron master."

Must not this mean that the American who is brought up with the idea of political liberty must surrender what every citizen deems far more important, his industrial liberty? Can this contradiction—our grand political liberty and this industrial slavery—long coexist? Either political liberty will be extinguished or industrial liberty must be restored.

The real cause that is disturbing business today is not the uncertainty as to the interpretation of "reasonable" or "unreasonable" restraint of trade; it is this social unrest of our people in this struggle with which none in our history save the Revolution and the Civil War can be compared.

"TRUSTS, EFFICIENCY AND THE
NEW PARTY," SEPTEMBER 14, 1912

Woodrow Wilson ran for president in 1912 as a progressive on the Democratic ticket, opposed to the continued existence of the trusts. Theodore Roosevelt ran against him, as the candidate of the newly formed Progressive party, on a platform of destruction only of the trusts whose social policies somehow made them hopeless but retention of large business entities regulated by government. Wilson, coached by Brandeis, argued that there came a point at which bigness itself was the problem, and there was no such thing as a "good" trust. It is the difference between these two strains of progressivism that Brandeis attempted to spell out in the articles he wrote during the campaign.

Leaders of the Progressive Party argue that industrial monopolies should be legalized, lest we lose the efficiency of large-scale production and distribution. No argument could be more misleading. The issue of competition *versus* monopoly presents no such alternative as "Shall we have small concerns or large?" "Shall we have ill-equipped plants or well-equipped?"

In the first place, neither the Sherman law nor any of the proposed perfecting amendments (La Follette–Lenroot bill or Stanley bill) contain any prohibition of mere size. Under them a business may *grow* as large as it will or can—without any restriction or without any presumption arising against it. It is only when a monopoly is attempted, or when a business, instead of being allowed to *grow* large, *is made* large by combining competing businesses in restraint of trade, that the Sherman law and the proposed perfecting amendments can have any application. And even then the Sherman law and the proposed amendments would not necessarily restrict size. They merely declare that *if there has been such a combination in restraint of trade* the combiners have the burden of showing that it was reasonable, or, in other words, consistent with the public welfare; and that if such a combination controls more than thirty per cent of the country's business it will, in the absence of explanation, be deemed unreasonable.

In the second place, it may safely be asserted that in America there is no line of business in which all or most concerns or plants must be concentrated in order to attain the size of greatest efficiency. For, while a business may be too small to be efficient, efficiency does not grow indefinitely with increasing size. There is in every line of business a unit of greatest efficiency. What the size of that unit is cannot be determined in advance by a general rule. It will vary in different lines of business and with different concerns in the same line. It will vary with the same concern at different times because of different conditions. What the most efficient size is can be learned definitely only by experience. The unit of greatest efficiency is reached when the disadvantages of size counterbalance the advantages. The unit of greatest efficiency is exceeded when the disadvantages of size outweigh the advantages. For a unit of business may be too large to be efficient as well as too small. And in no American industry is monopoly an essential condition of the greatest efficiency.

The history of American trusts makes this clear. That history shows:

First. No conspicuous American trust owes its existence to the desire for increased efficiency. "Expected economies from combination" figure largely in promoters' prospectuses; but they have never been a compelling motive in the formation of any trust. On the contrary, the purpose of combining has often been to curb efficiency or even to preserve inefficiency, thus frustrating the natural law of survival of the fittest.

Second. No conspicuously profitable trust owes its profits largely to superior efficiency. Some trusts have been very efficient, as have some independent concerns; but conspicuous profits have been secured mainly through control of the market—through the power of monopoly to fix prices—through this exercise of the taxing power.

Third. No conspicuous trust has been efficient enough to maintain long, as against the independents, its proportion of the business of the country without continuing to buy up, from time to time, its successful competitors.

These three propositions are also true of most of the lesser trusts. If there is any exception, the explanation will doubtless be found in extraordinary ability on the part of the managers or unusual trade conditions.

And this further proposition may be added:

Fourth. Most of the trusts which did not secure monopolistic positions have failed to show marked success or efficiency, as compared with independent competing concerns.

THE MOTIVES FOR TRUST BUILDING

The first proposition is strikingly illustrated by the history of the Steel Trust. The main purpose in forming that trust was to eliminate from the steel business the most efficient manufacturer the world has ever known—Andrew Carnegie. The huge price paid for his company was merely the bribe required to induce him to refrain from exercising his extraordinary ability to make steel cheaply. Carnegie could make and sell steel several dollars a ton cheaper than any other concern. Because his competitors were unable to rise to his remarkable efficiency, his business career was killed; and the American people were deprived of his ability—his genius—to produce steel cheaply. As the Stanley Investigating Committee found, the acquisition of the Carnegie Company by the promoters of the Steel Trust was *"not the purchase of a mill, but the retirement of a man."*

Herbert Knox Smith, Commissioner of Corporations, after elaborate investigation, declared:

"The conclusion is inevitable, therefore, that the price paid for the Carnegie Company was largely determined by fear on the part of the organizers of the Steel Corporation of the competition of that concern.

Mr. Carnegie's name in the steel industry had been long synonymous with aggressive competition, and there can be little doubt that the huge price paid for the Carnegie concern was, in considerable measure, for the specific purpose of eliminating a troublesome competitor, and Mr. Carnegie in particular."

. . . The bribe paid to eliminate Carnegie's efficiency was . . . at least $250,000,000. It was paid, as the Stanley Committee finds, to prevent a contest "between fabricators of steel and fabricators of securities; between makers of billets and of bonds." It was paid to save the huge paper values which George W. Perkins and others had recently created by combining into eight grossly overcapitalized corporations a large part of the steel mills of America. No wonder that J. P. Morgan & Co. were panic-stricken at the rumor that Carnegie was to build a tube mill which might reduce the cost of making tubes $10 a ton, when those bankers had recently combined seventeen tube mills (mostly old) of the aggregate value of $19,000,000, had capitalized them at $80,000,000 and taken $20,000,000 of the securities for themselves as promotion fees. The seven other similar consolidations of steel plants floated about the same time had an aggregate capitalization of $437,825,800, of which $43,306,811 was taken by the promoters for their fees.

As Commissioner Herbert Knox Smith reported to the President:

"A steel war might have meant the sudden end of the extraordinary period of speculative activity and profit. On the other hand, an averting of this war, and the coalition of the various great consolidations, if successfully financed, would be a tremendous 'bull' argument. It would afford its promoters an opportunity for enormous stock-market profits through the sale of securities."

So Carnegie was eliminated, and efficiency in steel making was sacrificed in the interest of Wall Street; the United States Steel Corporation was formed; and J. P. Morgan & Co. and their associates took for their services as promoters the additional sum of $62,500,000 in cash values.

THE SOURCES OF MOST PROFITS

The second proposition—that conspicuous trust profits are due mainly to monopoly control of the market—is supported by abundant evidence equally conclusive.

Next to the Standard Oil, the Tobacco Trust is, perhaps, the most prominent of the excessive profit takers . . . In 1908, when the trust earned only 4 per cent on its cigar business, it controlled only about one-eighth of the cigar business of the country. When it earned 103.5 per cent on its smoking tobacco subsidiaries, it controlled three-quarters of the smoking tobacco business of the country.

"The combination's ability to establish and maintain prices without much regard to competition in the principal branches of the business [says Commissioner Smith] . . . is vividly illustrated by the fact that when the internal-revenue tax on tobacco was reduced in 1901 and 1902, the combination maintained its prices at the level which had been established when the tax was increased some years earlier. As a result of this policy it appropriated practically the entire reduction in the tax as additional profit in succeeding years."

That is the kind of efficiency in which trusts particularly excel.

BUYING COMPETITORS

The third proposition—that trusts are not efficient enough to hold their relative positions in the trade as compared with the independents without buying up successful competitors—is also supported by abundant evidence . . .

UNSUCCESSFUL TRUSTS

Of the truth of the fourth proposition, stated above—that most of the trusts which did not secure monopolistic positions have failed to show marked success or efficiency as compared with the independent competing concerns—every reader familiar with business must be able to supply evidence. Let him who doubts examine the stock quotations of long-established industrials and look particularly at the common stock which ordinarily represents the "expected economies" or "efficiency" of combination . . . perhaps the most conspicuous industrial trust which was not able to secure control of the market is the International Mercantile Marine. That company had behind it the ability and resources of J. P. Morgan & Co., and their great influence with the railroads . . . It could not secure control of the Atlantic trade, and in the seven years since its organization has not paid a dividend on its $100,000,000 of stock. Its common [stock] stands at 5 1/8, its preferred at 18 7/8 . . . On the other hand, the $120,000,000 stock of the Pullman Company, which has like influence with the railroads but succeeded in securing a monopoly, stands at 170 3/4.

Efficient or inefficient, every company which controls the market is a "money-maker." No, the issue of "Competition *versus* Monopoly" cannot be distorted into the issue of "Small Concerns *versus* Large." The unit in business may, of course, be too small to be efficient, and the larger unit has been a common incident of monopoly. But a unit too small for efficiency is by no means a necessary incident of competition. And a unit *too large* to be efficient is no uncommon incident of monopoly. Man's work often outruns the capacity of the individual man; and no matter how good the organization, the capacity of an individual man usually determines the success or failure of a particular enterprise—not only financially to the owners but in service to the community. Organization can do much to make concerns more efficient. Organization can do much to make larger units possible and profitable. But the efficacy even of organization has its bounds. There is a point where the centrifugal force necessarily exceeds the centripetal. And organization can never supply the combined judgment, initiative, enterprise and authority which must come from the chief executive officer. Nature sets a limit to his possible achievement.

As the Germans say: "Care is taken that the trees do not scrape the skies."

"THE NEW ENGLAND RAILROAD SITUATION," 1912

Brandeis fought a fierce nine-year war with the New Haven Railroad and the monopoly that it and its guiding spirit, J. P. Morgan, were gaining over public transportation throughout a large part of the country. Many battles were lost, but the war finally was won in 1914 when President Woodrow Wilson's attorney general forced the company to divest itself of the Boston & Maine Railroad as well as all its steamship and trolley lines. This article details the horrors Brandeis saw resulting from monopolies and from bigness in general.

The breakdown of transportation in New England under the New Haven monopoly has become obvious. Demoralized and curtailed freight service, antiquated equipment, frequent wrecks, discontented employees, heavy depreciation in the market value of securities, and huge borrowing on short-time notes at high interest are the accumulated evidences of that deterioration in our transportation system which has been in process during the past eight years of aggressive monopolization . . .

Truth *magazine received funds from the New Haven Railroad, a Brandeis target for almost a decade. In 1913, when Wilson was choosing his cabinet and the railroads feared Brandeis might be named attorney general,* Truth *ran a series of editorials claiming that he was dishonest, self-serving, and unethical and that if he was put in the cabinet his lack of real principles would show itself. One of the attacks was accompanied by this cartoon, labeled "The Substance and the Shadow," published on February 5, 1913. (University of Louisville Archives)*

While the policy of monopoly is the fundamental cause of the deterioration of our transportation system, it has itself bred subsidiary causes; and of these subsidiary causes excessive bigness is probably the most potent.

Excessive bigness often attends monopoly; but the evils of excessive bigness are something distinct from and additional to the evils of monopoly. A business may be too big to be efficient without being a monopoly; and it may be a monopoly and yet (so far as concerns size) may be well within the limits of efficiency. Unfortunately, the so-called New Haven system suffers from both excessive bigness and from monopoly.

THE MONOPOLY

The New Haven monopoly of transportation in New England, now substantially complete, rests upon ownership or legal control of an effective interest in:

Another Truth *cartoon from the same period. Brandeis's being labeled "Ishmael" in it is of course an oblique and negative reference to his Jewishness. (University of Louisville Archives)*

First. Substantially all the railroads in Maine, New Hampshire, Massachusetts, Rhode Island and Connecticut, except the Grand Trunk's line from Canada to New London and to Portland, the Canadian Pacific Line through northern Maine, and the Bangor and Aroostook.

Second. Substantially all the trolley lines in Rhode Island and Connecticut, the most important in western and central Massachusetts, and some in Maine, New Hampshire, Vermont and New York.

Third. Substantially all the steamship lines from any of the New England States to New York or Philadelphia or Baltimore . . .

All railroads entering Boston (unless the Boston, Revere Beach and Lynn be called a railroad and is independent) are either owned by the New Haven, or controlled legally or through an effective interest; for it has such a partnership interest also in the Boston and Albany. All the coastwise steamship lines sailing from Boston for New York, Philadelphia or Baltimore are owned or controlled legally or influenced through an effective interest.

THEY ALL WANT MR. BRANDEIS NOW

In 1910 Brandeis represented business organizations when the railroads asked the Interstate Commerce Commission for an increase in freight rates. He commented that if they were more efficient, the railroads could save $1 million a day. The cartoon shows executives of various railroads begging him to come to work for them. In fact, he offered to meet with them to discuss details of how they could save money but said he would accept no salary. The railroads ignored his offer. (Boston Post, *University of Louisville Archives*)

THE NEW HAVEN SUPERIOR TO OUR LAW

Between a [local] street railway, gas or electric light monopoly, existing under such conditions [of government regulation], and the New Haven monopoly in transportation there is no real resemblance. The New Haven claims rights under the laws of seven States and, in addition, under acts of Congress. Massachusetts has, except in strictly local matters, no effective legal control over the company. Neither the Massachusetts legislature, nor any commission it may create, can regulate the New Haven in any of its important functions. Any statute attempting to do so would be void as interfering with interstate commerce.

And Massachusetts cannot enforce her will even as to intrastate matters, as it does in the case of street railways, gas and other street-using corporations; because the railroad franchises cannot be taken without paying compensation. Massachusetts prohibited the New Haven from issuing stock without the consent of the railroad commissioners. The New Haven disobeyed the laws with impunity. Massachusetts laws prohibited the New Haven from issuing more bonds than stock. The New Haven disobeyed the laws with impunity. Massachusetts laws prohibited the New Haven from acquiring steamship lines. The New Haven disobeyed the laws with impunity. Massachusetts laws prohibited the New Haven from consolidating with other companies. The New Haven disobeyed the laws with impunity. In each instance these prohibitions were a part of Massachusetts' plan for regulating railroad companies; but the New Haven claimed the right to act under the laws of another State, and successfully defied Massachusetts . . . Regulation cannot produce efficient and enlightened railroad operation in the interests of the public; and without that the community cannot get satisfactory service . . . To abandon competition in transportation and rely upon regulation as a safeguard against the evils of monopoly would be like surrendering liberty and regulating despotism.

[A section follows listing the number and size of the railroads, trolleys, and steamship lines controlled by the New Haven.]

INTENSIVE RAILROADING

The bulk of the New Haven properties is huge; but it is not the huge bulk alone which renders impossible the task of efficient management. The New Haven properties are diverse in character and widely scattered; but lt is not these facts which present the most serious difficulty in their operation. The insuperable obstacle to efficient management of the New Haven properties, in addition to the status of monopoly, lies in the fact that almost each one of these many diverse properties, agglomerated into a so-called system, presents many problems which are not only important, but are individual to the particular property and to the particular community served by it. That results necessarily from the conditions surrounding transportation in New England.

For the solution of each of these problems there is required, not only separate investigation, but careful weighing of relevant facts. In order to secure unity of purpose and action, all these problems must be passed upon ultimately by the same chief executives. Now, the number of such decisions which any man can make, however able and hard-working he may be, and the extent of supervision which any man can effectively apply, are obviously very limited. Organization may accomplish much in extending the scope of work possible for an executive; but there is an obvious limit, also, to the efficiency of organization; for the success of the whole enterprise demands that the executive must be able to comprehend all the important facts bearing upon the properties. Real efficiency in any business in which conditions are ever changing must ultimately depend, in large measure, upon the correctness of judgment formed from day to day on the problems as they arise. And it is an essential of sound judgment that the executives have time to know and correlate the facts.

"INTERLOCKING DIRECTORATES," 1912

The continued success of the trusts, Brandeis found, was dependent on their access to huge amounts of capital. These came from banks, which invested heavily in the trusts and were tied to them through interlocking directorates. It was the series of articles about the Money Trust that Brandeis wrote in 1912 and that were published in Harper's Weekly *that had such an impact on presidential candidate Woodrow Wilson. Brandeis's ideas not only underlay the "new Freedom" platform on which Wilson campaigned against Theodore Roosevelt's "New Nationalism," but culminated in Wilson's creation of the Federal Reserve Board. Brandeis's articles were collected and published as a volume entitled* Other People's Money, *subsequently reprinted numerous times.*

The following passage concentrates on interlocking directorates and on Brandeis's bête noire, J. P. Morgan.

A single example will illustrate the vicious circle of control—the endless chain—through which our financial oligarchy now operates:

J. P. Morgan (or a partner), a director of the New York, New Haven, & Hartford Railroad, causes that company to sell to J. P. Morgan & Co. an issue of bonds. J. P. Morgan & Co. borrow the money with which to pay for the bonds from the Guaranty Trust Company, of which Mr. Morgan (or a partner) is a director. J. P. Morgan & Co. sell the bonds to the Penn Mutual Life Insurance Company, of which Mr. Morgan (or a partner) is a director. The New Haven spends the proceeds of the bonds in purchasing steel rails from the United States Steel Corporation, of which Mr. Morgan (or a partner) is a director. The United States Steel Corporation spends the proceeds of the rails in purchasing electrical supplies from the General Electric Company, of which Mr. Morgan (or a partner) is a director. The General Electric sells supplies to the Western Union Telegraph Company; and in both Mr. Morgan (or a partner) is a director. The Telegraph Company has an exclusive wire contract with the Reading, of which Mr. Morgan (or a partner) is a director. The Reading buys its passenger cars from the Pullman Company, of which Mr. Morgan (or a partner) is a director. The Pullman Company buys (for local use) locomotives from the Baldwin Locomotive Company, of which Mr. Morgan (or a partner) is a director. The Reading, the General Electric, the Steel Corporation and the New Haven, like the Pullman, buy locomotives from the Baldwin. The Steel Corporation, the Telephone Company, the New Haven, the Reading, the Pullman and the Baldwin Companies, like the Western Union, buy electrical supplies from the General Electric. The Baldwin, the Pullman, the Reading, the Telephone, the Telegraph and the General Electric companies, like the New Haven, buy steel products from the Steel Corporation. Each and every one of the companies last named markets its securities through J. P. Morgan & Co.; each deposits its funds with J. P. Morgan & Co.; and with these funds of each, the firm enters upon further operations.

NEW STATE ICE COMPANY V. LIEBMANN, 1932

An Oklahoma statute required new ice companies to obtain a certificate of public convenience and necessity from the state. The law's pur-

pose was to avoid the kind of duplication of plants and delivery service that resulted in higher costs for consumers. The Supreme Court struck it down as an undue interference with the right of property. Brandeis had long emphasized encouragement of competition, but substitution of judicial beliefs for the will of the majority in economic policy ran counter to his thinking about the nature of democracy, and he dissented here. Finding the briefs presented by Oklahoma insufficiently backed by facts, Brandeis wrote fourteen heavily footnoted pages to demonstrate the Oklahoma statute's rationality. As the footnotes were designed to include the relevant facts and the sources for them, they took up far more of the fourteen pages than did his text.

MR. JUSTICE BRANDEIS, dissenting.

Chapter 147 of the Session Laws of Oklahoma, 1925, declares that the manufacture of ice for sale and distribution is "a public business"; confers upon the Corporation Commission in respect to it the powers of regulation customarily exercised over public utilities; and provides specifically for securing adequate service. The statute makes it a misdemeanor to engage in the business without a license from the Commission; directs that the license shall not issue except pursuant to a prescribed written application, after a formal hearing upon adequate notice both to the community to be served and to the general public, and a showing upon competent evidence, of the necessity "at the place desired;" and it provides that the application may be denied, among other grounds, if "the facts proved at said hearing disclose that the facilities for the manufacture, sale and distribution of ice by some person, firm or corporation already licensed by said Commission at said point, community or place are sufficient to meet the public needs therein."

Under a license, so granted, the New State Ice Company is, and for some years has been, engaged in the manufacture, sale and distribution of ice at Oklahoma City, and has invested in that business $500,000. While it was so engaged, Liebmann, without having obtained or applied for a license, purchased a parcel of land in that city and commenced the construction thereon of an ice plant for the purpose of entering the business in competition with the plaintiff. To enjoin him from doing so this suit was brought by the Ice Company. Liebmann contends that the manufacture of ice for sale and distribution is not a public business; that it is a private business and, indeed, a common calling; that the right to engage in a common calling is one of the fundamental liberties guaranteed by the due process clause; and that to make his right to engage in that calling dependent upon a finding of public necessity deprives him of liberty and property in violation of the Fourteenth Amendment.

First. The Oklahoma statute makes entry into the business of manufacturing ice for sale and distribution dependent, in effect, upon a certificate of public convenience and necessity. Such a certificate was unknown to the common law. It is a creature of the machine age, in which plants have displaced tools and businesses are substituted for trades. The purpose of requiring it is to promote the public interest by preventing waste. Particularly in those businesses in which interest and depreciation charges on plant constitute a large element in the cost of production, experience has taught that the financial burdens incident to unnecessary duplication of facilities are likely to bring high rates and poor service. There, cost is usually dependent, among other things, upon volume; and division of possible patronage among competing concerns may so raise the unit cost of operation as to make it impossible to provide adequate service at reasonable rates. The introduction in the United States of the certificate of public convenience and necessity marked the growing conviction that under certain circumstances free competition might be harmful to the community and that, when it was so, absolute freedom to enter the business of one's choice should be denied.

Long before the enactment of the Oklahoma statute here challenged a like requirement had become common in the United States in some lines of business. The certificate was required first for railroads; then for street railways; then for other public utilities whose operation is dependent upon the grant of some special privilege . . .

Second. Oklahoma declared the business of manufacturing ice for sale and distribution a "public business;" that is, a public utility. So far as appears, it was the first State to do so. Of course, a legislature cannot by mere legislative fiat convert a business into a public utility. But the conception of a public utility is not static. The welfare of the community may require that the business of supplying ice be made a public utility, as well as the business of supplying water or any other necessary commodity or service. If the business is, or can be made, a public utility, it must be possible to make the issue of a certificate a prerequisite to engaging in it.

Whether the local conditions are such as to justify converting a private business into a public one is a matter primarily for the determination of the state legislature. Its determination is subject to judicial review; but the usual presumption of validity attends the enactment . . . The action of the State must be held valid unless clearly arbitrary, capricious or unreasonable. "The legislature being familiar with local conditions is, primarily, the judge of the necessity of such enactments. The mere fact that a court may differ with the legislature in its views of public policy, or that judges may hold views inconsistent with the propriety of the legislation in question, affords no ground for judicial interference." Whether the grievances are real or fancied, whether the remedies are wise or foolish, are not matters about which the Court may concern itself. "Our present duty is to pass upon the statute before us, and if it has been enacted upon a belief of evils that is not arbitrary we cannot measure their extent against the estimate of the legislature." A decision that the legislature's belief of evils was arbitrary, capricious and unreasonable may not be made without enquiry into the facts with reference to which it acted.

Third . . . The function of the Court is primarily to determine whether the conditions in Oklahoma are such that the legislature could not reasonably conclude (1) that the public welfare required treating the manufacture of ice for sale and distribution as a "public business"; and (2) that in order to ensure to the inhabitants of some communities an adequate supply of ice at reasonable rates it was necessary to give the Commission power to exclude the establishment of an additional ice plant in places where the community was already well served. Unless the Court can say that the Federal Constitution confers an absolute right to engage anywhere in the business of manufacturing ice for sale, it cannot properly decide that the legislature acted unreasonably without first ascertaining what was the experience of Oklahoma in respect to the ice business. The relevant facts appear, in part, of record. Others are matters of common knowledge to those familiar with the ice business. They show the actual conditions, or the beliefs, on which the legislators acted. In considering these matters we do not, in a strict sense, take judicial notice of them as embodying statements of uncontrovertible facts. Our function is only to determine the reasonableness of the legislature's belief in the existence of evils and in the effectiveness of the remedy provided. In performing this function we have no occasion to consider whether all the statements of fact which may be the basis of the prevailing belief are well-founded; and we have, of course, no right to weigh conflicting evidence.

(A) In Oklahoma a regular supply of ice may reasonably be considered a necessary of life, comparable to that of water, gas and electricity. The climate, which heightens the need of ice for comfortable and wholesome living, precludes resort to the natural product. There, as elsewhere, the development of the manufactured ice industry in recent years has been attended by deep-seated alterations in the economic structure and by radical changes in habits of popular thought and living. Ice has come to be regarded as a household necessity, indispensable to the preservation of food and so to economical household management and the maintenance of health. Its commercial uses are extensive. In urban communities, they absorb a large proportion of the total amount of ice manufactured for sale. The transportation, storage and distribution of a great part of the nation's food supply is dependent upon a continuous, and dependable supply of ice. It appears from the record that in certain parts of Oklahoma a large trade in dairy and other products has been built up as a result of rulings of the Corporation Commission under the Act of 1925, compelling licensed manufacturers to serve agricultural communities; and that this trade would be destroyed if the supply of ice were withdrawn. We cannot say that the legislature of Oklahoma acted arbitrarily in declaring that ice is an article of primary necessity, in industry and agriculture as well as in the household, partaking of the fundamental character of electricity, gas, water, transportation and communication . . .

In Oklahoma the mechanical household refrigerator is still an article of relative luxury. Legislation essential to the protection of individuals of limited or no means is not invalidated by the circumstance that other individuals are financially able to protect themselves. The businesses of power companies and of common carriers by street railway, steam railroad or motor vehicle fall within the field of public control, although it is possible, for a relatively modest outlay, to install individual power plants, or to purchase motor vehicles for private carriage of passengers or goods. The question whether in Oklahoma the means of securing refrigeration otherwise than by ice manufactured for sale and distribution has become so general as to destroy popular dependence upon ice plants is one peculiarly appropriate for the determination of its legislature and peculiarly inappropriate for determination by this Court, which cannot have knowledge of all the relevant facts.

The business of supplying ice is not only a necessity, like that of supplying food or clothing or shelter, but the legislature could also consider that it is one which lends itself peculiarly to monopoly. Characteristically the business is conducted in local plants with a market narrowly limited in area, and this for the reason that ice manufactured at a distance cannot effectively compete with a plant on the ground. In small towns and rural communities the duplication of plants, and in larger communities the duplication of delivery service, is wasteful and ultimately burdensome to consumers. At the same time the relative ease and cheapness with which an ice plant may be constructed exposes the industry to destructive and frequently ruinous competition. Competition in the industry tends to be destructive because ice plants have a determinate capacity, and inflexible fixed charges and operating costs, and because in a market of limited area the volume of sales is not readily expanded. Thus, the erection of a new plant in a locality already adequately served often causes managers to go to extremes in cutting prices in order to secure business. Trade journals and reports of association meetings of ice manufacturers bear ample witness to the hostility of the industry to such competition, and to its unremitting efforts, through trade associations, informal agreements, combination of delivery systems, and in particular through the consolidation of plants, to protect markets and prices against competition of any character.

That these forces were operative in Oklahoma prior to the passage of the Act under review, is apparent from the record. Thus, it was testified that in only six or seven localities in the State containing, in the aggregate, not more than 235,000 of the total population of approximately 2,000,000, was there "a semblance of competition"; and that even in those localities the prices of ice were ordinarily uniform. The balance of the population was, and still is, served by companies enjoying complete monopoly. Where there was competition, it often resulted to the disadvantage rather than the advantage of the public, both in respect to prices and to service. Some communities were without ice altogether, and the State was without means of assuring their supply. There is abundant evidence of widespread dissatisfaction with ice service prior to the Act of 1925, and of material improvement in the situation subsequently. It is stipulated in the record that the ice industry as a whole in Oklahoma has acquiesced in and accepted the Act and the status which it creates.

(B) The statute under review rests not only upon the facts just detailed but upon a long period of experience in more limited regulation dating back to the first year of Oklahoma's statehood. For 17 years prior to the passage of the Act of 1925, the Corporation Commission under §13 of the Act of June 10, 1908, had exercised jurisdiction over the rates, practices and service of ice plants, its action in each case, however, being predicated upon a finding that the company complained of enjoyed a "virtual monopoly" of the ice business in the community which it served . . . By formal orders, the Commission repeatedly fixed or approved prices to be charged in particular communities; required ice to be sold without discrimination and to be distributed as equitably as possible to the extent of the capacity of the plant; forbade short weights and ordered scales to be carried on delivery wagons and ice to be weighed upon the customer's request; and undertook to compel sanitary practices in the manufacture of ice and courteous service of patrons. Many of these regulations, other than those fixing prices, were embodied in a general order to all ice companies, issued July 15, 1921, and are still in effect. Informally, the Commission adjusted a much greater volume of complaints of a similar nature. It appears from the record that for some years prior to the Act of 1925 one day of each week was reserved by the Commission to hear complaints relative to the ice business . . .

Fourth. Can it be said in the light of these facts that it was not an appropriate exercise of legislative discretion to authorize the Commission to deny a license to enter the business in localities where necessity for another plant did not exist? The need of some remedy for the evil of destructive competition, where competition existed, had been and was widely felt. Where competition did not exist, the propriety of public regulation had been proven. Many communities were not supplied with ice at all. The particular remedy adopted was not enacted hastily. The statute was based upon a long-established state policy recognizing the public importance of the ice business, and upon 17 years' legislative and administrative experience in the regulation of it. The advisability of treating the ice business as a public utility and of applying to it the certificate of convenience and necessity had been under consideration for many years. Similar legislation had been enacted in Oklahoma under similar circumstances with respect to other public services. The measure bore a substantial relation to the evils found to exist. Under these circumstances, to hold the Act void as being unreasonable, would, in my opinion involve the exercise not of the function of judicial review, but the function of a super-legislature . . .

Fifth. The claim is that manufacturing ice for sale and distribution is a business inherently private, and, in effect, that no state of facts can justify denial of the right to engage in it. To supply one's self with water, electricity, gas, ice or any other article, is inherently a matter of private concern. So also may be the business of supplying the same articles to others for compensation. But the business of supplying to others, for compensation, any article or service whatsoever may become a matter of public concern. Whether it is, or is not, depends upon the conditions existing in the community affected. If it is a matter of public concern, it may be regulated, whatever the business. The public's concern may be limited to a single feature of the business, so that the needed protection can be secured by a relatively slight degree of regulation. Such is the concern over possible incompetence, which dictates the licensing of dentists, or the concern over possible dishonesty, which led to the licensing of auctioneers or hawkers. On the other hand, the public's concern about a particular business may be so pervasive and varied as to require constant detailed supervision and a very high degree of regulation. Where this is true, it is common to speak of the business as being a "public" one, although it is privately owned. It is to such businesses that the designation "public utility" is commonly applied; or they are spoken of as "affected with a public interest."

Sixth. It is urged specifically that manufacturing ice for sale and distribution is a common calling; and that the right to engage in a common calling is one of the fundamental liberties guaranteed by the due process clause. To think of the ice-manufacturing business as a common calling is difficult; so recent is it in origin and so peculiar in character . . .

It is settled that the police power commonly invoked in aid of health, safety and morals, extends equally to the promotion of the public welfare . . . While, ordinarily, free competition in the common callings has been encouraged, the public welfare may at other times demand that monopolies be created. Upon this principle is based our whole modern practice of public utility regulation. It is no objection to the validity of the statute here assailed that it fosters monopoly. That, indeed, is its design. The certificate of public convenience and invention is a device a recent social-economic invention—through which the monopoly is kept under effective control by vesting in a commission the power to terminate it whenever that course is required in the public interest. To grant any monopoly to any person as a favor is forbidden even if terminable. But where, as here, there is reasonable ground for the legislative conclusion that in order to secure a necessary service at reasonable rates, it may be necessary to curtail the right to enter the calling, it is, in my opinion, consistent with the due process clause to do so, whatever the nature of the business. The existence of such power in the legislature seems indispensable in our ever-changing society . . .

Eighth. The people of the United States are now confronted with an emergency more serious than war. Misery is wide-spread, in a time, not of scarcity, but of over-abundance. The long-continued depression has brought unprecedented unemployment, a catastrophic fall in commodity prices and a volume of economic losses which threatens our financial institutions. Some people believe that the existing conditions threaten even the stability of the capitalistic system. Economists are searching for the causes of this disorder and are reexamining the bases of our industrial structure. Business men are seeking possible remedies. Most of them realize that failure to distribute widely the profits of industry has been a prime cause of our present plight. But rightly or wrongly, many persons think that one of the major contributing causes has been unbridled competition. Increasingly, doubt is expressed whether it is economically wise, or morally right, that men should be permitted to add to the producing facilities of an industry which is already suffering from over-capacity. In justification of that doubt, men point to the excess-capacity of our productive facilities resulting from their vast expansion without corresponding increase in the consumptive capacity of the people. They assert that through improved methods of manufacture, made possible by advances in science and invention and vast accumulation of capital, our industries had become capable of producing from thirty to one hundred per cent. more than was consumed even in days of vaunted prosperity; and that the present capacity will, for a long time, exceed the needs of business. All agree that irregularity in employment—the greatest of our evils—cannot be overcome unless production and consumption are more nearly balanced. Many insist there must be some form of economic control. There are plans for proration. There are many proposals for stabilization. And some thoughtful men of wide business experience insist that all projects for stabilization and proration must prove futile unless, in some way, the equivalent of the certificate of public convenience and necessity is made a prerequisite to embarking new capital in an industry in which the capacity already exceeds the production schedules.

Whether that view is sound nobody knows. The objections to the proposal are obvious and grave. The remedy might bring evils worse than the present disease. The obstacles to success seem insuperable. The economic and social sciences are largely uncharted seas. We have been none too successful in the modest essays in economic control already entered upon. The new proposal involves a vast extension of the area of control. Merely to acquire the knowledge essential as a basis for the exercise of this multitude of judgments would be a formidable task; and each of the thousands of these judgments would call for some measure of prophecy. Even more serious are the obstacles to success inherent in the demands which execution of the project would make upon human intelligence and upon the character of men. Man is weak and his judgment is at best fallible.

Yet the advances in the exact sciences and the achievements in invention remind us that the seemingly impossible sometimes happens. There are many men now living who were in the habit of using the age-old expression: "It is as impossible as flying." The discoveries in physical science, the triumphs in invention, attest the value of the process of trial and error. In large measure, these advances have been due to experimentation. In those fields experimentation has, for two centuries, been not only free but encouraged. Some people assert that our present plight is due, in part, to the limitations set by courts upon experimentation in the fields of social and economic science; and to the discouragement to which proposals for betterment there have been subjected otherwise. There must be power in the States and the Nation to remould, through experimentation, our economic practices and institutions to meet changing social and economic needs. I cannot believe that the framers of the Fourteenth Amendment, or the States which ratified it, intended to deprive us of the power to correct the evils of technological unemployment and excess productive capacity which have attended progress in the useful arts.

To stay experimentation in things social and economic is a grave responsibility. Denial of the right to experiment may be fraught with serious consequences to the Nation. It is one of the happy incidents of the federal system that a single courageous State may, if its citizens choose, serve as a laboratory; and try novel social and economic experiments without risk to the rest of the country. This Court has the power to prevent an experiment. We may strike down the statute which embodies it on the ground that, in our opinion, the measure is arbitrary, capricious or unreasonable. We have power to do this, because the due process clause has been held by the Court applicable to matters of substantive law as well as to matters of procedure. But in the exercise of this high power, we must be ever on our guard, lest we erect our prejudices into legal principles. If we would guide by the light of reason, we must let our minds be bold.

LIGGETT CO. V. LEE, 1932

Florida imposed heavier license fees on stores that were part of multi-county chains than on independent shops or groups of independently owned stores that operated as cooperatives. Brandeis was convinced that both businesses and consumers ought to be organized into cooperatives. He used the occasion of his dissent to reiterate the social and economic problems caused by corporations by presenting a parade of facts, backed up by copious quotes from and references to books and articles by economists, congressional hearings, and government reports.

MR. JUSTICE BRANDEIS, dissenting in part.

The Florida law is general in its terms. It prohibits the operation . . . of any retail store without securing annually a license; and provides, among other things, for annual fees which are in part graduated. If the owner operates only one store the state fee is $5; if more than one, the fee for the additional stores rises by step increases, dependent upon both the number operated and whether all operated are located in a single county. The highest fee is for a store in excess of 75. If all of the stores are located in a single county, the fee for each store in excess of 75 is $40; if all are not located in the same county the fee is $50. Under this law, the owner of 100 stores not located in a single county pays for each store operated, on the average, $33.65; and if they were located in a single county the owner would pay for each store, on the average, $25.20. If the 100 stores were independently owned (although operated cooperatively as a so-called "voluntary chain") the annual fee for each would be only $5 . . .

The plaintiffs are thirteen corporations which engage in Florida exclusively in intrastate commerce. Each (except one) owns and operates a chain of retail stores within the State and some operate stores in more than one county . . .

If a State believes that adequate protection against harm apprehended or experienced can be secured, without revoking the corporate privilege, by imposing thereafter upon corporations the handicap of higher, discriminatory license fees as compensation for the privilege, I know of nothing in the Fourteenth Amendment to prevent it from making the experiment . . .

Whether the citizens of Florida are wise in seeking to discourage the operation of chain stores is, obviously, a matter with which this Court has no concern. Nor need it, in my opinion, consider whether the differences in license fees employed to effect such discouragement are inherently reasonable, since the plaintiffs are at liberty to refuse to pay the compensation demanded for the corporate privilege and withdraw from the State, if they consider the price more than the privilege is worth. But a review of the legislation of the several States by which all restraints on corporate size and activity were removed, and a consideration of the economic and social effects of such removal, will help to an understanding of Anti–Chain Store Laws; and will show that the discriminatory license fees prescribed by Florida, even if treated merely as a form of taxation, were laid for a purpose which may be appropriately served by taxation, and that the specific means employed to favor the individual retailer are not constitutionally objectionable.

Second. The prevalence of the corporation in America has led men of this generation to act, at times, as if the privilege of doing business in corporate form were inherent in the citizen; and has led them to accept the evils attendant upon the free and unrestricted use of the corporate mechanism as if these evils were the inescapable price of civilized life and, hence, to be borne with resignation. Throughout the greater part of our history a different view prevailed. Although the value of this instrumentality in commerce and industry was fully recognized, incorporation for business was commonly denied long after it had been freely granted for religious, educational and charitable purposes. It was denied because of fear. Fear of encroachment upon the liberties and opportunities of the individual. Fear of the subjection of labor to capital. Fear of monopoly. Fear that the absorption of capital by corporations, and their perpetual life, might bring evils similar to those which attended mortmain.

There was a sense of some insidious menace inherent in large aggregations of capital, particularly when held by corporations. So, at first, the corporate privilege was granted sparingly; and only when the grant seemed necessary in order to procure for the community some specific benefit otherwise unattainable. The later enactment of general incorporation laws does not signify that the apprehension of corporate domination had been overcome. The desire for business expansion created an irresistible demand for more charters; and it was believed that under general laws embodying safeguards of universal application the scandals and favoritism incident to special incorporation could be avoided. The general laws, which long embodied severe restrictions upon size and upon the scope of corporate activity, were, in part, an expression of the desire for equality of opportunity . . .

(a) Limitation upon the amount of the authorized capital of business corporations was long universal . . . (b) Limitations upon the scope of a business corporation's powers and activity were also long universal . . . (c) The removal by the leading industrial States of the limitations upon the size and powers of business corporations appears to have been due, not to their conviction that maintenance of the restrictions was undesirable in itself, but to the conviction that it was futile to insist upon them; because local restriction would be circumvented by foreign incorporation. Indeed, local restriction seemed worse than futile. Lesser States, eager for the revenue derived from the traffic in charters, had removed safeguards from their own incorporation laws. Companies were early formed to provide charters for corporations in states where the cost was lowest and the laws least restrictive. The states joined in advertising their wares. The race was not one of diligence but of laxity. Incorporation under such laws was possible; and the great industrial States yielded in order not to lose wholly the prospect of the revenue and the control incident to domestic incorporation.

Third. Able, discerning scholars have pictured for us the economic and social results of thus removing all limitations upon the size and activities of business corporations and of vesting in their managers vast powers once exercised by stockholders—results not designed by the States and long unsuspected. They show that size alone gives to giant corporations a social significance not attached ordinarily to smaller units of private enterprise. Through size, corporations, once merely an efficient tool employed by individuals in the conduct of private business, have become an institution—an institution which has brought such concentration of economic power that so-called private corporations are sometimes able to dominate the State. The typical business corporation of the last century, owned by a small group of individuals, managed by their owners, and limited in size by their personal wealth, is being supplanted by huge concerns in which the lives of tens or hundreds of thousands of employees and the property of tens or hundreds of thousands of investors are subjected, through the corporate mechanism, to the control of a few men. Ownership has been separated from control; and this separation has removed many of the checks which formerly operated to curb the misuse of wealth and power. And as ownership of the shares is becoming continually more dispersed, the power which formerly accompanied ownership is becoming increasingly concentrated in the hands of a few. The changes thereby wrought in the lives of the workers, of the owners and of the general public, are so fundamental and far-reaching as to lead these scholars to compare the evolving "corporate system" with the feudal system; and to lead other men of insight and experience to assert that this "master institution of civilised life" is committing it to the rule of a plutocracy.

The data submitted in support of these conclusions indicate that in the United States the process of absorption has already advanced so far that perhaps two-thirds of our industrial wealth has passed from individual possession to the ownership of large corporations whose shares are dealt in on the stock exchange; that 200 non-banking corporations, each with assets in excess of $90,000,000, control directly about one-fourth of all our national wealth, and that their influence extends far beyond the assets under their direct control; that these 200 corporations, while nominally controlled by about 2,000 directors are actually dominated by a few hundred persons—the negation of industrial democracy. Other writers have shown that, coincident with the growth of these giant corporations, there has occurred a marked concentration of individual wealth, and that the resulting disparity in incomes is a major cause of the existing depression. Such is the Frankenstein monster which States have created by their corporation laws.

Fourth. Among these 200 corporations, each with assets in excess of $90,000,000, are five of the plaintiffs. These five have in the aggregate, $820,000,000 of assets; and they operate, in the several States, an aggregate of 19,718 stores. A single one of these giants operates nearly 16,000. Against these plaintiffs, and other owners of multiple stores, the individual retailers of Florida are engaged in a struggle to preserve their independence—perhaps a struggle for existence. The citizens of the State, considering themselves vitally interested in this seemingly unequal struggle, have undertaken to aid the individual retailers by subjecting the owners of multiple stores to the handicap of higher license fees. They may have done so merely in order to preserve competition. But their purpose may have been a broader and deeper one. They may have believed that the chain store, by furthering the concentration of wealth and of power and by promoting absentee ownership, is thwarting American ideals; that it is making impossible equality of opportunity; that it is converting independent tradesmen into clerks; and that it is sapping the resources, the vigor and the hope of the smaller cities and towns . . .

The purpose of the Florida statute is not, like ordinary taxation, merely to raise revenue. Its main purpose is social and economic. The chain store is treated as a thing menacing the public welfare. The aim of the statute, at the lowest, is to preserve the competition of the independent stores with the chain stores; at the highest, its aim is to eliminate altogether the corporate chain stores from retail distribution . . . The legislation reminds of that by which Florida and other States, in order to eliminate the "premium system" in merchandising, exacted high license fees of merchants who offered trading stamps with their goods.

The plaintiffs discuss the broad question whether the power to tax may be used for the purpose of curbing, or of exterminating, the chain stores by whomsoever owned. It is settled that a State "may carry out a policy" by "adjusting its revenue laws and taxing system in such a way as to favor certain industries or forms of industry." And since the Fourteenth Amendment "was not intended to compel the State to adopt an iron rule of equal taxation," it may exempt from taxation kinds of business which it wishes to promote; and may burden more heavily kinds of business which it wishes to discourage. It protects, by the oleomargarine laws, our farmers and dairymen from the competition of other Americans. It eliminated, by a prohibitive tax, the issue of state bank notes in competition with those of national banks. Such is the constitutional power of Congress and of the state legislatures. The wisdom of its exercise is not the concern of this Court . . .

The requirement of the equality clause that classification "must rest upon some ground of difference having a fair and substantial relation to the object of the legislation," is here satisfied . . . The size of estates, or of bequests, is the difference on which rest all the progressive inheritance taxes of the States and of the Nation. Differences in the size of incomes is the basis on which rest all progressive income taxes. Differences in the size of businesses present, likewise, an adequate basis for different rates of taxation. And so do differences in the extent or field of operation . . .

The State's power to apply discriminatory taxation as a means of preventing domination of intrastate commerce by capitalistic corporations is not conditioned upon the existence of economic need. It flows from the broader right of Americans to preserve, and to establish from time to time, such institutions, social and economic, as seem to them desirable; and, likewise, to end those which they deem undesirable. The State might, if conditions warranted, subject giant corporations to a control similar to that now exerted over public utility companies. Or, the citizens of Florida might conceivably escape from the domination of giant corporations by having the State engage in business. But Americans seeking escape from corporate domination have open to them under the Constitution another form of social and economic control—one more in keeping with our traditions and aspirations. They may prefer the way of cooperation, which leads directly to the freedom and the equality of opportunity which the Fourteenth Amendment aims to secure. That way is clearly open. For the fundamental difference between capitalistic enterprise and the cooperative between economic absolutism and industrial democracy—is one which has been commonly accepted by legislatures and the courts as justifying discrimination in both regulation and taxation.

There is a widespread belief that the existing unemployment is the result, in large part, of the gross inequality in the distribution of wealth and income which giant corporations have fostered; that by the control which the few have exerted through giant corporations, individual initiative and effort are being paralyzed, creative power impaired and human happiness lessened; that the true prosperity of our past came not from big business, but through the courage, the energy and the resourcefulness of small men; that only by releasing from corporate control the faculties of the unknown many, only by reopening to them the opportunities for leadership, can confidence in our future be restored and the existing misery be overcome; and that only through participation by the many in the responsibilities and determinations of business, can Americans secure the moral and intellectual development which is essential to the maintenance of liberty. If the citizens of Florida share that belief, I know of nothing in the Federal Constitution which precludes the State from endeavoring to give it effect and prevent domination in intrastate commerce by subjecting corporate chains to discriminatory license fees. To that extent, the citizens of each State are still masters of their destiny.

6 / Zionism: Progressives and Pilgrims in Palestine

Brandeis's Zionism was largely an application of the ideas that illuminated his approach to democracy in general. He viewed Zionism as a struggle for the kind of moral society and justice that he had thought had existed in Periclean Athens and that had been among the dreams of the American Pilgrims. To him, the Zionists were the ideological descendants of the Pilgrims, and he frequently referred to them as such. Zionism embodied the values of his progressive attitudes toward education, civic participation, community control of resources, and political equality of all human beings. He turned ancient Jews into the forerunners of Americans, proclaiming that "twentieth century ideals of America have been the ideals of the Jew for more than twenty centuries." Nationalism was a communal longing that paralleled the desire for individual liberty, and he argued that Jews had as much right as the Belgians or Italians to a territory of their own. He added that the creation of a Jewish homeland was necessary because of the anti-Semitic forces that seemed ineradicable in Europe.

There were contradictions in his Zionism. Although he accepted the nationalist argument that the Jewish culture could develop only in a homeland, he did not consider Palestine an attractive home for American Jews, who were unaffected by European anti-Semitism, and did not reconcile his assumption that a national home was a prerequisite of the continued development of a particularistic culture with the reality of a dynamic Jewish culture in the United States. This may be in part because he himself had so little interest in Jewish culture. In fact, while his earlier speeches referred to the importance of the Jewish heritage to a more democratic United States, he later grew impatient with attempts to revive Jewish culture in the United States or anywhere else outside Palestine and urged Jews to become not more Jewish but more Zionistic. He claimed that "Jews gave to the world its three greatest religions, reverence for law, and the highest conceptions of morality," but he found the same lawfulness and morality in ancient Greece.

Some of the contradictions may have existed because Brandeis was a problem-solver, and his Zionism was in part his reaction to the problem of European anti-Semitism. That was the reason he saw no disloyalty in American Zionism; American Zionists would give their primary loyalty to the United States and would further its values by helping to create a homeland in Palestine where other Jews could be as free as they were.

As soon as he became chairman of the Provisional Executive Committee for General Zionist Affairs in 1914, Brandeis did what he had with all his public service causes. He threw himself into every conceivable detail of organization and insisted that everyone else working with the movement had to be equally committed. He frequently sent a dozen or more letters a day, issuing directives and exhorting more strenuous efforts. The continuous stream of communications displayed his interest in and knowledge of details: how many members and sympathizers the movement had in every American city, how much money had been raised at virtually every meeting held, the names of people who could be persuaded to contribute or do more, and the contents of every American Zionist publication. During the last few months of 1914 he lectured about Zionism in New York, Boston, Cincinnati, Chicago, Milwaukee, Rochester, Buffalo, Philadelphia, Pittsburgh, St. Louis, and Springfield, Massachusetts. In 1915 he added Portland, Maine; New Haven; Atlantic City; Salem, Massachusetts; Baltimore; Washington; Providence; and Louisville to his itinerary. He created the American Jewish Congress as well as a multiplicity of Palestine-geared organizations such as the Palestine Development Leagues, the Palestine Co-operative Fund, and the Palestine Economic Corporation. His energy was prodigious and he simply assumed that the rest of the world could match his pace if it really tried.

"THE JEWISH PROBLEM: HOW TO SOLVE IT," 1915

"The Jewish Problem" is included here slightly out of chronological order because it was Brandeis's most important Zionist address. It is also a major statement of "progressive" Zionism and provides a context for his other speeches on the subject. It includes his explanation of why he considered Zionism necessary, emphasized that it was an attempt to create a democratic society, and drew links between the Jewish community in Palestine and both ancient Greece and the colonies

Brandeis chairing a Zionist conference in London, 1920. (Zionist Archives and Library)

established by the American Pilgrims. References in this and subsequent speeches to land purchase, as well as his entire philosophy, indicate that Brandeis believed that the land needed by the Jewish community had to be bought—not, as would happen after Israel gained statehood in 1948, be confiscated—and that it simply did not occur to him that anything the Zionists were doing implied that Palestinian Arabs were to be treated as less than equal.

The suffering of the Jews due to injustices continuing throughout nearly twenty centuries is the greatest tragedy in history. Never was the aggregate of such suffering larger than today. Never were the injustices more glaring. Yet the present is pre-eminently a time for hopefulness. The current of world thought is at last preparing the way for our attaining justice. The war is developing opportunities which may make possible the solution of the "Jewish Problem." But to avail of these opportunities we must understand both them and ourselves. We must recognize and accept facts. We must consider our course with statesmanlike calm. We must pursue resolutely the course we shall decide upon, and be ever ready to make the sacrifices which a great cause demands. Thus only can liberty be won.

For us the Jewish Problem means this: How can we secure for Jews, wherever they may live, the same rights and opportunities enjoyed by non-Jews? How can we secure for the world the full contribution which Jews can make, if unhampered by artificial limitations?

The problem has two aspects: that of the individual Jew—and that of Jews collectively. Obviously, no individual should be subjected anywhere, by reason of the fact that he is a Jew, to a denial of any common right or opportunity enjoyed by non-Jews. But Jews collectively should likewise enjoy the same right and opportunity to live and develop as do other groups of people. This right of development on the part of the group is essential to the full enjoyment of rights by the individual. For the individual is dependent for his development (and his happiness) in large part upon the development of the group of which he forms a part. We can scarcely conceive of an individual German or Frenchman living and developing without some relation to the contemporary German or French life and culture. And since death is not a solution of the problem of life, the solution of the Jewish Problem necessarily involves the continued existence of the Jews as Jews . . .

The meaning of the word Jewish in the term "Jewish Problem" must be accepted as coextensive with the disabilities which it is our problem to remove. It is the non-Jews who create the disabilities and in so doing give definition to the term Jew. Those disabilities extend substantially to all of Jewish blood. The disabilities do not end with a renunciation of faith, however sincere. They do not end with the elimination, however complete, of external Jewish mannerisms. The disabilities do not end ordinarily until the Jewish blood has been so thoroughly diluted by repeated intermarriages as to result in practically obliterating the Jew.

And we Jews, by our own acts, give a like definition to the term Jew. When men and women of Jewish blood suffer—because of that fact— and even if they suffer from quite different causes—our sympathy and our help goes out to them instinctively in whatever country they may live and without inquiring into the shades of their belief or unbelief. When those of Jewish blood exhibit moral or intellectual superiority, genius or special talent, we feel pride in them, even if they have abjured the faith like Spinoza, Marx, Disraeli, or Heine. Despite the meditations of pundits or the decrees of councils, our own instincts and acts, and those of others, have defined for us the term Jew.

Half a century ago the belief was still general that Jewish disabilities would disappear before growing liberalism. When religious toleration was proclaimed, the solution of the Jewish Problem seemed in sight. When the so-called rights of man became widely recognized, and the equal right of all citizens to life, liberty, and the pursuit of happiness began to be enacted into positive law, the complete emancipation of the Jew seemed at hand. The concrete gains through liberalism were indeed large. Equality before the law was established throughout the western hemisphere. The Ghetto walls crumbled; the ball and chain of restraint were removed in central and western Europe. Compared with the cruel discrimination to which Jews are now subjected in Russia and Roumania, their advanced condition in other parts of Europe seems almost ideal.

But anti-Jewish prejudice was not exterminated even in those countries of Europe in which the triumph of civil liberty and democracy extended fully to Jews "the rights of man." The anti-Semitic movement arose in Germany a year after the granting of universal suffrage. It broke out violently in France, and culminated in the Dreyfus case, a century after the French Revolution had brought "emancipation." It expressed itself in England through the Aliens Act, within a few years after the last of Jewish disabilities had been there removed by law. And in the United States the Saratoga incident reminded us, long ago, that we too have a Jewish question.

The disease is universal and endemic. There is, of course, a wide difference between the Russian disabilities with their Pale of Settlement, their denial of opportunity for education and choice of occupation, and their recurrent pogroms, and the German disabilities curbing university, bureaucratic, and military careers. There is a wide difference also between these German disabilities and the mere social disabilities of other lands. But some of those now suffering from the severe disabilities imposed by Russia and Roumania are descendants of men and women who in centuries before our modern liberalism enjoyed both legal and social equality in Spain and southern France. The manifestations of the Jewish Problem vary in the different countries, and at different periods in the same country, according to the prevailing degree of enlightenment and other pertinent conditions. Yet the differences, however wide, are merely in degree and not in kind. The Jewish Problem is single and universal. But it is not necessarily eternal. It may be solved.

Why is it that liberalism has failed to eliminate the anti-Jewish prejudice? It is because the liberal movement has not yet brought full liberty. Enlightened countries grant to the individual equality before the law; but they fail still to recognize the equality of whole peoples or nationalities. We seek to protect as individuals those constituting a minority; but we fail to realize that protection cannot be complete unless group equality also is recognized.

Deeply imbedded in every people is the desire for full development—

the longing, as Mazzini phrased it, ''to elaborate and express their idea, to contribute their stone also to the pyramid of history.'' Nationality like democracy has been one of the potent forces making for man's advance during the past hundred years. The assertion of nationality has infused whole peoples with hope, manhood, and self-respect. It has ennobled and made purposeful millions of lives. It offered them a future, and in doing so revived and capitalized all that was valuable in their past. The assertion of nationality raised Ireland from the slough of despondency. It roused southern Slavs to heroic deeds. It created gallant Belgium. It freed Greece. It gave us united Italy. It manifested itself even among free peoples—like the Welsh who had no grievance, but who gave expression to their nationality through the revival of the old Cymric tongue. Each of these peoples developed because, as Mazzini said, they were enabled to proclaim ''to the world that they also live, think, love, and labor for the benefit of all.''

In the past it has been generally assumed that the full development of one people necessarily involved its domination over others. Strong nationalities are apt to become convinced that by such domination only, does civilization advance. Strong nationalities assume their own superiority, and come to believe that they possess the divine right to subject other peoples to their sway. Soon the belief in the existence of such a right becomes converted into a conviction that a duty exists to enforce it. Wars of aggrandizement follow as a natural result of this belief.

This attitude of certain nationalities is the exact correlative of the position which was generally assumed by the strong in respect to other individuals before democracy became a common possession. The struggles of the eighteenth and nineteenth centuries both in peace and in war were devoted largely to overcoming that position as to individuals. In establishing the equal right of every person to development, it became clear that equal opportunity for all involves this necessary limitation: each man may develop himself so far, but only so far, as his doing so will not interfere with the exercise of a like right by all others. Thus liberty came to mean the right to enjoy life, to acquire property, to pursue happiness in such manner and to such extent as the exercise of the right in each is consistent with the exercise of a like right by every other of our fellow citizens. Liberty thus defined underlies twentieth-century democracy. Liberty thus defined exists in a large part of the western world. And even where this equal right of each individual has not yet been accepted as a political right, its ethical claim is gaining recognition. Democracy rejected the proposal of the superman who should rise through sacrifice of the many. It insists that the full development of each individual is not only a right, but a duty to society, and that our best hope for civilization lies not in uniformity, but in wide differentiation.

The movements of the last century have proved that whole peoples have individuality no less marked than that of the single person, that the individuality of a people is irrepressible, and that the misnamed internationalism which seeks the obliteration of nationalities or peoples is unattainable. The new nationalism proclaims that each race or people, like each individual, has a right and duty to develop, and that only through such differentiated development will high civilization be attained. Not until these principles of nationalism, like those of democracy, are generally accepted, will liberty be fully attained, and minorities be secure in their rights. But there is ground for hope that the establishment of these principles will come as one of the compensations of the present war—and, with it, the solution of the Jewish Problem.

The difference between a nation and a nationality is clear; but it is not always observed. Likeness between members is the essence of nationality; but the members of a nation may be very different. A nation may be composed of many nationalities, as some of the most successful nations are. An instance of this is the British nation, with its division into English, Scotch, Welsh, and Irish at home; with the French in Canada; and, throughout the Empire, scores of other nationalities. Other examples are furnished by the Swiss nation with its German, French, and Italian sections; by the Belgian nation composed of Flemings and Walloons; and by the American nation which comprises nearly all the white nationalities. The unity of a nationality is a fact of nature. The unity into a nation is largely the work of man. The false doctrine that nation and nationality must be made co-extensive is the cause of some of our greatest tragedies. It is, in large part, the cause also of the present war. It has led, on the one hand, to cruel, futile attempts at enforced assimilation, like the Russianizing of Finland and Poland, and the Prussianizing of Posen, Schleswig-Holstein, and Alsace-Lorraine. It has led, on the other hand, to those Panistic movements which are a cloak for territorial ambitions. As a nation may thrive though composed of many nationalities, so a nationality may thrive though forming parts of several nations. The essential in either case is recognition of the equal rights of each nationality . . .

Common race is only one of the elements which determine nationality. Conscious community of sentiments, common experiences, common qualities are equally, perhaps more, important. Religion, traditions, and customs bound us together though scattered throughout the world. The similarity of experiences tended to produce similarity of qualities and community of sentiments. Common suffering so intensified the feeling of brotherhood as to overcome largely all the influences making for diversification. The segregation of the Jews was so general, so complete, and so long continued as to intensify our "peculiarities" and make them almost ineradicable.

We recognize that with each child the aim of education should be to develop his own individuality, not to make him an imitator, not to assimilate him to others. Shall we fail to recognize this truth when applied to whole peoples? And what people in the world has shown greater individuality than the Jews? Has any a nobler past? Does any possess common ideas better worth expressing? Has any marked traits worthier of development? Of all the peoples in the world those of two tiny states stand pre-eminent as contributors to our present civilization—the Greeks and the Jews. The Jews gave to the world its three greatest religions, reverence for law, and the highest conceptions of morality. Never before has the value of our contribution been so generally recognized. Our teaching of brotherhood and righteousness has, under the name of democracy and social justice, become the twentieth-century striving of America and of western Europe. Our conception of law is embodied in the American constitutions which proclaim this to be a "government of laws and not of men." And for the triumph of our other great teaching—the doctrine of peace, this cruel war is paving the way.

While every other people is striving for development by asserting its nationality, and a great war is making clear the value of small nations, shall we voluntarily yield to anti-Semitism, and instead of solving our "problem" end it by ignoble suicide? Surely this is no time for Jews to despair. Let us make clear to the world that we too are a nationality clamoring for equal rights, to life and to self-expression . . . Standing upon this broad foundation of nationality, Zionism aims to give it full development. Let us bear clearly in mind what Zionism is, or rather what it is not.

It is not a movement to remove all the Jews of the world compulsorily to Palestine. In the first place there are 14,000,000 Jews, and Palestine would not accommodate more than one-fifth of that number. In the second place, it is not a movement to compel anyone to go to Palestine. It is essentially a movement to give to the Jew more, not less, freedom—it aims to enable the Jews to exercise the same right now exercised by practically every other people in the world: To live at their option either in the land of their fathers or in some other country; a right which members of small nations as well as of large—which Irish, Greek, Bulgarian, Servian, or Belgian, may now exercise as fully as Germans or English.

Zionism seeks to establish in Palestine, for such Jews as choose to go and remain there, and for their descendants, a legally secured home, where they may live together and lead a Jewish life; where they may expect ultimately to constitute a majority of the population, and may look forward to what we should call home rule. The Zionists seek to establish this home in Palestine because they are convinced that the undying longing of Jews for Palestine is a fact of deepest significance; that it is a manifestation in the struggle for existence by an ancient people which had established its right to live—a people whose three thousand years of civilization has produced a faith, culture, and individuality which enable them to contribute largely in the future, as they had in the past, to the advance of civilization; and that it is not a right merely, but a duty of the Jewish nationality to survive and develop. They believe that there only can Jewish life be fully protected from the forces of disintegration; that there alone can the Jewish spirit reach its full and natural development; and that by securing for those Jews who wish to settle in Palestine the opportunity to do so, not only those Jews, but all other Jews will be benefited and that the long perplexing Jewish Problem will, at last, find solution.

They believe that to accomplish this, it is not necessary that the Jewish population of Palestine be large as compared with the whole number of Jews in the world; for throughout centuries when the Jewish influence was greatest—during the Persian, the Greek, and the Roman Empires, only a relatively small part of the Jews lived in Palestine; and only a small part of the Jews returned from Babylon when the Temple was rebuilt.

Since the destruction of the Temple, nearly two thousand years ago, the longing for Palestine has been ever present with the Jew. It was the hope of a return to the land of his fathers that buoyed up the Jew amidst persecution, and for the realization of which the devout ever prayed. Until a generation ago this was a hope merely—a wish piously prayed for, but not worked for. The Zionist movement is idealistic, but it is also essentially practical. It seeks to realize that hope; to make the dream of a Jewish life in a Jewish land come true as other great dreams of the world have been realized—by men working with devotion, intelligence, and self-sacrifice. It was thus that the dream of Italian independence and unity, after centuries of vain hope, came true through the efforts of Mazzini, Garibaldi, and Cavour; that the dream of Greek, of Bulgarian, and of Servian independence became facts; that the dream of home rule in Ireland has just been realized.

The rebirth of the Jewish nation is no longer a mere dream. It is in process of accomplishment in a most practical way, and the story is a wonderful one. A generation ago a few Jewish emigrants from Russia and from Roumania, instead of proceeding westward to this hospitable country where they might easily have secured material prosperity, turned eastward for the purpose of settling in the land of their fathers.

To the worldly wise these efforts at colonization appeared very foolish. Nature and man presented obstacles in Palestine which appeared almost insuperable; and the colonists were in fact ill-equipped for their task, save in their spirit of devotion and self-sacrifice. The land, harassed by centuries of misrule, was treeless and apparently sterile; and it was infested with malaria. The government offered them no security, either as to life or property. The colonists themselves were not only unfamiliar with the character of the country, but were ignorant of the farmer's life which they proposed to lead; for the Jews of Russia and Roumania had been generally denied the opportunity of owning or working land. Furthermore, these colonists were not inured to the physical hardships to which the life of a pioneer is necessarily subjected. To these hardships and to malaria many succumbed. Those who survived were long confronted with failure. But at last success came. Within a generation these Jewish Pilgrim Fathers, and those who followed them, have succeeded in establishing these two fundamental propositions:

First, that Palestine is fit for the modern Jew.

Second, that the modern Jew is fit for Palestine.

Nearly fifty self-governing Jewish colonies attest to this remarkable achievement.

This land, treeless a generation ago, supposed to be sterile and hopelessly arid, has been shown to have been treeless and sterile only because of man's misrule. It has been shown to be capable of becoming again a land "flowing with milk and honey." Oranges and grapes, olives and almonds, wheat and other cereals are now growing there in profusion.

This material development has been attended by a spiritual and social development no less extraordinary; a development in education, in health, and in social order; and in the character and habits of the population. Perhaps the most extraordinary achievement of Jewish nationalism is the revival of the Hebrew Language, which has again become a language of the common intercourse of men. The Hebrew tongue, called a dead language for nearly two thousand years, has, in the Jewish colonies and in Jerusalem, become again the living mother-tongue. The effect of this common language in unifying the Jews is, of course, great; for the Jews of Palestine came literally from all the lands of the earth, each speaking, except for the use of Yiddish, the language of the country from which he came, and remaining in the main, almost a stranger to the others. But the effect of the renaissance of the Hebrew tongue is far greater than that of unifying the Jews. It is a potent factor in reviving the essentially Jewish spirit.

Our Jewish Pilgrim Fathers have laid the foundation. It remains for us to build the superstructure.

Let no American imagine that Zionism is inconsistent with patriotism. Multiple loyalties are objectionable only if they are inconsistent. A man is a better citizen of the United States for being also a loyal citizen of his state, and of his city; for being loyal to his family, and to his profession or trade; for being loyal to his college or his lodge. Every Irish-American who contributed towards advancing home rule was a better man and a better American for the sacrifice he made. Every American Jew who aids in advancing the Jewish settlement in Palestine, though he feels that neither he nor his descendants will ever live there, will likewise be a better man and a better American for doing so . . .

America's fundamental law seeks to make real the brotherhood of man. That brotherhood became the Jewish fundamental law more than twenty-five hundred years ago. America's insistent demand in the twentieth century is for social justice. That also has been the Jews' striving for ages. Their affliction as well as their religion has prepared the Jews for effective democracy. Persecution broadened their sympathies; it trained them in patient endurance, in self-control, and in sacrifice. It made them think as well as suffer. It deepened the passion for righteousness.

Indeed, loyalty to America demands rather that each American Jew become a Zionist. For only through the ennobling effect of its strivings can we develop the best that is in us and give to this country the full benefit of our great inheritance. The Jewish spirit, so long preserved, the character developed by so many centuries of sacrifice, should be preserved and developed further, so that in America as elsewhere the sons of the race may in future live lives and do deeds worthy of their ancestors . . .

In the Jewish colonies of Palestine there are no Jewish criminals; because everyone, old and young alike, is led to feel the glory of his race and his obligation to carry forward its ideals. The new Palestinian Jewry produces instead of criminals, great scientists like Aaron Aaronsohn, the discoverer of wild wheat; great pedagogues like David Yellin; craftsmen like Boris Schatz, the founder of the Bezalel; intrepid *Shomrim*, the Jewish guards of peace, who watch in the night against marauders and doers of violent deeds . . .

Since the Jewish Problem is single and universal, the Jews of every country should strive for its solution. But the duty resting upon us of America is especially insistent. We number about 3,000,000, which is more than one-fifth of all the Jews in the world—a number larger than that comprised within any other country, except the Russian Empire. We are representative of all the Jews in the world; for we are composed of immigrants, or descendants of immigrants coming from every other country, or district. We include persons from every section of society, and of every shade of religious belief. We are ourselves free from civil or political disabilities, and are relatively prosperous. Our fellow Americans are infused with a high and generous spirit, which insures approval of our struggle to ennoble, liberate, and otherwise improve the condition of an important part of the human race; and their innate manliness makes them sympathize particularly with our efforts at self help. America's detachment from Old World problems relieves us from suspicions and embarrassments frequently attending the activities of Jews of rival European countries. And a conflict between American interests or ambitions and Jewish aims is not conceivable. Our loyalty to America can never be questioned.

Let us therefore lead—earnestly, courageously, and joyously—in the struggle for liberation. Let us all recognize that we Jews are a distinct nationality of which every Jew, whatever his country, his station, or shade of belief is necessarily a member. Let us insist that the struggle for liberty shall not cease until equality of opportunity is accorded to nationalities as to individuals. Let us insist also that full equality of opportunity cannot be obtained by Jews until we, like members of other nationalities, shall have the option of living elsewhere or of returning to the land of our forefathers.

The fulfillment of these aspirations is clearly demanded in the interest of mankind, as well as in justice to the Jews. They cannot fail of attainment if we are united and true to ourselves. But we must be united not only in spirit but in action. To this end we must organize. Organize, in the first place, so that the world may have proof of the extent and the intensity of our desire for liberty. Organize, in the second place, so that our resources may become known and be made available. But in mobilizing our forces it will not be for war. The whole world longs for the solution of the Jewish Problem. We have but to lead the way, and we may be sure of ample co-operation from non-Jews. In order to lead the way, we need, not arms, but men; men with those qualities for which Jews should be peculiarly fitted by reason of their religion and life: men of courage, of high intelligence, of faith and public spirit, of indomitable will and ready self-sacrifice; men who will both think and do, who will devote high abilities to shaping our course, and to overcoming the many obstacles which must from time to time arise. And we need other, many, many other men—officers commissioned and non-commissioned, and common soldiers in the cause of liberty, who will give of their effort and resources, as occasion may demand, in unfailing and ever-strengthening support of the measures which may be adopted. Organization, thorough and complete, can alone develop such leaders and the necessary support.

Organize, organize, organize—until every Jew in America must stand up and be counted—counted with us—or prove himself, wittingly or unwittingly, of the few who are against their own people.

"A CALL TO THE EDUCATED JEW," JANUARY 1915

Speaking to the Intercollegiate Menorah Association, Brandeis tried to show why secular Jews ought to be Zionists, again making the connection between the values contained in his versions of Zionism and Americanism. He discussed the Jewish love of learning, which he considered a major element of Jewish character. Learning was of value because it could be used to better existence and especially to make society more democratic. Just as the possession of civil liberties carried the

concomitant obligation of civic responsibility, so possession of learn-
ing implied a duty to help those in need.

While I was in Cleveland a few weeks ago, a young man who has won
distinction on the bench told me this incident from his early life. He
was born in a little village of Western Russia where the opportunities
for schooling were meager. When he was thirteen his parents sent him
to the nearest city in search of an education. There, in Bialystok, were
good secondary schools and good high schools; but the Russian law,
which limits the percentage of Jewish pupils in any school, barred his
admission. The boy's parents lacked the means to pay for private tui-
tion. He had neither relative nor friend in the city. But soon three men
were found who volunteered to give him instruction. None of them was
a teacher by profession. One was a newspaper man; another was a
chemist; the third, as I recall, was a tradesman; all were educated men.
And throughout five long years these men took from their leisure the
time necessary to give a stranger an education.

The three men of Bialystok realized that education was not a thing of
one's own to do with what one pleases, that it was not a personal privilege to be merely enjoyed by the possessor, but a precious treasure
transmitted; a sacred trust to be held, used and enjoyed, and if possible
strengthened, then passed on to others upon the same trust. Yet the
treasure which these three men held and which the boy received in
trust was much more than an education. It included that combination
of qualities which enabled and impelled these three men to give, and
the boy to seek and to acquire, an education. These qualities embrace:
first, intellectual capacity; second, an appreciation of the value of education; third, indomitable will; fourth, capacity for hard work. It was
these qualities which enabled the lad, not only to acquire but to so utilize an education that, coming to America, ignorant of our language
and of our institutions he attained in comparatively few years the important office he has so honorably filled. [*The reference apparently is to
Judge Manuel Levine (1881–1939), chief justice of the Court of Appeals
of the Eighth Ohio District.*]

Whence comes this combination of qualities of mind, body and character? These are qualities with which every one of us is familiar, singly
and in combination; which you find in friends and relatives; and which
others doubtless discover in you. They are qualities possessed by most
Jews who have attained distinction or other success. In combination,

they may properly be called Jewish qualities. For they have not come to us by accident; they were developed by three thousand years of civilization and nearly two thousand years of persecution; developed through our religion and spiritual life; through our traditions; and through the social and political conditions under which our ancestors lived. They are, in short, the product of Jewish life.

Our intellectual capacity was developed by the almost continuous training of the mind throughout twenty-five centuries. The Torah led the "People of the Book" to intellectual pursuits at times when most of the Aryan peoples were illiterate. Religion imposed the use of the mind upon the Jews, indirectly as well as directly. It demanded of the Jew not merely the love, but also the understanding of God. This necessarily involved a study of the Law. The conditions under which the Jews were compelled to live during the last two thousand years promoted study in a people among whom there was already considerable intellectual attainment. Throughout the centuries of persecution practically the only life open to the Jew which could give satisfaction was the intellectual and spiritual life. Other fields of activity and of distinction which divert men from intellectual pursuits were closed to Jews. Thus they were protected by their privations from the temptations of material things and worldly ambitions. Driven by circumstances to intellectual pursuits their mental capacity gradually developed. And as men delight in that which they do well, there was an ever-widening appreciation of things intellectual. And finally, the Jewish capacity for hard work is also the product of Jewish life, a life characterized by temperate, moral living continued throughout the ages, and protected by those marvelous sanitary regulations which were enforced through the religious sanctions. Remember, too, that amidst the hardship to which our ancestors were exposed it was only those with endurance who survived.

So let us not imagine that what we call our achievements are wholly or even largely our own. The phrase "self-made man" is most misleading. We have power to mar but we alone cannot make. The relatively large success achieved by Jews wherever the door of opportunity was opened to them is due, in the main, to this product of Jewish life, to this treasure which we have acquired by inheritance, and which we are in duty bound to transmit unimpaired, if not augmented, to coming generations . . . Our Jewish trust comprises also that which makes the living worthy and success of value. It brings us that body of moral and intellectual perceptions, the point of view and the ideals, which are expressed in the term Jewish spirit; and therein lies our richest inheritance.

Is it not a striking fact that a people coming from Russia, the most autocratic of countries, to America, the most democratic of countries, comes here, not as to a strange land, but as to a home? The ability of the Russian Jew to adjust himself to America's essentially democratic conditions is not to be explained by Jewish adaptability. The explanation lies mainly in the fact that the twentieth century ideals of America have been the ideals of the Jew for more than twenty centuries. We have inherited these ideals of democracy and of social justice as we have the qualities of mind, body and character to which I referred. We have inherited also that fundamental longing for truth on which all science, and so largely the civilization of the twentieth century, rests; although the servility incident to persistent oppression has in some countries obscured its manifestation.

Among the Jews democracy was not an ideal merely. It was a practice, a practice made possible by the existence among them of certain conditions essential to successful democracy, namely:

First: An all-pervading sense of duty in the citizen. Democratic ideals cannot be attained through emphasis merely upon the rights of man. Even a recognition that every right has a correlative duty will not meet the needs of democracy. Duty must be accepted as the dominant conception in life. Such were the conditions in the early days of the colonies and states of New England, when American democracy reached there its fullest expression; for the Puritans were trained in implicit obedience to stern duty by constant study of the Prophets.

Second: Relatively high intellectual attainments. Democratic ideals cannot be attained by the mentally undeveloped. In a government where everyone is part sovereign, everyone should be competent, if not to govern, at least to understand the problems of government; and to this end education is an essential. The early New Englanders appreciated fully that education is an essential of potential equality. The founding of their common school system was coincident with founding of the colonies; and even the establishment of institutions for higher education did not lag far behind. Harvard College was founded but six years after the first settlement of Boston.

Third: Submission to leadership as distinguished from authority . . .

Fourth: A developed community sense. The sense of duty to which I have referred was particularly effective in promoting democratic ideals among the Jews, because of their deep-seated community feeling. To describe the Jew as an individualist is to state a most misleading half-truth. He has to a rare degree merged his individuality and his interests in the community of which he forms a part. As Ahad Ha'am [a Jewish poet who immigrated to Palestine] so beautifully said: "Judaism did not turn heavenward and create in Heaven an eternal habitation of souls. It found 'eternal life' on earth, by strengthening the social feeling in the individual; by making him regard himself not as an isolated being with an existence bounded by birth and death, but as part of a larger whole, as a limb of the social body. This conception shifts the center of gravity of the ego not from the flesh to the spirit, but from the individual to the community; and concurrently with this shifting, the problem of life becomes a problem not of individual, but of social life . . . When the individual thus values the community as his own life, and strives after its happiness as though it were his individual wellbeing, he finds satisfaction, and no longer feels so keenly the bitterness of his individual existence, because he sees the end for which he lives and suffers." Is not that the very essence of the truly triumphant twentieth-century democracy?

Such is our inheritance; such the estate which we hold in trust. And what are the terms of that trust; what the obligations imposed? The short answer is *noblesse oblige*; and its command is twofold. It imposes duties upon us in respect to our own conduct as individuals; it imposes no less important duties upon us as part of the Jewish community or people . . .

But from the educated Jew far more should be exacted. In view of our inheritance and our present opportunities, self-respect demands that we live not only honorably but worthily; and worthily implies nobly. The educated descendants of a people which in its infancy cast aside the Golden Calf and put its faith in the invisible God cannot worthily in its maturity worship worldly distinction and things material. "Two men he honors and no third," says Carlyle, "the toil-worn craftsman who conquers the earth and him who is seen toiling for the spiritually indispensable."

And yet, though the Jew make his individual life the loftiest, that alone will not fulfill the obligations of his trust. We are bound not only to use worthily our great inheritance, but to preserve, and if possible, augment it; and then transmit it to coming generations. The fruit of three thousand years of civilization and a hundred generations of suffering may not be sacrificed by us. It will be sacrificed if dissipated. Assimilation is national suicide. And assimilation can be prevented only by preserving national characteristics and life as other peoples, large and small, are preserving and developing their national life. Shall we with our inheritance do less than the Irish, the Serbians, or the Bulgars? And must we not, like them, have a land where the Jewish life may be naturally led, the Jewish language spoken, and the Jewish spirit prevail? Surely we must, and that land is our fathers' land; it is Palestine.

The undying longing for Zion is a fact of deepest significance, a manifestation in the struggle for existence.

The establishment of the legally secured Jewish home is no longer a dream. For more than a generation brave pioneers have been building the foundations of our new-old home. It remains for us to build the super-structure. The Ghetto walls are now falling. Jewish life cannot be preserved and developed, assimilation cannot be averted, unless there be reestablished in the fatherland a center from which the Jewish spirit may radiate and give to the Jews scattered throughout the world that inspiration which springs from the memories of a great past and the hope of a great future.

The glorious past can really live only if it becomes the mirror of a glorious future; and to this end the Jewish home in Palestine is essential. We Jews of prosperous America above all need its inspiration.

"AN ESSENTIAL OF LASTING PEACE," 1915

Although this address to the Economic Club of Boston technically was not about Zionism or given to a Zionist audience, Brandeis used it to explain his concept of nationalism as an essential element of human equality and its acceptance as a prerequisite of peace. World War I had begun, although the United States was not yet involved in it.

Those discussing the possibilities of a lasting peace usually emphasize one or the other of the following means of securing it:

First. The creation of a Congress of the Nations to determine what should be their relative rights, of an International Court to decide any disputed claims, and of an International Police to enforce the laws of this Congress and the decisions of this Court.

Second. The democratization of the nations, and particularly of the war-making power; so that the people, who must ultimately bear the burdens of war, may decide whether war shall be entered upon.

Third. Disarmament—so that unpreparedness may prevent precipitate action—and encourage sober second thought.

Fourth. The removal of economic causes of war, and pre-eminently the prohibition of preferential tariffs.

These suggestions, if carried out, would undoubtedly tend to preserve peace; for together they would reduce the provocations of war and lessen the facility of conducting it. But is there not a cause of war which is more fundamental than any of those which it is sought thus to remove?

Deeply imbedded in every nation and people is the desire for full development—the longing for self-expression. In the past it has been generally assumed that the full development of one people necessarily involved its domination over others. Strong nations are apt to become convinced that by such domination only does civilization advance. Strong nations assume their own superiority, and come to believe that they possess the divine right to subject other peoples to their sway. Soon the belief in the existence of such a right becomes converted into a conviction that a duty exists to enforce it. Wars of aggrandizement follow as a natural result of this belief.

This attitude of nations and peoples is the exact correlative of the position generally assumed by the strong in respect to other individuals before democracy became a common possession. The struggles of the eighteenth and nineteenth centuries, both in peace and in war, were devoted largely to overcoming that position as to individuals, to establishing the equal right to development of every person, and in making clear that equal opportunity for all involves this necessary limitation: each man may develop himself so far, but only so far, as his doing so will not interfere with the exercise of a like right by all others. Thus liberty has come to mean the right to enjoy life, to acquire property, to pursue happiness, in such manner that the exercise of the right in each is consistent with the exercise of a like right by every other of our fellow citizens. Liberty thus defined underlies twentieth-century democracy. Liberty thus defined exists in a large part of the western world. And even where this equal right of all has not yet been accepted as a political right, its ethical value is becoming recognized.

The movements of the last century have proved that whole peoples have individuality no less marked than that of the single person; that the individuality of a people is irrepressible, and that internationalism which seeks the obliteration of nations or peoples is unattainable. As democracy rejects the proposal of the superman who shall rise through sacrifice of the many and insists that the full development of each individual is not only a right but a duty to society; so the new nationalism proclaims the right and the duty of each race or people to develop itself fully.

The history of the last century shows the persistence and intensity of this feeling. It made a great and united country out of the Italy which had been declared by Metternich to be but a "geographical expression." It freed Greece. It created the kingdoms of Roumania, Bulgaria, and Servia. It made little Montenegro an independent state. It established home rule in Ireland. It revived the Cymric language in Wales. It has kept alive the struggle for a free Poland. It made a dual monarchy out of Austria; and the demands of its many other peoples subjected to the German-Hungarian rule have kept it in constant turmoil. If we wish to find the true explanation of the readiness of the European peoples to sacrifice their best in man and property—of their joyousness amid losses which cannot be repaired in generations—we must look deeper for the war's causes than economic ambitions or treaty violations. The fundamental cause is the longing of the people for self-development—for self-expression; and the mistaken belief on one side or the other that this self-development justly requires the subjection of other peoples.

No peace which is lasting can ever come until the nations, great and small, accept the democratic principle that there is and shall be no supernation, to rise through subjection of others, and the truth that each people has in it something of peculiar value which it can contribute to that civilization for which we are all striving. And until that principle is accepted—and that truth recognized, unrest must be unending. Whatever economic arrangement may be made, however perfect and comprehensive may become the machinery for enforcing the treaties of the nations, those people who are not accorded equality of opportunity for full development will prove a source of irritation; injustice will bring its inevitable penalty; and the peace of the world will be broken again and again, as those little nations of the Balkans have taught us in recent years.

Equal opportunity for all people as for all individuals—that is the essential of international as well as of national justice upon which a peace which is to be permanent must rest. Unless that fundamental right is recognized and granted universally, there will be discord and war in the future, as there has been in the past.

"PALESTINE AND THE JEWISH DEMOCRACY," 1915

Perhaps the most notable thing about this speech is the way in which Brandeis equated problems and institution building among the Palestinian Jews with the drive for greater democracy in the United States. It reiterates some of the themes of "The Jewish Problem" but also emphasizes gender equality, education, civic cooperation, and an attack on the problem of unemployment.

Three centuries ago Elder Brewster, reviewing the first year after the landing of the Pilgrims at Plymouth Rock, said: "It is not with us as with men whom small things can discourage or small discontents make them wish themselves home again." Small discontents! Out of the hundred who came in the *Mayflower* fifty-one had died before the close of the year, and at times out of the forty-nine survivors only seven were fit to work. Yet the spirit of the Pilgrim Fathers did not falter. To that spirit we owe in large part the Commonwealth of Massachusetts and that which we prize most in American life.

With a like spirit the Jewish Pilgrim Fathers turned a generation ago to Palestine, and began to establish those settlements called colonies, through which Zionism is becoming a reality.

To avoid misunderstanding, let me say at the outset what Zionism is, and particularly what it is not.

First, it is not a movement to transport all the Jews in the world to Palestine . . .

Secondly, it is not a movement to transport compulsorily a single Jew to Palestine . . .

Thirdly, neither is it a movement to wrest the sovereignty of Palestine from the Turkish Government. Zionism is a movement to give the Jews a home in the land of their fathers where the Jewish life may be lived normally and naturally, and where the Jews may in time hope to constitute a majority of the population and look forward to what we have come to call home rule . . .

The first years of these Jewish settlers resembled the first years of the Pilgrim Fathers at Plymouth. They had to fight death and disease. Misgovernment of the country had brought malaria into it. The land appeared to be exhausted, and they knew not how to enrich and till it. Many died, and those who survived lived only to be confronted by obstacle after obstacle. Failure followed failure; but they were determined, and every failure meant new effort; every mistake was a teacher. Plowing as they did in the field of faith and reaping experience, these men and those who joined them succeeded at the end of twenty-five years in establishing the two great propositions upon which practical Zionism rests: (1) that Palestine is fit for the modern Jew, and (2) that the modern Jew is fit for Palestine . . .

Education has ever been treasured by the Jewish people. Civilization without education is inconceivable to them. And so they have established a school system almost complete. But for this war it would have been capped with the establishment of the first department of the University of Jerusalem—the medical department. The war interrupted that forward step, and also the opening of the Institute of Technology at Haifa. But before the war there had been established high schools in which were fitted, not only Jews of Palestine, but hundreds who came from Russia and Roumania, so thoroughly that they could enter, on equal terms with the European students, any of the great universities of Austria, Germany, and France. But it is not only in things material and intellectual that the Zionists undertook to develop civilization in Palestine. They sought otherwise to carry forward the work of the Jewish spirit. Carlyle has said: "Two men he honors and no third. The toilworn craftsman who conquers the earth; and him who is seen striving for the spiritually indispensable." Had Carlyle lived he would have sent greetings to those Jewish settlers of Palestine; for they have both tilled the soil and have sought to establish the principles of democracy and social justice for which we of America are now striving. In their self-governing colonies, over forty in number, ranging in population from a few families to some two thousand, they have pure democracy, and, since those self-governing colonies were establishing a true democracy, they gave women equal rights with men, without so much as a doubt on the part of any settler. And women contributed, like the men, not only in the toil of that which is narrowly called the home, but in the solution of broader difficult problems. One of these problems was law and order. For the Jewish settlers in Palestine had in some respects problems similar to those of our own early settlers—the Bedouins taking the place of the Indians. Their farms and settlements needed protection. The Turkish Government does not, among its functions, assume that of policing. The Jews therefore hired Arabs to guard their colonies, and mounted Arabs protected their land. But after a number of years a woman—one of the women voters—said: "We must protect ourselves. We must establish our own mounted police." And the Jewish young men, largely sons of the original immigrants, responded; and out of the suggestion of a woman came the great Palestine institution, a Guild of Honor among the Jewish youth of the land.

The Jews carried out otherwise principles of democracy. Among the problems which they undertook to solve is one with which we have been particularly concerned this last year—the problem of unemployment. The prosperity of the Palestine colonies had depended largely upon its export trade. The orange crop, grapes, the olives, the almonds, are the crops from which money had been brought into Palestine. Even wheat has been exported in considerable quantities, and sold principally to Italy, because it is well suited to the manufacture of macaroni.

When the war came, their trade practically ceased, because the export markets were closed to them. It ceased wholly later because, when Turkey entered the war, it prohibited all exports. This stoppage of trade naturally brought on unemployment. The industries dependent on the export business closed down. Moreover, there had been almost a boom in building in Palestine just before the war, because the immigration had increased largely, the last year before the war being the most prosperous the colonies had ever had.

But when the war began the Zionists found themselves confronted with this situation: builders, planters, and manufacturers, employing comparatively large numbers of Jewish workmen, were forced to close or curtail operations and the workmen were thrown out of employment. The Zionists recognized that the burdens consequent on this common disaster ought not to fall on that part of the Jewish population alone, but should be borne by the entire Jewish people. They undertook to find employment for those who had lost their jobs. In part they did this by going on courageously with public works, with road-building and drainage work, with the construction of a public hospital, and similar undertakings. That helped some. They suggested that the farmers look ahead and do upon their farms work that would add ultimately to the value of these farms. That took care of a large part of the workmen in the country districts. But there were many unemployed Jewish workmen in the cities, which had been growing incident to the growth of the colonies. What could be done there? The Zionists studied the problem, and found that the reason many of the industries closed down was not that the owners wished to do so, but that they were unable to get the money to continue to carry on their business. They therefore undertook, to the extent of the available funds, to lend money to those industries which were relatively large employers of labor, to the end that those for whom they held themselves responsible should not be put in the position of takers of charity. To this end those who had steady jobs suffered their salaries to be cut one-fourth, one-third, and in some cases even more, and those who had not steady jobs were enabled to work at least part of the time under a fair distribution of that work which it was possible to provide for them. Thus did this people, struggling again the hardships of the war, without the ability to call upon a government to aid them, dependent largely only upon themselves for help, undertake to do what social justice demands. And what they did in this emergency they have long been doing, or attempting to do, through their institutions in various fields of public activity.

Notable among the Zionist institutions is the Jewish National Fund, formed to purchase land as the inalienable property of the Jewish people in Palestine. A large part of the settlers own individual property, but the Zionist organization determined that the land it acquired should be the property of the Jewish people, remaining national domain and leased to the settlers at a rent which would not allow of unearned increment. That Jewish National Fund, besides being used for acquiring land, has been devoted to afforestation and to securing proper housing conditions for Jewish working-people. Funds have thus been lent for the purpose of erecting proper workingmen's dwellings in the colonies and cities.

This Jewish National Fund, used thus for the Jewish people, is, in the most exact sense, a fund of the people. Hundreds of thousands of persons have contributed to that fund. They have contributed also to another fund—the Jewish Colonial Trust, of which the Anglo-Palestine Company is the leading bank of Palestine. To purchase the shares of that bank hundreds of thousands of people have contributed. I have been told that in Russia and Galicia, where for centuries poverty has been so deep, there are people who pawned their coats to raise money to buy a share in the Jewish Colonial Trust, in order to help carry out the national ideal. The bank, founded on strictly business principles, is managed also on strictly humanitarian and social principles. Through that bank the Jewish colonists have been aided in many ways. It has enabled them to establish co-operative societies dealing with almost every activity of Jewish life. It has enabled communities to avoid the heavy burdens of tax farming. It has enabled villages to establish a system of irrigation and water supply. And, while thus serving the public welfare, it became the leading bank of deposits and financial institution of Palestine.

In other fields likewise Zionists have undertaken functions which governments should assume, but generally do not. Among their institutions is the Palestine Office, so called, an exalted information bureau and intelligence office for the prospective settler, which helps to place him in his new home with the minimum of self-sacrifice and suffering on his part, and which acts in many ways as friend and adviser of the Jewish inhabitants in the land of their fathers . . .

I was talking not long ago with one of the men who went as a pioneer to Palestine. He referred in discussion to another Palestinian, and, as a word of severest censure, he said: "Yes, he is a Zionist, but he thinks of his own interests first. That is all right in other countries, but in Palestine it is all wrong." And as he spoke he made me think of the words which Mazzini uttered when entering Rome in 1849: "In Rome we may not be moral mediocrities." That is the feeling of the Palestinian Pilgrim Fathers. That should be the feeling of their brethren throughout the world when they think of their great inheritance, of their glorious past—the mirror of the future.

PITTSBURGH PLATFORM, JUNE 25, 1918

The statement adopted at the Pittsburgh convention of the Federation of American Zionists became the basis of the formal American Zionist agenda. It includes not only the primacy Brandeis invariably gave to the interrelated phenomena of democracy, education, and civil liberties but, in addition, his application to Palestine of the policy toward use of land, other natural resources, and public utilities that he had developed during the Pinchot-Ballinger Alaskan land scandal.

In 1897 the first Zionist Congress at Basle defined the object of Zionism to be "the establishment of a publicly recognized and legally secured homeland for the Jewish people in Palestine." The recent declarations of Great Britain, France, Italy and others of the allied democratic states, have established this public recognition of the Jewish National Home as an international fact. Therefore, we desire to affirm anew the principles which have guided the Zionist movement since its inception and which were the foundation of the ancient Jewish state and of the living Jewish law embodied in the traditions of two thousand years of exile.

First: We declare for political and civil equality irrespective of race, sex, or faith of all the inhabitants of the land.

Second: To insure in the Jewish National Home in Palestine equality of opportunity we favor a policy which, with due regard to existing rights, shall tend to establish the ownership and control by the whole people of the land, of all natural resources and of all public utilities.

Third: All land, owned or controlled by the whole people, should be leased on such conditions as will insure the fullest opportunity for development and continuity of possession.

Fourth: The cooperative principle should be applied so far as feasible in the organization of all agricultural, industrial, commercial, and financial undertakings.

Fifth: The system of free public instruction which is to be established should embrace all grades and departments of education.

LETTERS FROM PALESTINE

Brandeis's only trip to Palestine took place during the summer of 1919. By then he was the acknowledged leader of American Zionism and the Jewish settlers turned his visit into a triumphal tour. There were groups of singing children, flying flags, honor guards, delegations of Hadassah doctors and members of the Jewish Brigade, and roads lined with residents in their holiday best. His ecstatic reaction to the progress he found in the settlements and cities he visited, as well as his enhanced awareness of their problems, is clear in the letters below.

Letter to Alice Goldmark Brandeis,
July 10, 1919, from Jerusalem

We have been in Palestine 48 hours. The first day was spent on the way to Jerusalem; the second here. It is a wonderful country, a wonderful city. [Aaron] Aaronsohn [the agronomist who had piqued Brandeis's interest in Palestine—see Introduction] was right. It is a miniature California, but a California endowed with all the interest which the history of man can contribute and the deepest emotions which can stir a

Brandeis on his only trip to Palestine, 1919. (Zionist Archives and Library)

people. The ages-long longing, the love is all explicable now. It has also the great advantage over California of being small. The marvellous contrasts of nature are in close juxtaposition. Not only the mind but the eye may grasp them within a single picture, and the marvelous quality of the air brings considerable distances into it. What I saw of California and the Grand Canyon seemed less beautiful than the view from the Mount of Olives upon the Dead Sea and the country beyond. And yet all say that northern Palestine is far more beautiful, and that in this extra-dry season we are seeing the country at its worst.

It was a joy from the moment we reached it at Rafia. Many enter south of Gaza, and even in the hot plains the quality of the air was bracing. To my surprise, I have experienced no inconvenience from the altitude (about 2500 feet) here, and I have seen nothing in the country yet which should deter even such lovers as you of the cool to avoid summering here. The nights are always cool. In Jerusalem it is comfortable at mid-day in the shade, and there is almost constant breeze.

We are living here most pleasantly . . . and I am taken care of much in the manner of a Swiss landlady. Living conditions couldn't be better.

The problems are serious and numerous. The way is long, the path difficult and uncertain; but the struggle is worthwhile. It is indeed a Holy Land.

Letter to Chaim Weizmann,
July 20, 1919, from Haifa, Palestine

It is fine to be able to send you our greetings from your brother's and sister's charming house. Palestine has won our hearts . . . It is no wonder that the Jews love her so.

Letter to Alice Goldmark Brandeis,
July 6, 1919, from Alexandria, Egypt

Our Palestine stay—only 16 1/2 days—was crowded with impressions and most informing. I feel that we really know the main problems and the difficulties and possibilities. What we saw and heard there has been supplement[ed] by the constant conferences since with our associates; also all my previous reading has become vitalized; so that the 16 days represent in some respects years of acquisitiveness. We saw practically all the country; all the cities and 23 of the 43 Jewish Colonies. I have been converted to the food & found long auto travel agreeable and not fatiguing.

My opinion as to the future was summed up in a letter to General Allenby substantially as follows: "What I have seen and heard strengthen greatly my conviction that Palestine can and must become the Jewish Homeland as promised in the Balfour Declaration. The problems and the difficulties are serious and numerous, even more so than I had anticipated; but there is none which will not be solved & overcome by the indomitable spirit of the Jews here and elsewhere."

. . . Felix [Frankfurter] was very wise in insisting upon our coming.

MESSAGES TO ZIONIST LEADERS AND OTHERS
WORKING IN THE ZIONIST MOVEMENT

Telegram to Benjamin Perlstein, September 19, 1914

Request [Louis] Lipsky to caution organizers of my meetings to select rather small halls. Overcrowded small hall meeting better than large hall nearly full. Every man turned away for lack of room is worth two who get in.

Letter to Richard Gottheil, October 2, 1914

I trust that you are making good progress in organizing a band of speakers among the intellectuals. It seems to me very important that this work should be pressed forward as rapidly as possible, and that intensive work of educating through small groups and meetings should be undertaken.

Telegram to Louis Lipsky, October 3, 1914

Yes, will arrive Cleveland in time for afternoon luncheon, but should favor luncheon only if Committee convinced it will be financially profitable. Cleveland ought to produce at least five thousand dollars.

Letter to Israel J. Biskind, November 6, 1914

I find upon my return here that up to date, $2,000 has been received from Cleveland. We have hoped that Cleveland would contribute at least $5,000 . . . Will you kindly confer with your associates and let me know when we may expect further remittances from Cleveland.

Letter to Benjamin Perlstein, November 9, 1914

Send to members of each of the Committee having matters in hand not yet disposed of, a request to send a report to the office in writing not later than next Monday and let me have carbons of letters that you send.

Letter to Max Mitchell, November 17, 1914

I hope you have already undertaken to get the large subscriptions about which you spoke to me. Try to make them at least $500 a piece; and one or two $1000 subscriptions would go a long way towards giving the proper impetus to the work throughout the Country and in putting Massachusetts where it belongs in this movement.

I hope that you will have these checks in hand before Friday, when I start for Chicago.

I venture to suggest that the collections from Chicago ought to reach in the aggregate $20,000. In Boston we raised about $7,000 at our meeting on the 27th.

Letter to Jacob deHaas, January 25, 1915

Please arrange that I receive not later than the 5th of each month a report covering the activities of the Zionist Bureau during the preceding month.

I should be glad if you would give some care to the form of the report, so that it may be possible, by a comparison of the reports from month to month, to note readily the progress that has been made in each line of activity, and serve as a current reference to the achievements of the Bureau.

Letter to Louis Lipsky, January 27, 1915

First: The format of the Maccabaean seems to me a great improvement, but the smallness of the print seems to me most objectionable . . .

Letter to Henrietta Szold, March 4, 1915

You . . . are to be congratulated on the February number of the Hadassah Bulletin.

(Please send me for my files Nos. 1,2,3, and 4 of the Hadassah Bulletin.) . . . if you could arrange to have Miss Leon, who made an excellent impression here, or some of your other members, here for a series of conferences, a very considerably increased Hadassah membership might be expected.

Letter to Joseph L. Cohen, May 1, 1915

. . . *Second:* We must make available for our members an adequate Zionist library, directing our efforts:

(a) to having the desirable works on Zionism in leading public libraries . . . and the main universities.

(b) to have some works in public libraries in all communities where there are many Jews.

c) to provide a reasonable working library at Zionist headquarters, and at any Zionist Bureau that may be established . . .

"Members, Money, Discipline": Note to Morris Rothenberg, February 18, 1917

Please extend my greetings to your Council [the Zionist Council of Greater New York, of which Rothenberg was chairman] at its annual meeting [the Eleventh Annual Convention] and tell them that they can prove themselves good Zionists only by producing Members, Money, Discipline.

Letter to Robert Szold, August 19, 1930

Our crying need is a body of competent and willing speakers and writers . . . The conditions of Jews in the Diaspora in 1930—as compared with 1920 and 1914—has worsened to such a degree, that the belief of thinking Jews that the Jewish problem would be solved by growing enlightenment in the Diaspora must have been seriously shaken—if not shattered.

A speaker sufficiently familiar with Jewish history, could, in the light of recent events, demolish these objectors. The anti-Semitic outbreaks in Europe, the closing of the doors to immigrants by practically all the new countries, the rise of anti-Semitism even in the new countries, remove the old alternatives from consideration. The question now presented is largely Palestine—or Despair? . . .

The social life and strivings of the Jews as reflected in official reports and serious economic and political discussion, and as interpreted in literary productions, affords abundant material for appeal to Jewish liberals—with or without religious faith and to idealists of any race or creed . . .

Every opportunity to speak which offers, however modest or unpromising it may appear, should be availed of; and effort should be continuously and persistently made to create opportunities. Lodges, Club societies, gatherings—social or serious—should be sought—whatever their character . . .

The available material affords also ample evidence in support of the argument that with a proper British attitude Jews can live in harmony with the Arabs; that friendly relations are being developed in many places; and that raising of the level of Arab existence has been, and is, not only a necessary incident of the Jewish upbuilding of P.—but the Jewish desire; that the Jews recognize that raising the Arab level is essential to attain the social end which the Jewish Labor especially is seeking to serve; and which Jewish industrialists desire in order to enlarge the home market.

Letter to Maurice B. Hexter, September 7, 1930

. . . the possibilities of Jewish urban immigration are practically unlimited; because its needs for land and water are small. Palestine has about the area of Massachusetts. The commerce and industry of the Commonwealth support nearly four million people. The essentials are a sea-port, a good harbor, a good climate and a population with brains, determination and character. When Haifa's harbor shall have been made good and malaria shall have been wholly eliminated, the Jews can provide Palestine with the other essential. Moreover, Massachusetts has no natural resources comparable to the Dead Sea salts—and no cheap supply of oil . . .

Nothing in Palestine development is more encouraging than the 1928 Census showing "3,505 producing enterprises." And happily their number is steadily growing. The new products of the "geo" and the "Lio" factories, the local production of the tins, the making of orange boxes of Hedera wood are notable events in the history of the country. We should do everything possible to promote such enterprises; to make Palestine self-sufficient; and to develop its exports of manufactured products. With the aid of these and the increasing orange production, the terrifying adverse trade balance can be overcome. The increase of £350,000 in the first four months of 1930 for exports and the decrease of £150,000 in imports is a most hopeful occurrence. The sale of £10,000 of artificial teeth to England is an indication of what Jewish ingenuity, courage and determination can achieve for Palestine. Even more should be possible.

Letter to Bernard Flexner, April 8, 1940

On general principles, we should promote Arab stockholding in Jewish enterprises and proportionate employment of Arab labor, but never more than such proportionate employment and never for the purpose of employing labor at lower rates.

7 / Government in a Democracy

Brandeis regarded democratic government as necessary because, without it, human fulfillment was impossible. The goal was the individual; the method was the organized community; the two were inextricably connected.

Government presented the same problem as all organizations: its effectiveness was dependent on its maintaining a size substantial enough to permit it to perform its functions, but it inevitably would be subject to the tendency to grow too big and too powerful. Brandeis was enthusiastic about the federal system because it kept many governmental powers in the states rather than in Washington and because the state governments could serve as laboratories for the constantly needed experimentation with public policies that were responsive to a changing society. He occasionally shocked young people eager to participate in the federal government by advising them to return to their states to ensure that the nurseries of democracy were functioning properly. Enthusiastic though he was about the presidencies of Woodrow Wilson and Franklin Roosevelt, he was opposed to those of their policies or actions that he considered to concentrate excessive power in their hands.

He would have liked to see the society's economic problems solved through voluntary action by individuals and organizations such as unions and corporations, but he recognized that in the modern world, there were already too many entrenched bastions of power for that to be possible. Government action was needed, all the more so after the economic crisis of the Depression. Nonetheless, all of his prescriptions were designed to minimize governmental involvement as much as possible. He dissented in the *Myers* case (below) and voted against the National Industrial Recovery Act of 1933, in both cases because he considered that to do otherwise would be to endorse dangerous concentrations of power in the executive. He returned to his theme of human fallibility and the recognition that the most talented and best-intentioned people must not be given more power than a human being could be expected to exercise intelligently. This limitation extended to the Supreme Court as well as to the other branches of government.

MYERS V. UNITED STATES, 1926

President Woodrow Wilson removed Frank Myers, a postmaster, without requesting the Senate's consent. The Court upheld the dismissal, and Brandeis wrote a lengthy dissent reflecting his fear of unaccountable power in any hands, including those of a president whose policies he supported. Separation of powers and checks and balances were as important to him as was federalism in helping to guarantee that governmental power would not be dangerously concentrated.

The Constitution gives the president power to appoint officials of the executive branch with the "advice and consent" of the Senate, which effectively means securing Senate confirmation of his nominees, but says nothing specific about the removal power. The question was whether the president's power as chief executive implied his right to remove officials, or whether Congress had the authority to define the terms, including possible removal, under which the Senate would agree to appointments. Brandeis's view was adopted by the Court some years later (1934) in Humphrey's Executor v. United States, *which effectively overruled* Myers *on the basis of his reasoning.*

MR. JUSTICE BRANDEIS, dissenting.

Postmasters are inferior officers. Congress might have vested their appointment in the head of the department. The Act of July 12, 1876, provided that "postmasters of the first, second, and third classes shall be appointed and may be removed by the President by and with the advice and consent of the Senate, and shall hold their offices for four years unless sooner removed or suspended according to law." That statute has been in force unmodified for half a century. Throughout the period, it has governed a large majority of all civil offices to which appointments are made by and with the advice and consent of the Senate. May the President, having acted under the statute in so far as it creates the office and authorizes the appointment, ignore, while the Senate is in session, the provision which prescribes the condition under which a removal may take place? . . .

The sole question is whether, in respect to inferior offices, Congress may impose upon the Senate both responsibilities, as it may deny to it participation in the exercise of either function.

In *Marbury v. Madison*, it was assumed, as the basis of decision, that the President, acting alone, was powerless to remove an inferior civil officer appointed for a fixed term with the consent of the Senate; and that case was long regarded as so deciding. In no case, has this Court determined that the President's power of removal is beyond control, limitation, or regulation by Congress. Nor has any lower federal court ever so decided. This is true of the power as it affects officers in the Army or the Navy and the high political officers like heads of departments, as well as of the power in respect to inferior statutory offices in the executive branch. Continuously for the last fifty-eight years, laws comprehensive in character, enacted from time to time with the approval of the President, have made removal from the great majority of the inferior presidential offices dependent upon the consent of the Senate. Throughout that period these laws have been continuously applied. We are requested to disregard the authority of *Marbury v. Madison* and to overturn this long established constitutional practice . . .

The ability to remove a subordinate executive officer, being an essential of effective government, will, in the absence of express constitutional provision to the contrary, be deemed to have been vested in some person or body. But it is not a power inherent in a chief executive. The President's power of removal from statutory civil inferior offices, like the power of appointment to them, comes immediately from Congress. It is true that the exercise of the power of removal is said to be an executive act; and that when the Senate grants or withholds consent to a removal by the President, it participates in an executive act. But the Constitution has confessedly granted to Congress the legislative power to create offices, and to prescribe the tenure thereof; and it has not in terms denied to Congress the power to control removals. To prescribe the tenure involves prescribing the conditions under which incumbency shall cease. For the possibility of removal is a condition or qualification of the tenure. When Congress provides that the incumbent shall hold the office for four years unless sooner removed with the consent of the Senate, it prescribes the term of the tenure . . .

The end to which the President's efforts are to be directed is not the most efficient civil service conceivable, but the faithful execution of the laws consistent with the provisions therefor made by Congress. A power essential to protection against pressing dangers incident to disloyalty in the civil service may well be deemed inherent in the executive office. But that need, and also insubordination and neglect of duty, are adequately provided against by implying in the President the constitutional power of suspension. Such provisional executive power is comparable to the provisional judicial power of granting a restraining order without notice to the defendant and opportunity to be heard. Power to remove, as well as to suspend, a high political officer, might conceivably be deemed indispensable to democratic government and, hence, inherent in the President. But power to remove an inferior administrative officer appointed for a fixed term cannot conceivably be deemed an essential of government.

To imply a grant to the President of the uncontrollable power of removal from statutory inferior executive offices involves an unnecessary and indefensible limitation upon the constitutional power of Congress to fix the tenure of inferior statutory offices. That such a limitation cannot be justified on the ground of necessity is demonstrated by the practice of our governments, state and national . . .

The assertion that the mere grant by the Constitution of executive power confers upon the President as a prerogative the unrestricted power of appointment and of removal from executive offices, except so far as otherwise expressly provided by the Constitution, is clearly inconsistent also with those statutes which restrict the exercise by the President of the power of nomination. There is not a word in the Constitution which in terms authorizes Congress to limit the President's freedom of choice in making nominations for executive offices. It is to appointment as distinguished from nomination that the Constitution imposes in terms the requirement of Senatorial consent. But a multitude of laws have been enacted which limit the President's power to make nominations, and which, through the restrictions imposed, may prevent the selection of the person deemed by him best fitted. Such restriction upon the power to nominate has been exercised by Congress continuously since the foundation of the Government. Every President has approved one or more of such acts. Every President has consistently observed them. This is true of those offices to which he makes appointments without the advice and consent of the Senate as well as of those for which its consent is required . . .

The practical disadvantage to the public service of denying to the President the uncontrollable power of removal from inferior civil offices would seem to have been exaggerated . . . for he can, at any time, exercise his constitutional right to suspend an officer and designate some other person to act temporarily in his stead; and he cannot, while the Senate is in session, appoint a successor without its consent. On the other hand, to the individual in the public service, and to the maintenance of its morale, the existence of a power in Congress to impose upon the Senate the duty to share in the responsibility for a removal is of paramount importance. The Senate's consideration of a proposed removal may be necessary to protect reputation and emoluments of office from arbitrary executive action. Equivalent protection is afforded to other inferior officers whom Congress has placed in the classified civil service and which it authorizes the heads of departments to appoint and to remove without the consent of the Senate. The existence of some such provision is a common incident of free governments. In the United States, where executive responsibility is not safeguarded by the practice of parliamentary interpellation, such means of protection to persons appointed to office by the President with the consent of the Senate is of special value.

Until the Civil Service Law, January 16, 1883, was enacted, the requirement of consent of the Senate to removal and appointment was the only means of curbing the abuses of the spoils system . . . the removal clause . . . had been recommended by Mr. Justice Story as a remedial measure, after the wholesale removals of the first Jackson administration. The Post Office Department was then the chief field for plunder. Vacancies had been created in order that the spoils of office might be distributed among political supporters. Fear of removal had been instilled in continuing office holders to prevent opposition or lukewarmness in support. Gross inefficiency and hardship had resulted . . .

The first substantial victory of the civil service reform movement, though a brief one, was the insertion of the removal clause in the Currency bill of 1863 . . . It was in the next Congress that the removal clause was applied generally by the Tenure of Office Act. The long delay in adopting legislation to curb removals was not because Congress accepted the doctrine that the Constitution had vested in the President uncontrollable power over removal. It was because the spoils system held sway . . .

The separation of the powers of government did not make each branch completely autonomous. It left each, in some measure, dependent upon the others, as it left to each power to exercise, in some respects, functions in their nature executive, legislative and judicial . . .

Checks and balances were established in order that this should be "a government of laws and not of men." As [Representative] White said in the House, in 1789, an uncontrollable power of removal in the Chief Executive "is a doctrine not to be learned in American governments" . . . The doctrine of the separation of powers was adopted by the Convention of 1787 not to promote efficiency but to preclude the exercise of arbitrary power. The purpose was, not to avoid friction, but, by means of the inevitable friction incident to the distribution of the governmental powers among three departments, to save the people from autocracy. In order to prevent arbitrary executive action, the Constitution provided in terms that presidential appointments be made with the consent of the Senate, unless Congress should otherwise provide; and this clause was construed by Alexander Hamilton in The Federalist, No. 77, as requiring like consent to removals. Limiting further executive prerogatives customary in monarchies, the Constitution empowered Congress to vest the appointment of inferior officers, "as they think proper, in the President alone, in the Courts of Law, or in the Heads of Departments." Nothing in support of the claim of uncontrollable power can be inferred from the silence of the Convention of 1787 on the subject of removal. For the outstanding fact remains that every specific proposal to confer such uncontrollable power upon the President was rejected. In America, as in England, the conviction prevailed then that the people must look to representative assemblies for the protection of their liberties. And protection of the individual, even if he be an official, from the arbitrary or capricious exercise of power was then believed to be an essential of free government.

ASHWANDER V. TENNESSEE VALLEY AUTHORITY,
1935

Although this case involved the power of the TVA to construct the Wheeler Dam, Brandeis considered the main issue to be the way the case had reached the Court. It had been brought as a stockholders' suit, a way of getting the courts to rule on the legitimacy of a statute that embodied a policy with which the plaintiffs disagreed. Brandeis would have upheld the TVA's authority without reaching the constitutional issue, because the plaintiffs had no real financial—as opposed to policy—interest in the case, and took the occasion to delineate what he considered to be the scope of the Court's authority in constitutional cases. It was his attempt to articulate the limited nature of judicial review, and it has been cited extensively in subsequent litigation.

MR. JUSTICE BRANDEIS, concurring.

The Court has frequently called attention to the "great gravity and delicacy" of its function in passing upon the validity of an act of Congress; and has restricted exercise of this function by rigid insistence that the jurisdiction of federal courts is limited to actual cases and controversies; and that they have no power to give advisory opinions . . .

The Court developed, for its own governance in the cases confessedly within its jurisdiction, a series of rules under which it has avoided passing upon a large part of all the constitutional questions pressed upon it for decision. They are:

1. The Court will not pass upon the constitutionality of legislation in a friendly, non-adversary, proceeding, declining because to decide such questions "is legitimate only in the last resort, and as a necessity in the determination of real, earnest and vital controversy between individuals. It never was the thought that, by means of a friendly suit, a party beaten in the legislature could transfer to the courts an inquiry as to the constitutionality of the legislative act."

2. The Court will not "anticipate question of constitutional law in advance of the necessity of deciding it."

3. The Court will not "formulate a rule of constitutional law broader than is required by the precise facts to which it is to be applied."

4. The Court will not pass upon a constitutional question although properly presented by the record, if there is also present some other ground upon which the case may be disposed of. This rule has found most varied application. Thus, if a case can be decided on either of two grounds, one involving a constitutional question, the other a question of statutory construction or general law, the Court will decide only the latter. Appeals from the highest court of a state challenging its decision of a question under the Federal Constitution are frequently dismissed because the judgment can be sustained on an independent state ground.

5. The Court will not pass upon the validity of a statute upon complaint of one who fails to show that he is injured by its operation. Among the many applications of this rule, none is more striking than the denial of the right of challenge to one who lacks a personal or property right. Thus, the challenge by a public official interested only in the performance of his official duty will not be entertained . . .

6. The Court will not pass upon the constitutionality of a statute at the instance of one who has availed himself of its benefits.

7. "When the validity of an act of the Congress is drawn in question, and even if a serious doubt of constitutionality is raised, it is a cardinal principle that this Court will first ascertain whether a construction of the statute is fairly possible by which the question may be avoided." [*Crowell v. Benson*, 285 U.S. 22, 62]

LETTER TO ELIZABETH BRANDEIS RAUSHENBUSH,
NOVEMBER 19, 1933

As had been the case during the Wilson administration, Brandeis was deeply involved in the New Deal. He invited a large number of the major policymakers to the weekly teas at his home that quickly became a regular part of Washington life. Mrs. Brandeis made certain that each person had an allotted time with the justice, and the list of members of Congress, executive branch officials, younger bureaucrats, labor leaders, diplomats, and journalists who spoke with him included the most powerful people in Washington. While he used the occasions to learn from them, he also made certain that they understood what he thought the government ought to be doing next. He did the same thing in a more concentrated way through Felix Frankfurter, Frankfurter's protégés Thomas Corcoran and Benjamin Cohen, and Brandeis's former clerk James Landis, the last three New Deal officials engaged in drafting much of the New Deal's most important statutes such as the Public Securities Act of 1933, the Securities Exchange Act of 1934, the Holding Company Act of 1935, and the Social Security Act of 1935. He had detailed ideas about how to pull the country out of the Depression and prepare it for the second half of the twentieth century, and he used every opportunity to urge them upon policymakers. His daughter, one of the creators of the Wisconsin unemployment plan that was the model for the federal Wagner Act, was working with a group of progressives planning to issue a manifesto about governmental policy. The manifesto never emerged, but the Brandeis letter provides additional details about what he thought the government should do.

Curb of bigness is indispensable to true Democracy & Liberty. It is the very foundation also of wisdom in things human

"Nothing too much"

I hope you can make your progressives see this truth. If they don't, we may get amelioration, but not a working "New Deal." And we are apt to get Fascist manifestations. Remember, the inevitable ineffectiveness of regulation, i.e. the limits of its efficiency in regulation.

If the Lord had intended things to be big, he would have made man bigger—in brains and character.

My "running waters" suggestion was this. My idea has been that the Depression can be overcome only by extensive public works.

(a) that no public works should be undertaken save those that would be effective in making the America of the future what it should be.

(b) that we should avail of the present emergency to get those public works which Americans would lack the insight & persistence to get for themselves in ordinary times.

These public works are, for every state,

(1) afforestation

(2) running water control

(3) adult education

(4) appropriate provision for dealing with defectives and delinquents.

By "running Water Control" I mean this:

In this country, where the rain fall is, in the main, between 35 and 50 inches, and the country largely blessed with hills or mountains, it is absurd to permit either floods or droughts, or waste of waters. We should so control all running waters, by reservoirs, etc., so

(a) as to prevent floods & soil erosion

(b) to make it possible to irrigate practically all land

(c) to utilize the water for power & inland navigation

(d) & for recreation

Every state should have its lakes and ponds galore. Doubtless, you will recall much discourse of mine on this subject.

HARRY SHULMAN, "MEMORANDUM OF TALK
WITH L.D.B. — DECEMBER 8, 1933"

Shulman had been Brandeis's law clerk during the Supreme Court's 1929-1930 term and subsequently became a professor at Yale Law School. Like all of Brandeis's clerks, he was a graduate of Harvard Law School and a protégé of Felix Frankfurter, to whom he sent this memo-

randum. *He noted that the memorandum actually was written on February 1, 1934, but the phrases used in it are Brandeisian and, taken in
conjunction with Brandeis's letter to his daughter and other letters
written during the early New Deal days, it can be assumed to reflect
Brandeis's thinking about the government's role in pulling the country
out of the Depression and planning for the years thereafter.*

L.D.B. asked . . . "do you want to know my program for recovery?" I expressed enthusiasm and he proceeded to tell it to me "in a few words":

The object is to make men free. The Government is to impose limitations in order to achieve that object. And in determining what to do we
should profit by our experience. This depression, unlike previous ones,
was not caused by flood, famine, plague or other public calamity. It
came about because of the failure of the Government to impose controls to prevent a breakdown.

First, I would take the Government out of the hands of the bankers. I
would do that by opening the postal savings department to all depositors without limitation of amount. I would establish in the post office
also a checking department, so that the post office could be used for
commercial accounts. I should also make the postal department the
agency for the issuance of securities. By appropriate federal taxation, I
would split up the banking business into its separate parts and prohibit
any bank from doing any more than one kind of banking business, so
that there would be separate savings banks, commercial banks, investment banks, etc. This would avoid the evil of great concentration of financial power in the hands of bankers.

Secondly, by appropriate federal taxation I would limit the amount of
property which any person could acquire or pass down upon death. I
would fix the maximum at, say, a million dollars, although that may be
too high.

Thirdly, by appropriate federal excise taxes I would limit the size of
corporations. I would do it not only with respect to corporations to be
formed in the future, but also for existing corporations. [Here I inter-
jected a statement about the renewed agitation for federal incorporation. Both L.D.B. and Mrs. B. quickly frowned upon it. I would leave a
lot of power to the states, said L.D.B. and have the federal government
help and direct the States by appropriate taxation. The federal government must not become too big just as corporations should not be permitted to become too big. You must remember that it is the littleness

of man that limits the size of things we can undertake. Too much bigness may break the federal government as it has broken business.]

Fourthly, I would establish a system of unemployment compensation similar to that adopted in Wisconsin. The system should be operated by the states but the federal Government by appropriate taxation and exemption from taxation should furnish the force which would compel the establishment of such systems. The purpose of unemployment compensation would be to bring stability, and it is the lack of this stability which has been a very important factor in the depression. The compensation system should be so framed that the business man will have to take into account the welfare of his employees as well as his investment when making plans for the future. The compensation system would not give us 100% stability but it will give it to us within a ten or fifteen per cent margin, and the resulting maintenance of purchasing power will tend to prevent the collapse which we are experiencing. I would do other things, of course, but these are the main points.

I suggested to L.D.B. that the first response, particularly to the third point, would be that it was attempting to do the impossible, to turn the clock back. His reaction was immediate and spirited: why shouldn't we turn the clock back? We just turned the clock back on a "noble experiment" [Prohibition] which was unanimously adopted in the country and was being tried for some time. At any rate whether the program can be executed or not is a separate question. To have that objection raised only confuses the proponent and directs his mind away from the real issue. First, we must determine what it is desirable to do and then we can find ways and means to do it. If Roosevelt would come out with this kind of a developed program, and if we could get spirit behind it, it could easily be put over.

At this point Mrs. B. pulled the Justice's trouser and I understood that time was up.

8 / The Right to Be Let Alone

Brandeis's first law partner was Samuel Warren, a member of a prominent Boston family. They remained on friendly terms after Warren left the partnership to help manage his family's business interests. In 1890, the two men became concerned about what they felt was the overly intrusive and lurid coverage being given to prominent Boston society figures by the local press. The result was an article, "The Right to Privacy," which they published in the *Harvard Law Review*. In it they argued that the law included a right to privacy that protected the individual's thoughts, statements, and emotions from undesired publicity. The article proved so influential that Dean Roscoe Pound of the Harvard Law School credited it with "nothing less than add[ing] a chapter to our law." It also made Judge Thomas M. Cooley's phrase "the right to be let alone" part of American political discourse.

Brandeis wrote about the article to his fiancee, Alice Goldmark, telling her among other things that when he glanced over the proofs, the article "did not strike me as being as good as I had thought it was." Goldmark's letters, since lost, apparently included some comments about privacy. On December 28, 1890, he continued the discussion in another letter, this time saying, "Of course you are right about Privacy and Public Opinion. All law is a dead letter without public opinion behind it. But law and public opinion interact—and they are both capable of being made. Most of the world is in more or less a hypnotic state—and it is comparatively easy to make people believe anything, particularly the right. Our hope is to make people see that invasions of privacy are not necessarily borne—and then make them ashamed of the pleasure they take in subjecting themselves to such invasions . . . The most perhaps that we can accomplish is to start a back-fire, as the woodmen or the prairie men do."

Although the privacy that was the subject of both the article and the letter was privacy against invasion by the press, Brandeis cared about privacy against governmental intrusion as well. This dovetailed with his emphasis on communication and discussion of ideas, for without privacy there could be no real freedom of speech. The right of the individual not to have his or her privacy violated by the government thus was a central element in his theory of democracy.

Brandeis was particularly distressed at the governmental invasions of privacy that accompanied World War I and the years immediately thereafter. He bombarded Frankfurter with letters about the subject, and two excerpts are included here. He also wrote at length about government and privacy in a number of cases heard by the Court during that period, excerpted below.

Brandeis found himself disagreeing with Justice Holmes about the right to privacy. Although they both dissented from a Court decision that permitted material stolen from an office and then turned over to public officials to be used in a criminal proceeding, they parted company in cases involving government entrapment and wiretapping. Brandeis was certain that government "espionage" and invasion of privacy ultimately would hurt democracy. Holmes, who had less faith in democratic processes, was more concerned with the undeniable fact that the people convicted had indeed committed the crimes.

While Brandeis's condemnation of government espionage perhaps unfortunately has not become part of mainstream American political thought, the right to privacy that he asserted in his 1890 article and his *Olmstead* dissent is now integral to it. It illuminates the case law upholding the constitutional right to privacy and is the basis for provisions in a number of state constitutions.

LETTERS TO FELIX FRANKFURTER

Frankfurter, a professor at the Harvard Law School, was involved with the Harvard Law Review, *and Brandeis inundated him with suggestions about articles on various topics. Frankfurter's connection to the* New Republic *led Brandeis to suggest other articles more appropriate for the popular press. The two men had been colleagues in liberal causes and in Zionism before Brandeis went onto the Court, and most of the matters that Brandeis cared about continued to be mentioned in the correspondence the two men maintained.*

November 26, 1920, Washington, D.C.

. . . the N[ew] R[epublic] ought to take up a continuous campaign against espionage . . . The fundamental objection to espionage is (1) that espionage demoralizes every human being who participates in or uses the results of espionage; (2) that it takes sweetness & confidence out of life; (3) that it takes away the special manly qualities of honor & generosity which were marked in Americans.

It is like the tipping system an import from Continental Europe & the Near East only a thousand times worse . . .

It is un-American. It is nasty. It is nauseating.

July 2, 1926, Chatham, Massachusetts
[The survey referred to is a study that Frankfurter was supervising on the "effect of legal control on the restraining of crime and the efficacy of the law's treatment of criminals" in Boston.]
I suggest that, as an incident of the current survey, special care be taken to ascertain and record:

(a) The character (ethical) of the evidence through which it is sought to obtain a conviction—e.g. to what extent it is of the character . . . [of] the many cases where fed[eral] crimes were prosecuted in U.S. courts with evidence illegally procured by state officials.

(b) The instruments through which the evidence [is] introduced— e.g. by policemen & (1) to what extent detectives & undercover men . . .

I have grave doubt whether we shall ever be able to effect more than superficial betterment unless we succeed in infusing a sense (A) of the dignity of the law among a free, self-governing people and (B) of the solemnity of the function of administering justice. Among the essentials is that the government must, in its methods, & means, & instruments, be ever the gentleman . . . There are times of ease & prosperity when the pressing danger is somnolence rather than litigiousness.

I think that, in respect to evidence as in other respects, there is a limit to what can be accomplished by the mercenary alone. There must be some point at which the ability of the citizen to shift the burdens of government upon the paid expert—be he policeman or executive— ends.

BURDEAU V. MCDOWELL, 1920

J. C. McDowell's office was broken into by an unknown person who stole various books, papers, and correspondence and then turned them over to Joseph A. Burdeau, the assistant attorney general in western Pennsylvania. McDowell sued for return of his materials, to prevent Burdeau from taking them before a grand jury that was investigating mail fraud. Justice William R. Day held for the Court that there had been no government wrongdoing and that Burdeau could use the materials in his grand jury proceeding.

MR. JUSTICE BRANDEIS dissenting, with whom MR. JUSTICE HOLMES concurs.

Plaintiff's private papers were stolen. The thief, to further his own ends, delivered them to the law officer of the United States. He, knowing them to have been stolen, retains them for use against the plaintiff. Should the court permit him to do so?

That the court would restore the papers to plaintiff if they were still in the thief's possession is not questioned. That it has power to control the disposition of these stolen papers, although they have passed into the possession of the law officer, is also not questioned. But it is said that no provision of the Constitution requires their surrender and that the papers could have been subpoenaed. This may be true. Still I cannot believe that action of a public official is necessarily lawful, because it does not violate constitutional prohibitions and because the same result might have been attained by other and proper means. At the foundation of our civil liberty lies the principle which denies to government officials an exceptional position before the law and which subjects them to the same rules of conduct that are commands to the citizen. And in the development of our liberty insistence upon procedural regularity has been a large factor. Respect for law will not be advanced by resort, in its enforcement, to means which shock the common man's sense of decency and fair play.

CASEY V. UNITED STATES, 1928

Casey, a Seattle attorney, was suspected by the warden of a county jail of supplying his clients with drugs. The warden informed federal narcotic agents, who induced two prisoners to offer Casey money for morphine and arranged to record their conversations. It was during these talks that a deal was struck, and a relative of one of the prisoners testified that she subsequently picked up the drugs from Casey's office.

Holmes wrote for the Court, upholding the conviction because there was no doubt about Casey's having violated the law.

As will be seen in the next chapter, Brandeis concurred rather than dissenting in the important case of Whitney v. California, *because of the Court's rule that it would not decide cases on the basis of issues not raised by the parties themselves. In* Casey, *however, he was sufficiently upset to ignore that rule in order to protect the government.*

MR. JUSTICE BRANDEIS, dissenting.

. . . In my opinion, the prosecution must fail because officers of the Government instigated the commission of the alleged crime.

These are facts disclosed by the Government's evidence. In the Western District of Washington, Northern Division, prisoners awaiting trial for federal offences are commonly detained at King County Jail. The prisoners' lawyers frequently come there for consultation with clients. At the request of prisoners, the jailer telephones the lawyers to come for that purpose. A small compartment—called the attorneys' cage—is provided. Prior to the events here in question, the jailer had, upon such request, telephoned Casey, from time to time, to come to see prisoners . . . To entrap him, [federal narcotic officers] installed a dictaphone in the attorneys' cage and arranged so that, from an adjacent room, they could both hear conversations in the cage and see occupants. Then they deposited with the superintendent of the jail $20 to [prisoner] Cicero's credit; arranged with him to request the jailer to summon Casey to come to the jail; and also that, when Casey came, Cicero would ask him to procure some morphine and would pay him the $20 for that purpose . . .

I am aware that courts—mistaking relative social values and forgetting that a desirable end cannot justify foul means—have, in their zeal to punish, sanctioned the use of evidence obtained through criminal violation of property and personal rights or by other practices of detectives even more revolting. But the objection here is of a different nature. It does not rest merely upon the character of the evidence or upon the fact that the evidence was illegally obtained. The obstacle to the prosecution lies in the fact that the alleged crime was instigated by officers of the Government; that the act for which the Government seeks to punish the defendant is the fruit of their criminal conspiracy to induce its commission. The Government may set decoys to entrap criminals. But it may not provoke or create a crime and then punish the criminal, its creature. If Casey is guilty of the crime of purchasing 3.4 grains of morphine, on December 31st, as charged, it is because he yielded to the temptation presented by the officers. Their conduct is not a defence to him . . . But it does not follow that the court must suffer a detective-made criminal to be punished. To permit that would be tantamount to a ratification by the Government of the officers' unauthorized and unjustifiable conduct.

This case is unlike those where a defendant confessedly intended to commit a crime and the Government having knowledge thereof merely presented the opportunity and set its decoy. So far as appears, the officers had, prior to the events on December 31st, no basis for a belief that Casey was violating the law, except that the jailer harbored a suspicion. Casey took the witness stand and submitted himself to cross-examination. He testified that he had "never bought, sold, given away or possessed a single grain of morphine or other opiate" and that he had "never procured, or suggested to anyone else to procure morphine or narcotics of any kind." He testified that the payments made on orders from Cicero and Roy Nelson were payments on account of services to be rendered as counsel for the defence in the prosecutions against them then pending. He denied every material fact testified to by witnesses for the prosecution and supported his oath by other evidence. The Government's witnesses admitted that the conversations in the attorneys' cage were carried on in the ordinary tone of voice; that there was no effort to lower the voice or to speak privately or secretly; and that they could have heard all that was said without the use of the dictaphone. They admitted that when the narcotic agents searched Casey's office under a search warrant, on the evening of December 31st, they did not find any narcotics or any trace of them or any other incriminating article; and that when, at about the same time, they arrested Casey, he was taking supper with his wife and daughter at his home seven miles from Seattle. Whether the charge against Casey is true, we may not enquire. But if under such circumstances, the mere suspicion of the jailer could justify entrapment, little would be left of the doctrine.

The fact that no objection on the ground of entrapment was taken by the defendant, either below or in this Court, is without legal significance. This prosecution should be stopped, not because some right of Casey's has been denied, but in order to protect the Government. To protect it from illegal conduct of its officers. To preserve the purity of its courts. In my opinion, the judgment should be vacated with direction to quash the indictment.

OLMSTEAD V. UNITED STATES, 1927

The facts of the wiretapping case appear in Brandeis's first paragraph. Chief Justice William Howard Taft wrote for the majority, upholding the convictions on the grounds that the Fourth Amendment's prohibition against governmental "searches and seizures" did not apply to wiretapping. There had been no physical trespass, nothing had been physically seized, and no one had forced the people involved to talk over their telephones. To Brandeis, who believed in the necessity for the law to reflect societal changes and who had written in Truax v. Corrigan (1921) that "rights of . . . the liberty of the individual must be remolded from time to time to meet the changing needs of society," this was as outrageous as the behavior of the government. It is in Olmstead that Brandeis penned the famous phrase calling privacy "the right to be let alone—the most comprehensive of rights and the right most valued by civilized men," and spoke of the importance of the example set for the people by its government. Discussing the case with a niece sometime later, he commented, "lying and sneaking are always bad, no matter what the ends," and "I don't care about punishing crime, but I am implacable in maintaining standards."

MR. JUSTICE BRANDEIS, dissenting.

The defendants were convicted of conspiring to violate the National Prohibition Act. Before any of the persons now charged had been arrested or indicted, the telephones by means of which they habitually communicated with one another and with others had been tapped by federal officers. To this end, a lineman of long experience in wire-tapping was employed, on behalf of the Government and at its expense. He tapped eight telephones, some in the homes of the persons charged, some in their offices. Acting on behalf of the Government and in their official capacity, at least six other prohibition agents listened over the tapped wires and reported the messages taken. Their operations extended over a period of nearly five months. The type-written record of the notes of conversations overheard occupies 775 typewritten pages. By objections seasonably made and persistently renewed, the defendants objected to the admission of the evidence obtained by wire-tapping, on the ground that the Government's wire-tapping constituted an unreasonable search and seizure, in violation of the Fourth Amendment; and that the use as evidence of the conversations overheard compelled the defendants to be witnesses against themselves, in violation of the Fifth Amendment.

The Government makes no attempt to defend the methods employed by its officers. Indeed, it concedes that if wire-tapping can be deemed a search and seizure within the Fourth Amendment, such wire-tapping as was practiced in the case at bar was an unreasonable search and seizure, and that the evidence thus obtained was inadmissible. But it relies on the language of the Amendment; and it claims that the protection given thereby cannot properly be held to include a telephone conversation.

"We must never forget," said Mr. Chief Justice Marshall in *McCulloch* v. *Maryland,* "that it is a constitution we are expounding." Since then, this Court has repeatedly sustained the exercise of power by Congress, under various clauses of that instrument, over objects of which the Fathers could not have dreamed. We have likewise held that general limitations on the powers of Government, like those embodied in the due process clauses of the Fifth and Fourteenth Amendments, do not forbid the United States or the States from meeting modern conditions by regulations which "a century ago, or even half a century ago, probably would have been rejected as arbitrary and oppressive." Clauses guaranteeing to the individual protection against specific abuses of power, must have a similar capacity of adaptation to a changing world. It was with reference to such a clause that this Court said in *Weems* v. *United States,* "Legislation, both statutory and constitutional, is enacted, it is true, from an experience of evils, but its general language should not, therefore, be necessarily confined to the form that evil had theretofore taken. Time works changes, brings into existence new conditions and purposes. Therefore a principle to be vital must be capable of wider application than the mischief which gave it birth. This is peculiarly true of constitutions . . . Under any other rule a constitution would indeed be as easy of application as it would be deficient in efficacy and power. Its general principles would have little value and be converted by precedent into impotent and lifeless formulas. Rights declared in words might be lost in reality." When the Fourth and Fifth Amendments were adopted, "the form that evil had theretofore taken," had been necessarily simple. Force and violence were then the only means known to man by which a Government could directly effect self-incrimination. It could compel the individual to testify—a compulsion effected, if need be, by torture. It could secure possession of his papers and other articles incident to his private life—a seizure effected, if need be, by breaking and entry. Protection against such invasion of "the sanctities of a man's home and the privacies of life" was provided in the Fourth and Fifth Amendments by specific language. But "time works changes, brings into existence new conditions and purposes." Subtler and more far-reaching means of invading privacy have become available to the Government. Discovery and invention have made it possible for the Government, by means far more effective than stretching upon the rack, to obtain disclosure in court of what is whispered in the closet.

Moreover, "in the application of a constitution, our contemplation cannot be only of what has been but of what may be." The progress of science in furnishing the Government with means of espionage is not likely to stop with wire-tapping. Ways may some day be developed by which the Government, without removing papers from secret drawers, can reproduce them in court, and by which it will be enabled to expose to a jury the most intimate occurrences of the home. Advances in the psychic and related sciences may bring means of exploring unexpressed beliefs, thoughts and emotions . . . Can it be that the Constitution affords no protection against such invasions of individual security?

In *Ex parte Jackson*, it was held that a sealed letter entrusted to the mail is protected by the Amendments. The mail is a public service furnished by the Government. The telephone is a public service furnished by its authority. There is, in essence, no difference between the sealed letter and the private telephone message . . . The evil incident to invasion of the privacy of the telephone is far greater than that involved in tampering with the mails. Whenever a telephone line is tapped, the privacy of the persons at both ends of the line is invaded and all conversations between them upon any subject, and although proper, confidential and privileged, may be overheard. Moreover, the tapping of one man's telephone line involves the tapping of the telephone of every other person whom he may call or who may call him.

Time and again, this Court in giving effect to the principle underlying the Fourth Amendment, has refused to place an unduly literal construction upon it . . . Literally, there is no "search" or "seizure" when a friendly visitor abstracts papers from an office; yet we held in *Gouled v. United States* that evidence so obtained could not be used. No court which looked at the words of the Amendment rather than at its underlying purpose would hold, as this Court did in *Ex parte Jackson*, that its protection extended to letters in the mails . . .

Decisions of this Court applying the principle of the *Boyd* case have settled these things. Unjustified search and seizure violates the Fourth Amendment, whatever the character of the paper; whether the paper when taken by the federal officers was in the home, in an office or elsewhere; whether the taking was effected by force, by fraud, or in the orderly process of a court's procedure. From these decisions, it follows necessarily that the Amendment is violated by the officer's reading the paper without a physical seizure, without his even touching it; and that use, in any criminal proceeding, of the contents of the paper so examined—as where they are testified to by a federal officer who thus saw the document or where, through knowledge so obtained, a copy has been procured elsewhere—any such use constitutes a violation of the Fifth Amendment.

The protection guaranteed by the Amendments is much broader in scope. The makers of our Constitution undertook to secure conditions favorable to the pursuit of happiness. They recognized the significance of man's spiritual nature, of his feelings and of his intellect. They knew that only a part of the pain, pleasure and satisfactions of life are to be found in material things. They sought to protect Americans in their beliefs, their thoughts, their emotions and their sensations. They conferred, as against the Government, the right to be let alone—the most comprehensive of rights and the right most valued by civilized men. To protect that right, every unjustifiable intrusion by the Government upon the privacy of the individual, whatever the means employed, must be deemed a violation of the Fourth Amendment. And the use, as evidence in a criminal proceeding, of facts ascertained by such intrusion must be deemed a violation of the Fifth.

Applying to the Fourth and Fifth Amendments the established rule of construction, the defendants' objections to the evidence obtained by wire-tapping must, in my opinion, be sustained. It is, of course, immaterial where the physical connection with the telephone wires leading into the defendants' premises was made. And it is also immaterial that the intrusion was in aid of law enforcement. Experience should teach us to be most on our guard to protect liberty when the Government's purposes are beneficent. Men born to freedom are naturally alert to repel invasion of their liberty by evil-minded rulers. The greatest dangers to liberty lurk in insidious encroachment by men of zeal, well-meaning but without understanding.

When these unlawful acts were committed, they were crimes only of the officers individually. The Government was innocent, in legal contemplation; for no federal official is authorized to commit a crime on its behalf. When the Government, having full knowledge, sought, through the Department of Justice, to avail itself of the fruits of these acts in order to accomplish its own ends, it assumed moral responsibility for the officers' crimes. And if this Court should permit the Government, by means of its officers' crimes, to effect its purpose of punishing the defendants, there would seem to be present all the elements of a ratification. If so, the Government itself would become a lawbreaker.

Decency, security, and liberty alike demand that government officials shall be subjected to the same rules of conduct that are commands to the citizen. In a government of laws, existence of the government will be imperilled if it fails to observe the law scrupulously. Our Government is the potent, the omnipresent teacher. For good or for ill, it teaches the whole people by its example. Crime is contagious. If the Government becomes a lawbreaker, it breeds contempt for law; it invites every man to become a law unto himself; it invites anarchy. To declare that in the administration of the criminal law the end justifies the means—to declare that the Government may commit crimes in order to secure the conviction of a private criminal—would bring terrible retribution. Against that pernicious doctrine this Court should resolutely set its face.

9 / The Right to Free Speech

The best-known statements about free speech made by a Supreme Court justice probably are those penned by Oliver Wendell Holmes. These include declarations that the Constitution mandates "the principle of free thought—not free thought for those who agree with us but freedom for the thought that we hate," "the ultimate good desired is better reached by free trade in ideas [and] the best test of truth is the power of the thought to get itself accepted in the competition of the market," and "Every idea is an incitement . . . The only difference between the expression of an opinion and an incitement in the narrower sense is the speaker's enthusiasm for the result." In fact, however, Holmes didn't consider free speech terribly important, as indicated by some of his opinions written as a member of the Massachusetts Judicial Court and various opinions he wrote for the Supreme Court. The latter included decisions upholding the convictions of various socialists for writing a little-known pamphlet and for giving a speech opposing World War I, and a dissent when the Court struck down post–World War I state laws that criminalized the teaching of German in public schools. Holmes's decisions in favor of speech resulted from his reading of the Constitution as embodying a directive from the people that the government not be permitted to interfere excessively with speech. It was actually Brandeis who wrote the opinions that declared free communication to be crucial to a democratic society and who thereby created a constitutional doctrine designed to keep governmental interference with speech to an absolute minimum.

The first speech case to reach the Supreme Court after Brandeis joined it was *Schenck* v. *United States* (1919), which the Court heard when the country was in the midst of World War I. The Court was asked to review the convictions of two Socialist party officials who had sent out a few leaflets to draftees urging them to oppose the draft and placed the remainder on a table for anyone who wandered into their obscure Philadelphia office to pick up. They had been charged and convicted under the section of the 1917 Espionage Act that made it illegal, "when the United States is at war . . . willfully [to] cause or attempt to cause insubordination, disloyalty, mutiny, or refusal of duty, in the military or naval forces of the United States, or . . . willfully [to] obstruct the recruiting or enlistment service of the United States." Upholding the conviction, Holmes enunciated what became known as the "clear and present danger" doctrine. What the socialists had done, Holmes wrote, might have been permissible had the country been at peace. But "when a nation is at war many things that might be said in time of peace are such a hindrance to its effort that their utterance will not be endured so long as men fight," and the Congress and trial court had acted within their respective constitutional powers when they enacted the Sedition Act and held that Schenck's leaflets presented the kind of "clear and present danger" against which the country could protect itself. There were times, Holmes suggested, when speech could become an act beyond the protection of the First Amendment. His famous example was that of "a man . . . falsely shouting fire in a theatre and causing a panic."

Brandeis, still relatively new to the Court and a great admirer of Holmes, went along with the unanimous decision. He later regretted that, telling Felix Frankfurter, "I have never been quite happy about my concurrence . . . I had not then thought the issues of speech out—I thought at the subject, not through it." In a series of subsequent opinions, Brandeis substantially altered the clear and present danger doctrine as well as the law of free speech.

One of the great disagreements between Holmes and Brandeis lay in their attitude toward speech and ideas. Holmes saw nothing special in speech. "Free speech stands no differently than freedom from vaccination," he wrote to Judge Learned Hand. A convinced Social Darwinist, Holmes thought that the development of society was the result of natural forces and had very little to do with any human being's ideas. Brandeis, to the contrary, believed that the expression of differences of opinion was paramount in a democracy, for "only through such differences do we secure the light and fuller understanding which are necessary to a wise decision" about public policies. In some ways, as he wrote in a section from *Gilbert v. Minnesota* included below, a citizen's engaging in political discussion is "more important to the Nation than it is to himself," adding elsewhere, "Differences in opinions are not only natural but desirable where the question is difficult; for only through such differences do we secure the light and fuller understanding which are necessary to a wise decision." If societal development was impossible without full access to ideas, so was the development of the individual, and Brandeis cared deeply about both. His clerk David Riesman said that Brandeis had "an extraordinary faith in the possibilities of human development." Holmes had no such faith.

Having "thought . . . through" the subject during the next few months, Brandeis dissented for himself and Holmes in *Schaefer* v. *United States*, when the Court upheld another conviction under the Espionage Act. Brandeis deliberately misread Holmes's opinion in *Schenck* v. *United States* and wrote, "The constitutional right of free speech has been declared to be the same in peace and in war." That was not what the Court had held in *Schenck*, but it was what Brandeis believed it should have said.

Brandeis went on to dissent, with Holmes, in *Pierce* v. *United States*, another Espionage Act case. He finally understood the issues involved in freedom of speech when he was faced with the *Schaefer* and *Pierce* cases, Brandeis told Frankfurter. Referring to Herbert Hoover's statement that criticism should end at the water's shore, Brandeis said he had written his dissents to argue that the opposite was true. It was at least as important for citizens to express their disagreements with governmental policy during war, when lives were at stake, as it was during quieter moments.

Holmes and Brandeis parted company when Brandeis dissented in *Gilbert* v. *Minnesota*, another case decided in 1920. Brandeis brought speech and privacy together in his dissent, asserting that the overly broad statute under which Gilbert had been convicted for interfering with the military enlistment effort actually criminalized the teaching of pacifism, even in the home. He dissented once more when the postmaster general, invoking the Espionage Act, denied the use of the second-class mails to the *Milwaukee Leader*.

In both *Gilbert* v. *Minnesota* and *Milwaukee Publishing* v. *Burleson*, Brandeis wrote angrily about the Court's willingness to use the Fourteenth Amendment's due process clause to strike down state legislation that interfered with property rights but to ignore the clause when the right of speech was at issue. Speaking to Frankfurter about "things that are fundamental," he mentioned "Right to Speech. Right to Education. Right to choice of profession. Right to locomotion." The "right to your education and to utter speech," he added, "is fundamental *except* clear and present danger." In other words, the Court should have been busy protecting free speech and education rather than property rights. His opinions indicate that by "speech" he meant "communication," including the right to a free press.

The most important of Brandeis's free speech opinions, and the last included in this chapter, undoubtedly was his concurrence in *Whitney v. California* (1927). This case is of significance not only because it delineates the role of speech in a free society but also because it presented an entirely different version of the clear and present danger doctrine. "Clear" became "serious"; "present" became "imminent." "Imminent" meant that there was no time whatsoever in which "to avert the evil by the processes of education," for if such time existed, "the remedy to be applied is more speech, not enforced silence." And "danger" was defined not as "some violence or . . . destruction of property," but "the probability of serious injury to the State." There could be no suppression of speech, according to Brandeis, unless the state itself, the creation of the sovereign people, was in danger. The *Whitney v. California* opinion is an extraordinary expression of faith in ideas and, equally, in the assumption that ultimately people will choose wisely in a democratic state that encourages the articulation of all ideas. Brandeis believed absolutely in the power of ideas. Nonetheless, what his opinions in these cases demonstrates is his certainty that the channels of communication had to be open to even the most heinous ideas, for only through education and free discussion could such ideas be negated.

SCHAEFER V. UNITED STATES, 1920

Five officers and editors of the Tageblatt, a German-language newspaper, were convicted under the Espionage Act for helping the enemies of the United States by publishing false material designed to interfere with recruitment into the armed services. Justice Joseph McKenna, speaking for the Court, struck down the convictions of two of the men but upheld the convictions of three others. Brandeis's statement in the dissent he wrote for Justice Holmes and himself that "the nature and possible effect of a writing cannot be properly determined by culling here and there a sentence and presenting it separated from the context," and his reprinting of the publications in their entirety, was in keeping with his insistence upon examining all the relevant facts. Most of the articles nonetheless have been omitted here, although the gist and tone of them can be gathered from what follows.

MR. JUSTICE BRANDEIS delivered the following opinion in which MR. JUSTICE HOLMES concurred.

The extent to which Congress may, under the Constitution, interfere with free speech was in *Schenck* v. *United States* declared by a unanimous court to be this:—"The question in every case is whether the words used are used in such circumstances and are of such a nature as to create a clear and present danger that they will bring about the substantive evils that Congress has a right to prevent. It is a question of proximity and degree."

This is a rule of reason. Correctly applied, it will preserve the right of free speech both from suppression by tyrannous, well-meaning majorities and from abuse by irresponsible, fanatical minorities. Like many other rules for human conduct, it can be applied correctly only by the exercise of good judgment; and to the exercise of good judgment, calmness is, in times of deep feeling and on subjects which excite passion, as essential as fearlessness and honesty. In my opinion, no jury acting in calmness could reasonably say that any of the publications set forth in the indictment was of such a character or was made under such circumstances as to create a clear and present danger either that they would obstruct recruiting or that they would promote the success of the enemies of the United States. That they could have interfered with the military or naval forces of the United States or have caused insubordination, disloyalty, mutiny, or refusal of duty in its military or naval services was not even suggested; and there was no evidence of conspiracy except the cooperation of editors and business manager in issuing the publications complained of.

The nature and possible effect of a writing cannot be properly determined by culling here and there a sentence and presenting it separated from the context. In making such determination, it should be read as a whole; at least if it is short like these news items and editorials. Fifteen publications were set forth in the indictment; and others were introduced in evidence. To reproduce all of them would unduly prolong this opinion. Four are selected which will illustrate the several contentions of the Government. That at least three of these four were deemed by it of special importance is shown by the fact that each of the three was made the subject of a separate count.

First: There were convictions on three counts of wilfully obstructing the recruiting and enlistment service. The conviction of the news editor of so obstructing rested wholly upon his having inserted the following reprint from a Berlin paper in the Tageblatt:

"Berlin, Aug. 5.—In the 'Taglishe Rundschau,' Professor Jenny writes under the title 'Americanism' as follows:—Americans think in exaggerations and talk in superlatives. Even Ambassador Andrew White in his Memoirs falls into superlatives in comparatively insignificant cases. He speaks of them as the most important events of his life and maintains that certain people have made an indelible impression on him, whom others consider to be ordinary average men.

"The army of ten million men has dwindled to a voluntary army of 120,000; while the new conscripted army of 565,000 will not even be ready to begin drilling for the front in six months. The hundred thousand air ships were reduced to 20,000 and then to 3,000, which the Americans hope to have ready for next summer if they find the right model for them. As for the thousands of ships that were to be sent across the ocean, America, six months after the declaration of war, has not yet decided whether they are to be wood or steel ships; so far not even the keel of one ship has been laid. It amounts to this, that now when the Americans can scrape some tonnage together, the troops are not ready, and when they have the troops ready, the tonnage will not be available.

"The army of ten million and the hundred thousand airships which were to annihilate Germany, have proved to be American boasts which will not stand washing. It is worthy to note how much the Yankees can yell their throats out without spraining their mouths. This is in accord with their spiritual quality. They enjoy a capacity for Lying, which is able to conceal to a remarkable degree a lack of thought behind a superfluity of words.

"But some fine day, if they do not stop their boasting and bluffing, it might happen to them that they get the lockjaw, for which there is no better relief than a good box on the ear. Moreover it is not to be assumed that the Americans are really in earnest with the war. No one would be surprised if they found a thousand and one excuses for taking no active part in the European War."

It is not apparent on a reading of this article—which is not unlike many reprints from the press of Germany to which our patriotic societies gave circulation in order to arouse the American fighting spirit—how it could rationally be held to tend even remotely or indirectly to obstruct recruiting. But as this court has declared and as Professor Chafee has shown in his "Freedom of Speech in War Time," the test to be applied—as in the case of criminal attempts and incitement—is not the remote or possible effect. There must be the clear and present danger. Certainly men judging in calmness and with this test presented to them could not reasonably have said that this coarse and heavy humor immediately threatened the success of recruiting.

Second: There were convictions on three counts of wilfully conveying false reports and statements with intent to promote the success of the enemies of the United States. The Tageblatt, like many of the smaller newspapers, was without a foreign or a national news service of any kind and did not purport to have any. It took such news usually from items appearing in some other paper theretofore published in the German or the English language. It did not in any way indicate the source of its news. The item, if taken from the English press, was of course translated. Sometimes it was copied in full; sometimes in part only; and sometimes it was rewritten; or editorial comment was added. The Government did not attempt to prove that any statement made in any of the news items published in the Tageblatt was false in fact. Its evidence, under each count, was limited to showing that the item as published therein varied in some particular from the item as it appeared in the paper from which it had been copied; and no attempt was made to prove the original despatch to the latter paper. The Government contended that solely because of variation from the item copied it was a false report, although the item in the Tageblatt did not purport to reproduce an item from another paper, and in no way indicated the source of the news. Each of the three items following illustrates a different method by which the variation was effected:

1. The publication for which the news editor was convicted on the fifth count by reason of an addition to the item copied:
(The translation of the Tageblatt item as set forth in the indictment.)

"Further Economies.

"Amsterdam, September 2. It has been reported here that permission to export the wheat and flour on the ships held in New York has been refused. Information to this effect is contained in an official proclamation of the latest cut in bread rations and of the need for economy which has reached the civil authorities: This document says: 'We know now with certainty that we cannot count upon the import of breadstuffs from America and that we must strive to make our own provisions suffice. In initiated circles it is said that under no conditions can the new American proposal be accepted, and that the foodstuffs may rot before the ships will be unloaded.' "[*Brandeis had the German version printed side by side with the translation.*]

The falsification charged is said to consist in having added to the despatch which was copied from the Staatszeitung the words: "In initiated circles it is said that under no conditions can the new American proposal be accepted, and that the foodstuffs may rot before the ships will be unloaded." But it is obvious, upon comparing the English translation with the German original, that the defendant did no such thing. The sentence referred to was not made a part of the despatch in the Tageblatt. It followed the despatch; it was not within the quotation marks; and was separated from it by a dash,—a usual method of indicating that what follows is comment or an addition made by the editor. In the English translation as set forth in the indictment, this sentence, through some inadvertence of the Government's translator or draftsman, was included as part of the despatch and brought with the quotation therein. Evidently both the jury and the trial judge failed to examine the German original.

3. The publication for which the news editor was convicted on the sixth count because of the change of a word in the item copied: [*Brandeis then quotes a lengthy article about a speech made by Senator La Follette, prophesying that Liberty Bonds "would eventually find their way into the hands of the rich," arguing that the war should be paid for by higher taxes, and predicting that if current prices continue to be hard there will be breadlines.*]

Falsification is charged solely because the word "Brot-riots" (translated as "bread-riots") was used in the twelfth line of the article instead of the word "Brotreihen" (translated as "breadlines").

The act punishes the wilful making and conveying of "false reports or false statements with intent to interfere with the operation or success of the military or naval forces of the United States or to promote the success of its enemies." Congress sought thereby to protect the American people from being wilfully misled to the detriment of their cause by one actuated by the intention to further the cause of the enemy. Wilfully untrue statements which might mislead the people as to the financial condition of the Government and thereby embarrass it; as to the adequacy of the preparations for war or the support of the forces; as to the sufficiency of the food supply; or wilfully untrue statements or reports of military operations which might mislead public opinion as to the competency of the army or navy or its leaders (See "The Relation Between the Army and the Press in War Time," War College Publication, 1916); or wilfully untrue statements or reports which might mislead officials in the execution of the law, or military authorities in the disposition of the forces. Such is the kind of false statement and the only kind which, under any rational construction, is made criminal by the act. Could the military and naval forces of the United States conceivably have been interfered with or the success of the enemy conceivably have been promoted by any of the three publications set forth above? Surely, neither the addition to the first, nor the omission from the second constituted the making of a false statement or report. The mistranslation of "breadlines" in one passage of the third, if it can be deemed a false report, obviously could not have promoted the success of our enemies. The other publications set out in the indictment were likewise impotent to produce the evil against which the statute aimed.

Darkow, the news editor, and Werner, the editor, were each sentenced to five years in the penitentiary; Lemke, the business manager, to two years. The jury which found men guilty for publishing news items or editorials like those here in question must have supposed it to be within their province to condemn men not merely for disloyal acts but for a disloyal heart; provided only that the disloyal heart was evidenced by some utterance. To hold that such harmless additions to or omissions from news items, and such impotent expressions of editorial opinion, as were shown here, can afford the basis even of a prosecution will doubtless discourage criticism of the policies of the Government. To hold that such publications can be suppressed as false reports, subjects to new perils the constitutional liberty of the press, already seriously curtailed in practice under powers assumed to have been conferred upon the postal authorities. Nor will this grave danger end with the passing of the war. The constitutional right of free speech has been declared to be the same in peace and in war. In peace, too, men may differ widely as to what loyalty to our country demands; and an intolerant majority, swayed by passion or by fear, may be prone in the future, as it has often been in the past, to stamp as disloyal opinions with which it disagrees. Convictions such as these, besides abridging freedom of speech, threaten freedom of thought and of belief.

PIERCE V. UNITED STATES, 1920

Pierce *was another case involving Espionage Act convictions for distribution of leaflets that had allegedly interfered with the operation of the war effort and caused insubordination. Speaking with Frankfurter, Brandeis attributed Justice Mahlon Pitney's opinion for the Court upholding the convictions to "Pitney's Presbyterian doctrine of freedom of will," which led Pitney to believe that "those individuals having free choice of right and wrong, choose wrong" and so should not be exposed to wrong ideas. Brandeis added that he thought Pitney was "very kindly" but "wholly without knowledge." As his opinion indicates, Brandeis was incredulous at the government's finding the publications threatening, which is no doubt one reason he reprinted them at length and talked about the kinds of witnesses produced by the prosecution. All the 1920 cases excerpted here give some sense of the hysteria that gripped the nation during World War I and of Brandeis's awareness of the negative impact such emotion could have on the democratic process.*

MR. JUSTICE BRANDEIS, dissenting, delivered the following opinion in which MR. JUSTICE HOLMES concurred.

What is called "distributing literature" is a means commonly used by the Socialist Party to increase its membership and otherwise to advance the cause it advocates. To this end the national organization with headquarters at Chicago publishes such "literature" from time to time and sends sample copies to the local organizations. These, when they approve, purchase copies and call upon members to volunteer for service in making the distribution locally. Sometime before July 11, 1917, a local of the Socialist Party at Albany, New York, received from the national organization sample copies of a four-page leaflet entitled "The Price We Pay," written by Irwin St. John Tucker, an Episcopal clergyman and a man of sufficient prominence to have been included in the 1916–1917 edition of "Who's Who in America." The proposal to distribute this leaflet came up for action at a meeting of the Albany local held on July 11, 1917. A member who was a lawyer called attention to the fact that the question whether it was legal to distribute this leaflet was involved in a case pending in Baltimore in the District Court of the United States; and it was voted "not to distribute 'The Price We Pay' until we know if it is legal." The case referred to was an indictment under the Selective Draft Act for conspiracy to obstruct recruiting by means of distributing the leaflet. Shortly after the July 11th meeting it became known that District Judge Rose had directed an acquittal in that case; and at the next meeting of the local, held July 25th, it was voted to rescind the motion "against distributing 'The Price We Pay' and call for distributors." Four members of the local . . . volunteered as distributors. They distributed about five thousand copies by hand in Albany.

In New York a different view [from that in Baltimore] was taken; and an indictment was found against the four distributors. [Those counts not already eliminated include] count three, which charges a violation of 3 of the Espionage Act by making false reports and false statements, with the intent "to interfere with the operation and success of the military and naval forces"; and counts two and six, also involving 3 of the Espionage Act, the one for conspiring, the other for attempting, "to cause insubordination, disloyalty and refusal of duty in the military and naval forces." . . . Although the uttering or publishing of the words charged be admitted, there necessarily arises in every case . . . the question whether the words were used "in such circumstances and are of such a nature as to create a clear and present danger that they will bring about the substantive evil that Congress has a right to prevent," *Schenck* v. *United States*; and also the question whether the act of uttering or publishing was done willfully, that is, with the intent to produce the result which the Congress sought to prevent. But in cases of the first class [of crimes under the Act] three additional elements of the crime must be established, namely:

(1) The statement or report must be of something capable of being proved false in fact. The expression of an opinion, for instance, whether sound or unsound, might conceivably afford a sufficient basis for the charge of attempting to cause insubordination, disloyalty or refusal of duty, or for the charge of obstructing recruiting; but, because an opinion is not capable of being proved false in fact, a statement of it cannot be made the basis of a prosecution of the first class.

(2) The statement or report must be proved to be false.

(3) The statement or report must be known by the defendant to be false when made or conveyed.

In the case at bar the alleged offence consists wholly in distributing leaflets which had been written and published by others . . . With unimportant exceptions to be discussed later, the only evidence introduced to establish the several elements of both of the crimes charged is the leaflet itself; and the leaflet is unaffected by extraneous evidence which might give to words used therein special meaning or effect. In order to determine whether the leaflet furnishes any evidence to establish any of the above enumerated elements of the offences charged, the whole leaflet must necessarily be read. It is as follows:

THE PRICE WE PAY.
by Irwin St. John Tucker.
I.

Conscription is upon us: the draft law is a fact!
Into your homes the recruiting officers are coming. They will take your sons of military age and impress them into the army;
Stand them up in long rows, break them into squads and platoons, teach them to deploy and wheel;
Guns will be put into their hands; they will be taught not to think, only to obey without questioning.
Then they will be shipped thru the submarine zone by the hundreds of thousands to the bloody quagmire of Europe.
Into that seething, heaving swamp of torn flesh and floating entrails they will be plunged, in regiments, divisions and armies, screaming as they go.
Agonies of torture will rend their flesh from their sinews, will crack their bones and dissolve their lungs; every pang will be multiplied in its passage to you.
Black death will be a guest at every American fireside. Mothers and fathers and sisters, wives and sweethearts will know the weight of that awful vacancy left by the bullet which finds its mark.
And still the recruiting officers will come; seizing age after age, mounting up to the elder ones and taking the younger ones as they grow to soldier size;
And still the toll of death will grow.
Let them come! Let death and desolation make barren every Home! Let the agony of war crack every parent's heart! Let the horrors and miseries of the world-downfall swamp the happiness of every hearthstone!
Then perhaps you will believe what we have been telling you! For war is the price of your stupidity, you who have rejected Socialism!

III.

Food prices go up like skyrockets; and show no sign of bursting and coming down.

Wheat, corn, potatoes, are far above the Civil War mark; eggs, butter, meat: all these things are almost beyond a poor family's reach.

The Attorney General of the United States is so busy sending to prison men who do not stand up when the Star Spangled Banner is played, that he has no time to protect the food supply from gamblers.

Starvation begins to stare us in the face—and we, people of the richest and most productive land on earth are told to starve ourselves yet further because our allies must be fed.

Submarines are steadily sending to the fishes millions of tons of food stuffs; and still we build more ships, and send more food, and more and more is sunk;

Frantically we grub in the earth and sow and tend and reap; and then as frantically load the food in ships, and then as frantically sink with them—

The poor folks are growling and muttering with savage side-long glances and are rolling up their sleeves.

For the price they pay for their stupidity is getting beyond their power to pay!

IV.

Frightful reports are being made of the ravages of venereal diseases in the army training camps, and in the barracks where the girl munition workers live.

One of the great nations lost more men thru loathsome immoral diseases than on the firing line, during the first 18 months of the war.

Back from the Mexican border our boys come, spreading the curse of the great Black Plague among hundreds of thousands of homes; blasting the lives of innocent women and unborn babes,

Future generations of families are made impossible; blackness and desolation instead of happiness and love will reign where the homes of the future should be;

And all because you believed the silly lie, that 'Socialism would destroy the home!'

Pound on, guns of the embattled host; wreck yet more homes, kill yet more husbands and fathers, rob yet more maidens of their sweethearts, yet more babies of their fathers;

That is the price the world pays for believing the monstrous, damnable, outrageous lie that Socialism would destroy the home!

Now the homes of the world are being destroyed; every one of them would have been saved by Socialism. But you would not believe. Now pay the price!

v.

This war began over commercial routes and ports and rights; and underneath all the talk about democracy versus autocracy, you hear a continual note, and undercurrent, a subdued refrain;
'Get ready for the commercial war that will follow this war.'
Commercial war preceded this war; it gave rise to this war; it now gives point and meaning to this war;
And as soon as the guns are stilled and the dead are buried, commercial forces will prepare for the next bloody struggle over routes and ports and rights, coal mines and railroads;
For these are the essence of this, as of all other wars!
But go to it! Believe everything you are told—you always have and doubtless always will, believe them.
Only do retain this much reason; when you have paid the price, the last and uttermost price; and have not received what you were told you were fighting for—namely Democracy—
Then remember that the price you paid was not the purchase price for justice, but the penalty price for your stupidity!

vi.

We have been telling you for, lo, these many years that the whole nation could be mobilized and every man, woman and child induced to do his bit for the service of humanity but you have laughed at us.
Now you call every person traitor, slacker, pro-enemy who will not go crazy on the subject of killing; and you have turned the whole energy of the nations of the world into the service of their kings for the purpose of killing—killing—killing.
Why did you ridicule us and call us impractical dreamers when we prophesied a world-state of fellow workers, each man creating for the benefit of all the world, and the whole world creating for the benefit of each man?
Those idle taunts; those thoughtless jeers, that refusal to listen, to be fair-minded—you are paying for them now.
—Lo, the price you pay! Lo, the price your children will pay. Lo, the agony, the death, the blood, the unforgettable sorrow,—

The price of your stupidity!

For this war—as every one who thinks or knows anything will say, whenever truth-telling becomes safe and possible again,— This war is to determine the question, whether the chambers of commerce of the allied nations or of the Central Empires have the superior right to exploit undeveloped countries.

It is to determine whether interest, dividends and profits shall be paid to investors speaking German or those speaking English and French.

Our entry into it was determined by the certainty that if the allies do nothing, J. P. Morgan's loans to the Allies will be repudiated, and those American investors who bit on his promises would be hooked.

Socialism would have settled that question; it would determine that to every producer shall be given all the value of what he produces; so that nothing would be left over for exploiters or investors.

With that great question settled there would be no cause for war.

IF THIS INTERESTS YOU, PASS IT ON.

Subscribe to The American Socialist, Published weekly by the National Office, Socialist Party, 803 West Madison Street, Chicago, Ill., 50 cents per year, 25 cents for 6 months. It is a paper without a muzzle.

First: From this leaflet, which is divided into six chapters, there are set forth in count three, five sentences as constituting the false statements or reports wilfully conveyed by defendants with the intent to interfere with the operation and success of the military and naval forces of the United States.

(a) Two sentences are culled from the first chapter. They follow immediately after the words: "Conscription is upon us; the draft law is a fact"—and a third sentence culled follows a little later. They are:

"Into your homes the recruiting officers are coming. They will take your sons of military age and impress them into the army . . . And still the recruiting officers will come; seizing age after age, mounting up to the elder ones and taking the younger ones as they grow to soldier size."

To prove the alleged falsity of these statements the Government gravely called as a witness a major in the regular army with 28 years' experience, who has been assigned since July 5, 1917, to recruiting work. He testified that "recruiting" has to do with the volunteer service and has nothing to do with the drafting system and that the word impress has no place in the recruiting service. The subject of his testimony was a matter not of fact but of law; and as a statement of law it was erroneous. That "recruiting is gaining fresh supplies for the forces, as well by draft as otherwise" had been assumed by the Circuit Court of Appeals for that circuit in *Masses Publishing Co.* v. *Patten* (decided eleven days before this testimony was given), and was later expressly held by this court in *Schenck* v. *United States*. The third of the sentences charged as false was obviously neither a statement nor a report, but a prediction; and it was later verified. That the prediction made in the leaflet was later verified is, of course, immaterial; but the fact shows the danger of extending beyond its appropriate sphere the scope of a charge of falsity.

(b) The fourth sentence set forth in the third count as a false statement was culled from the third chapter of the leaflet and is this:

"The Attorney General of the United States is so busy sending to prison men who do not stand up when the Star Spangled Banner is played, that he has not time to protect the food supply from gamblers."

To prove the falsity of this statement the Government called the United States Attorney for that district who testified that no federal law makes it a crime not to stand up when the "Star Spangled Banner" is played and that he has no knowledge of any one being prosecuted for failure to do so. The presiding judge supplemented this testimony by a ruling that the Attorney General, like every officer of the Government, is presumed to do his duty and not to violate his duty and that this presumption should obtain unless evidence to the contrary was adduced. The Regulations of the Army provide that if the National Anthem is played in any place those present, whether in uniform or in civilian clothes, shall stand until the last note of the anthem. The regulation is expressly limited in its operation to those belonging to the military service, although the practice was commonly observed by civilians throughout the war. There was no federal law imposing such action upon them. The Attorney General, who does not enforce Army Regulations, was, therefore, not engaged in sending men to prison for that offence. But when the passage in question is read in connection with the rest of the chapter, it seems clear that it was intended, not as a statement of fact, but as a criticism of the Department of Justice for devoting its efforts to prosecutions for acts or omissions indicating lack of sympathy with the war, rather than to protecting the community from profiteering by prosecuting violators of the Food Control Act. Such criticisms of governmental operations, though grossly unfair as an interpretation of facts or even wholly unfounded in fact, are not "false reports or false statements with intent to interfere with the operation or success of the military or naval forces."

(c) The remaining sentence, set forth in count three as a false statement, was culled from the sixth chapter of the leaflet and is this:

"Our entry into it was determined by the certainty that if the allies do not win, J. P. Morgan's loans to the allies will be repudiated, and those American investors who bit on his promises would be hooked."

To prove the falsity of this statement the Government introduced the address made by the President to Congress on April 2, 1917, which preceded the adoption of the Joint Resolution of April 6, 1917, declaring that a state of war exists between the United States and The Imperial German Government. This so-called statement of fact—which is alleged to be false—is merely a conclusion or a deduction from facts . . . In its essence it is the expression of a judgment—like the statements of many so-called historical facts . . . The cause of a war—as of most human action—is not single. War is ordinarily the result of many cooperating causes, many different conditions, acts and motives. Historians rarely agree in their judgment as to what was the determining factor in a particular war, even when they write under circumstances where detachment and the availability of evidence from all sources minimize both prejudice and other sources of error. For individuals, and classes of individuals, attach significance to those things which are significant to them. And, as the contributing causes cannot be subjected, like a chemical combination in a test tube, to qualitative and quantitative analysis so as to weigh and value the various elements, the historians differ necessarily in their judgments. One finds the determining cause of war in a great man, another in an idea, a belief, an economic necessity, a trade advantage, a sinister machination, or an accident. It is for this reason largely that men seek to interpret anew in each age, and often with each new generation, the important events in the world's history.

That all who voted for the Joint Resolution of April 6, 1917, did not do so for the reasons assigned by the President in his address to Congress on April 2, is demonstrated by the discussions in the House and in the Senate. That debate discloses also that both in the Senate and in the House the loans to the Allies and the desire to ensure their repayment in full were declared to have been instrumental in bringing about in our country the sentiment in favor of the war. However strongly we may believe that these loans were not the slightest makeweight, much less a determining factor, in the country's decision, the fact that some of our representatives in the Senate and the House declared otherwise on one of the most solemn occasions in the history of the Nation, should help us to understand that statements like that here charged to be false are in essence matters of opinion and judgment, not matters of fact to be determined by a jury upon or without evidence; and that even the President's address, which set forth high moral grounds justifying our entry into the war, may not be accepted as establishing beyond a reasonable doubt that a statement ascribing a base motive was criminally false. All the alleged false statements were an interpretation and discussion of public facts of public interest . . . To hold that a jury may make punishable statements of conclusions or of opinion, like those here involved, by declaring them to be statements of facts and to be false would practically deny members of small political parties freedom of criticism and of discussion in times when feelings run high and the questions involved are deemed fundamental. There is nothing in the act compelling or indeed justifying such a construction of it; and I cannot believe that Congress in passing, and the President in approving, it conceived that such a construction was possible.

Second: But, even if the passages from the leaflet set forth in the third count could be deemed false statements within the meaning of the act, the convictions thereon were unjustified because evidence was wholly lacking to prove any one of the other essential elements of the crime charged. Thus there was not a particle of evidence that the defendants knew that the statements were false. They were mere distributors of the leaflet. It had been prepared by a man of some prominence. It had been published by the national organization. Not one of the defendants was an officer even of the local organization. One of them, at least, was absent from the meetings at which the proposal to distribute the leaflet was discussed. There is no evidence that the truthfulness of the statements contained in the leaflet had ever been questioned before this indictment was found. The statement mainly relied upon to sustain the conviction—that concerning the effect of our large loans to the Allies—was merely a repetition of what had been declared with great solemnity and earnestness in the Senate and in the House while the Joint Resolution was under discussion. The fact that the President had set forth in his noble address worthy grounds for our entry into the war, was not evidence that these defendants knew to be false the charge that base motives had also been operative. The assertion that the great financial interests exercise a potent, subtle and sinister influence in the important decisions of our Government had often been made by men high in authority. Mr. Wilson, himself a historian, said before he was President and repeated in the New Freedom that: "The masters of the Government of the United States are the combined capitalists and manufacturers of the United States." We may be convinced that the decision to enter the great war was wholly free from such base influences but we may not, because such is our belief, permit a jury to find, in the absence of evidence, that it was proved beyond a reasonable doubt that these defendants *knew* that a statement in this leaflet to the contrary was false.

. . . The fact that the local refused to distribute the pamphlet until Judge Rose had directed a verdict of acquittal in the Baltimore case shows that its members desired to do only that which the law permitted. The tenor of the leaflet itself shows that the intent of the writer and of the publishers was to advance the cause of Socialism; and each defendant testified that this was his only purpose in distributing the pamphlet. Furthermore, the nature of the words used and the circumstances under which they were used showed affirmatively that they did not "create a clear and present danger," that thereby the operations or success of our military and naval forces would be interfered with . . .

The third count is the charge of wilfully conveying in time of war false statements with the intent to interfere with the operation and success of our military or naval forces. One who did that would be called a traitor to his country. The defendants, humble members of the Socialist Party, performed as distributors of the leaflet what would ordinarily be deemed merely a menial service. To hold them guilty under the third count is to convict not them alone, but, in effect, their party, or at least its responsible leaders, of treason, as that word is commonly understood. I cannot believe that there is any basis in our law for such a condemnation on this record.

Third: To sustain a conviction on the second or on the sixth count it is necessary to prove that by cooperating to distribute the leaflet the defendants conspired or attempted wilfully to "cause insubordination, disloyalty, mutiny, or refusal of duty, in the military or naval forces" . . . The leaflet contains lurid and perhaps exaggerated pictures of the horrors of war. Its arguments as to the causes of this war may appear to us shallow and grossly unfair. The remedy proposed may seem to us worse than the evil which, it is argued, will be thereby removed. But the leaflet, far from counselling disobedience to law, points to the hopelessness of protest, under the existing system, pictures the irresistible power of the military arm of the Government, and indicates that acquiescence is a necessity. Insubordination, disloyalty, mutiny and refusal of duty in the military or naval forces are very serious crimes. It is not conceivable that any man of ordinary intelligence and normal judgment would be induced by anything in the leaflet to commit them and thereby risk the severe punishment prescribed for such offences. Certainly there was no clear and present danger that such would be the result.

The fundamental right of free men to strive for better conditions through new legislation and new institutions will not be preserved, if efforts to secure it by argument to fellow citizens may be construed as criminal incitement to disobey the existing law—merely, because the argument presented seems to those exercising judicial power to be unfair in its portrayal of existing evils, mistaken in its assumptions, unsound in reasoning or intemperate in language. No objections more serious than these can, in my opinion, reasonably be made to the arguments presented in "The Price We Pay."

GILBERT V. STATE OF MINNESOTA, 1920

The facts of the case are contained in Brandeis's opinion. Holmes, who disagreed with Brandeis's assumption that permitting the states almost any economic experimentations they chose would result in progress, voted with the majority to uphold the conviction. The last part of Brandeis's dissent was meant as a blast against a Court that had used the Fourteenth Amendment's due process clause to strike down legislation protective of workers' rights, alleging that it interfered with the employer's "liberty of contract" that the Court had read into the clause, but declined to apply it to a state's interference with speech.

MR. JUSTICE BRANDEIS, dissenting.

Joseph Gilbert, manager of the organization department of the Non-partisan League, was sentenced to fine and imprisonment for speaking on August 18, 1917, at a public meeting of the League, words held to be prohibited by c. 463 of the laws of Minnesota, approved April 20, 1917.

The Minnesota statute was enacted during the World War; but it is not a war measure. The statute is said to have been enacted by the State under its police power to preserve the peace,—but it is in fact an act to prevent teaching that the abolition of war is possible. Unlike the Federal Espionage Act of June 15, 1917, it applies equally whether the United States is at peace or at war. It abridges freedom of speech and of the press, not in a particular emergency, in order to avert a clear and present danger, but under all circumstances. The restriction imposed relates to the teaching of the doctrine of pacifism and the legislature in effect prescribes it for all time. The statute does not in terms prohibit the teaching of the doctrine. Its prohibition is more specific and is directed against the teaching of certain applications of it. This specification operates, as will be seen, rather to extend, than to limit the scope of the prohibition.

Sections 1 and 2 prohibit teaching or advocating by printed matter, writing or word of mouth, that men should not enlist in the military or naval forces of the United States. The prohibition is made to apply whatever the motive, the intention, or the purpose of him who teaches. It applies alike to the preacher in the pulpit, the professor at the university, the speaker at a political meeting, the lecturer at a society or club gathering. Whatever the nature of the meeting and whether it be public or private, the prohibition is absolute, if five persons are assembled. The reason given by the speaker for advising against enlistment is immaterial. Young men considering whether they should enter these services as a means of earning a livelihood or as a career, may not be told that, in the opinion of the speaker, they can serve their country and themselves better by entering the civil service of State or Nation, or by studying for one of the professions, or by engaging in the transportation service, or in farming or in business, or by becoming a workman in some productive industry. Although conditions may exist in the Army or the Navy which are undermining efficiency, which tend to demoralize those who enter the service and would render futile their best efforts, the State forbids citizens of the United States to advocate that men should not enlist until existing abuses or defects are remedied. The prohibition imposed by the Minnesota statute has no relation to existing needs or desires of the government. It applies although recruiting is neither in process nor in contemplation. For the statute aims to prevent not acts but beliefs. The prohibition imposed by 3 is even more far-reaching than that provided in 1 and 2. Section 3 makes it punishable to teach in any place a single person that a citizen should not aid in carrying on a war, no matter what the relation of the parties may be. Thus the statute invades the privacy and freedom of the home. Father and mother may not follow the promptings of religious belief, of conscience or of conviction, and teach son or daughter the doctrine of pacifism. If they do any police officer may summarily arrest them.

That such a law is inconsistent with the conceptions of liberty hitherto prevailing seems clear. But the matter is not one merely of state concern. The state law affects directly the functions of the Federal Government. It affects rights, privileges and immunities of one who is a citizen of the United States; and it deprives him of an important part of his liberty. These are rights which are guaranteed protection by the Federal Constitution; and they are invaded by the statute in question.

Congress has the exclusive power to legislate concerning the Army and the Navy of the United States, and to determine, among other things, the conditions of enlistment . . . Congress, legislating for a people justly proud of liberties theretofore enjoyed and suspicious or resentful of any interference with them, might conclude that even in times of grave danger, the most effective means of securing support from the great body of citizens is to accord to all freedom to criticise the acts and administration of their country, although such freedom may be used by a few to urge upon their fellow-citizens not to aid the Government in carrying on a way, which reason or faith tells them is wrong and will, therefore, bring misery upon their country.

The right of a citizen of the United States to take part, for his own or the country's benefit, in the making of federal laws and in the conduct of the Government, necessarily includes the right to speak or write about them; to endeavor to make his own opinion concerning laws existing or contemplated prevail; and, to this end, to teach the truth as he sees it . . . Full and free exercise of this right by the citizen is ordinarily also his duty; for its exercise is more important to the Nation than it is to himself. Like the course of the heavenly bodies, harmony in national life is a resultant of the struggle between contending forces. In frank expression of conflicting opinion lies the greatest promise of wisdom in governmental action; and in suppression lies ordinarily the greatest peril. There are times when those charged with the responsibility of Government, faced with clear and present danger, may conclude that suppression of divergent opinion is imperative; because the emergency does not permit reliance upon the slower conquest of error by truth. And in such emergencies the power to suppress exists . . . As exclusive power over enlistments in the Army and Navy of the United States and the responsibility for the conduct of war is vested by the Federal Constitution in Congress, legislation by a State on this subject is necessarily void unless authorized by Congress.

I have difficulty in believing that the liberty guaranteed by the Constitution, which has been held to protect against state denial the right of an employer to discriminate against a workman because he is a member of a trade union, the right of a business man to conduct a private employment agency, or to contract outside the State for insurance of his property, although the legislature deems it inimical to the public welfare, does not include liberty to teach, either in the privacy of the home or publicly, the doctrine of pacifism; so long, at least, as Congress has not declared that the public safety demands its suppression. I cannot believe that the liberty guaranteed by the Fourteenth Amendment includes only liberty to acquire and to enjoy property.

MILWAUKEE SOCIAL DEMOCRATIC PUBLISHING COMPANY V. BURLESON, 1920

Another Espionage Act conviction, this one involved the section that gave the postmaster general the right to deny use of the second-class mails to newspapers he found unacceptable under the act. The first-class cost of mailing newspapers and magazines has always been prohibitive. Brandeis once again dissented from the Court's upholding of the conviction, this time because he read the act as permitting the postmaster general to prohibit subversive second-class mail but not to enjoin future mailings on the basis of past articles. He also reiterated his opposition to the Court's willingness to use the Constitution to protect property but not speech, adding that the right to send the product of one's business through the mails is a property right. Holmes wrote his own dissent, apparently to disassociate himself from Brandeis's angry words about the Court's interpretation of the due process clause.

MR. JUSTICE BRANDEIS, dissenting.

This case arose during the World War; but it presents no legal question peculiar to war. It is important, because what we decide today may determine in large measure whether in times of peace our press shall be free.

The denial to a newspaper of entry as second-class mail, or the revocation of an entry previously made, does not deny to the paper admission to the mail; nor does it deprive the publisher of any mail facility. It merely deprives him of the very low postal rates, called second class, and compels him to pay postage for the same service at the rate called third class, which was, until recently, from eight to fifteen times as high as the second-class rate. Such is the nature and the only effect of an order denying or revoking the entry. In this case entry to the second-class mail was revoked because the paper had, in the opinion of the Postmaster General, systematically inserted editorials and news items which he deemed unmailable. The question presented is: Did Congress confer upon the Postmaster General authority to deny second-class postal rates on that ground? The question of the scope of the Postmaster General's power is presented to us on the following record:

Some years prior to 1917 The Milwaukee Leader, a daily newspaper published by the Milwaukee Social Democratic Publishing Company, made application to use the second-class mail, was declared entitled to do so, and thereafter used it continuously. It built up a large circulation, of which about 9,000 copies were distributed daily through the second-class mail. In September, 1917, its publisher was directed to show cause "why the authorization of admission . . . to the second class mail matter . . . should not be revoked upon the following ground:

"The publication was . . . in conflict with the provisions of the law embodied in section 481 1/2 Postal Laws and Regulations" . . . On this notice to show cause the Third Assistant Postmaster General held the customary informal hearing. The publisher of The Milwaukee Leader had not been convicted by any court of violating the Espionage Law; and its representative denied that it had ever committed any act in violation of it. But the Third Assistant Postmaster General issued on October 3, 1917, to the postmaster at Milwaukee the instruction that The Milwaukee Leader "is not entitled to transmission in the mails at the second-class rates."

This determination and action were confirmed by the Postmaster General; and the postmaster at Milwaukee thereafter denied to the publication transmission at the rates provided by law for second-class mail. The order did not forbid to The Milwaukee Leader all use of the mails; nor did it limit in any way the use of the mail facilities; it merely revoked the so-called second-class mailing permit; and the effect of this was to impose a higher rate of postage on every copy of the newspaper thereafter mailed.

The Postmaster General . . . gives this justification for his action:

"By representations and complaints from sundry good and loyal citizens of the United States and from personal reading and consideration of the issues of the said relator's publication, from the date of the declaration of war down to the time of service of the citation upon it, and the hearing granted in pursuance thereof, it seemed to this respondent, in the exercise of his judgment and discretion and in obedience to the duty on him reposed as well by the general statutes as by the special provisions of said Espionage Law, that the provisions of the latter act were systematically and continually violated by the relator's publication.''

It thus appears that the Postmaster General, in the exercise of a supposed discretion, refused to carry at second class mail rates all future issues of The Milwaukee Leader, solely because he believed it had systematically violated the Espionage Act in the past. It further appears that this belief rested partly upon the contents of past issues of the paper filed with the return and partly upon ''representations and complaints from sundry good and loyal citizens,'' whose statements are not incorporated in this record and which do not appear to have been called to the attention of the publisher of The Milwaukee Leader at the hearing or otherwise. It is this general refusal thereafter to accept the paper for transmission at the second-class mail rates which is challenged as being without warrant in law.

First. Power to exclude from the mails has never been conferred in terms upon the Postmaster General . . . If such power were possessed by the Postmaster General, he would, in view of the practical finality of his decisions, become the universal censor of publications. For a denial of the use of the mail would be for most of them tantamount to a denial of the right of circulation.

Second . . . It is insisted that a citizen uses the mail at second-class rates not as of right—but by virtue of a privilege or permission, the granting of which rests in the discretion of the Postmaster General. Because the payment made for this governmental service is less than it costs, it is assumed that a properly qualified person has not the right to the service so long as it is offered; and may not complain if it is denied to him. The service is called the second-class privilege. But, in fact, the right to the lawful postal rates is a right independent of the discretion of the Postmaster General.

Third . . . A publisher must deposit with the local postmaster, before the first mailing of every issue, a copy of the publication which is now examined for matter subject to a higher rate and in order to determine the portion devoted to advertising. If there is illegal material in the newspaper, here is ample opportunity to discover it and remove the paper from the mail. Indeed, of the four classes of mail, it is the second alone which affords to the postal official full opportunity of ascertaining, before deposit in the mail, whether that which it is proposed to transmit is mailable matter. [To read the statutes differently] would in practice seriously abridge the freedom of the press.

(a) The power to police the mails is an incident of the postal power. Congress may, of course, exclude from the mails matter which is dangerous or which carries on its face immoral expressions, threats or libels . . . The postal power, like all its other powers, is subject to the limitations of the Bill of Rights. Congress may not through its postal police power put limitations upon the freedom of the press which if directly attempted would be unconstitutional.

How dangerous to liberty of the press would be the holding that the second-class mail service is merely a privilege, which Congress may deny to those whose views it deems to be against public policy . . .

(b) The right which Congress has given to all properly circumstanced persons to distribute newspapers and periodicals through the mails is a substantial right. It is of the same nature as, indeed, it is a part of, the right to carry on business which this court has been jealous to protect against what it has considered arbitrary deprivations. A law by which certain publishers were unreasonably or arbitrarily denied the low rates would deprive them of liberty or property without due process of law; and it would likewise deny them equal protection of the laws.

(e) The punishment inflicted is not only unusual in character; it is, so far as known, unprecedented in American legal history. Every fine imposed by a court is definite in amount. Every fine prescribed by Congress is limited in amount. Statutes frequently declare that each day's continuation of an offence shall constitute a new crime. But here a fine imposed for a past offence is made to grow indefinitely each day—perhaps throughout the life of the publication. Already, having grown at the rate of say $150 a day, it may aggregate, if the circulation has been maintained, about $180,000 for the three years and four months since the order was entered; and its growth continues.

In conclusion I say again—because it cannot be stressed too strongly—that the power here claimed is not a war power. There is no question of its necessity to protect the country from insidious domestic foes. To that end Congress conferred upon the Postmaster General the enormous power contained in the Espionage Act of entirely excluding from the mails any letter, picture or publication which contained matter violating the broad terms of that act. But it did not confer—and the Postmaster General concedes that it did not confer—the vague and absolute authority practically to deny circulation to any publication which in his opinion is likely to violate in the future any postal law . . . If, under the Constitution, administrative officers may, as a mere incident of the peace time administration of their departments, be vested with the power to issue such orders as this, there is little of substance in our Bill of Rights and in every extension of governmental functions lurks a new danger to civil liberty.

LETTERS TO FELIX FRANKFURTER

Brandeis's concern about the invasions of speech embodied in the kinds of federal and state legislation involved in these cases was reflected in a number of letters he sent to Frankfurter during the 1920s. As mentioned in the preceding chapter, Brandeis regularly suggested topics for articles he thought might appear in the Harvard Law Review *or the* New Republic. *The letters also indicate the close relationship Brandeis perceived between speech and privacy.*

June 25, 1926, Chatham, Massachusetts
2. Wouldn't it be possible to interest Bohlen and Dickinson [two law professors] directly & through them students, to make the necessary investigation & present in the Law Review articles bearing on the redress for the invasion of civil and political rights through arbitrary etc. governmental action, by means of civil suits?

I think the failure to attempt such redress as against government officials for the multitude of invasions during the war and post-war period is also as disgraceful as the illegal acts of the government and the pusillanimous action of our people in acting the statutes which the state and the nation put on the books. Americans should be reminded of the duty to litigate.

July 16, 1926, Chatham, Massachusetts
We need a John Quincy Adams to persistently press forward the right to free speech.

Brandeis and the Supreme Court in 1937, two years before his retirement. Standing, left to right: Benjamin Cardozo, Harlan Fiske Stone, Owen J. Roberts, Hugo Black. Seated: George Sutherland, James McReynolds, Chief Justice Charles Evans Hughes, Brandeis, Pierce Butler. (Harris and Ewing, Collection of the Supreme Court of the United States)

ORAL ARGUMENT IN *NEAR V. MINNESOTA*,
JANUARY 30, 1931

The Saturday Press, *a newspaper published in Minneapolis by J. M. Near and Howard A. Guilford, was infamous for being virulently anti-Semitic, anti-Catholic, and anti-black. When the paper published an article accusing specific public officials of participating in a gambling ring, it was enjoined from further publication under a Minnesota statute that permitted suspension of periodicals that were "malicious, scandalous and defamatory." The* Chicago Tribune *quickly offered to subsidize legal costs, and Near and Guilford appealed. When the case reached the Supreme Court, Court-watchers expected its first Jewish member, also well known as a major Zionist leader, to be hostile to the publication. Minnesota Deputy Attorney General James E. Markham contended during oral argument that the law did not constitute prior restraint or other violation of the rights of a free press. Brandeis interrupted with remarks that indicate the depth of his commitment to free*

Brandeis and his economist daughter Elizabeth Raushenbush, November 1936. (Collection of the Supreme Court of the United States)

communication of ideas. Chief Justice Charles Evans Hughes later wrote for the Court overturning the injunction, and Brandeis added his name to Hughes's opinion.

Brandeis's comments refer to the Saturday Press articles in contention.

Brandeis: In these articles, the editors state that they seek to expose combinations between criminals and public officials in conducting and profiting from gambling hells. They name the Chief of Police and other officials. They state that they have been threatened with being, to use their own words, "bumped off."

They state that shortly after commencing publication Guilford was set upon by thugs and shot in the abdomen.

We do not know whether these allegations are true or false, but we do know that just such criminal combinations exist, to the shame of some of our cities.

What these men did seems like an effort to expose such a combination. Now, is that not a privileged communication, if there ever was one? How else can a community secure protection from that sort of thing, if people are not allowed to engage in free discussion in such matters?

Of course there was defamation. You cannot disclose evil naming the doers of evil. It is difficult to see how one can have a free press and the protection it affords in the democratic community without the privilege this act seeks to limit.

You are dealing here not with a sort of scandal too often appearing in the press, and which ought not to appear to the interest of any one, but with a matter of prime interest to every American citizen.

What sort of a matter could be more privileged?

Markham: Assuming it to be true.

Brandeis: No, a newspaper cannot always wait until it gets the judgement of a court. These men set out on a campaign to rid the city of certain evils.

Markham: So they say.

Brandeis: Yes, of course, so they say. They went forward with a definite program and certainly they acted with great courage. They invited suit for criminal libel if what they said was not true. Now, if that campaign was not privileged, if that is not one of the things for which the press chiefly exists, then for what does it exist?

As for such defamatory matter being issued regularly or customarily, how can such a campaign be conducted except by persistence and continued iteration?

WHITNEY V. CALIFORNIA, 1927

Anita Whitney was the fifty-two-year-old daughter of a California state senator and niece of former Supreme Court Justice Stephen Field. The incident leading to the charges against her was her presence at a Communist Labor party convention. Although she advocated a purely nonviolent role for the party, the convention adopted a more violence-oriented platform. In spite of having expressed her continuing disagreement with the platform, she was found guilty in 1920 of assisting in organizing and being a member of a party that advocated the use of unlawful force. It was a time when many states were reacting vehemently to the perceived threat of socialism. Apparently the Supreme Court of 1927 was no more immune to the general fears. Justice Edward T. Sanford, writing for the Court, upheld the conviction on the grounds that the kind of "united and joint action" implicit in the very existence of the party was much more dangerous than individual speech and could legitimately be punished for the "danger to the public peace and security" it presented to the state. Brandeis wrote a concurrence rather than a dissent because Whitney's lawyers had not argued that the statute was an unconstitutional limitation on speech that presented no clear and present danger to the state, which were the grounds on which he would have overturned the conviction. Brandeis felt constrained to follow the Court's rule that it would not decide a case on the basis of an argument not made by the attorneys. His eloquent defense of speech was so persuasive, however, that the governor of California cited it in pardoning Whitney.

MR. JUSTICE BRANDEIS, concurring.

All fundamental rights comprised within the term liberty are protected by the Federal Constitution from invasion by the States. The right of free speech, the right to teach and the right of assembly are, of course, fundamental rights. These may not be denied or abridged. But, although the rights of free speech and assembly are fundamental, they are not in their nature absolute. Their exercise is subject to restriction, if the particular restriction proposed is required in order to protect the State from destruction or from serious injury, political, economic or moral . . . This Court has not yet fixed the standard by which to determine when a danger shall be deemed clear; how remote the danger may be and yet be deemed present; and what degree of evil shall be deemed sufficiently substantial to justify resort to abridgement of free speech and assembly as the means of protection. To reach sound conclusions on these matters, we must bear in mind why a State is, ordinarily, denied the power to prohibit dissemination of social, economic and political doctrine which a vast majority of its citizens believes to be false and fraught with evil consequence.

Those who won our independence believed that the final end of the State was to make men free to develop their faculties; and that in its government the deliberative forces should prevail over the arbitrary. They valued liberty both as an end and as a means. They believed liberty to be the secret of happiness and courage to be the secret of liberty. They believed that freedom to think as you will and to speak as you think are means indispensable to the discovery and spread of political truth; that without free speech and assembly discussion would be futile; that with them, discussion affords ordinarily adequate protection against the dissemination of noxious doctrine; that the greatest menace to freedom is an inert people; that public discussion is a political duty; and that this should be a fundamental principle of the American government. They recognized the risks to which all human institutions are subject. But they knew that order cannot be secured merely through fear of punishment for its infraction; that it is hazardous to discourage thought, hope and imagination; that fear breeds repression; that repression breeds hate; that hate menaces stable government; that the path of safety lies in the opportunity to discuss freely supposed grievances and proposed remedies; and that the fitting remedy for evil counsels is good ones. Believing in the power of reason as applied through public discussion, they eschewed silence coerced by law—the argument of force in its worst form. Recognizing the occasional tyrannies of governing majorities, they amended the Constitution so that free speech and assembly should be guaranteed.

Fear of serious injury cannot alone justify suppression of free speech and assembly. Men feared witches and burnt women. It is the function of speech to free men from the bondage of irrational fears. To justify suppression of free speech there must be reasonable ground to fear that serious evil will result if free speech is practiced. There must be reasonable ground to believe that the danger apprehended is imminent. There must be a reasonable ground to believe that the evil to be prevented is a serious one. Every denunciation of existing law tends in some measure to increase the probability that there will be violation of it. Condonation of a breach enhances the probability. Expressions of approval add to the probability. Propagation of the criminal state of mind by teaching syndicalism increases it. Advocacy of law-breaking heightens it still further. But even advocacy of violation, however reprehensible morally, is not a justification for denying free speech where the advocacy falls short of incitement and there is nothing to indicate that the advocacy would be immediately acted on. The wide difference between advocacy and incitement, between preparation and attempt, between assembling and conspiracy, must be borne in mind. In order to support a finding of clear and present danger it must be shown either that immediate serious violence was to be expected or was advocated, or that the past conduct furnished reason to believe that such advocacy was then contemplated.

Those who won our independence by revolution were not cowards. They did not fear political change. The did not exalt order at the cost of liberty. To courageous self-reliant men, with confidence in the power of free and fearless reasoning applied through the processes of popular government, no danger flowing from speech can be deemed clear and present, unless the incidence of the evil apprehended is so imminent that it may befall before there is opportunity for full discussion. If there be time to expose through discussion the falsehood and fallacies, avert the evil by the processes of education, the remedy to be applied is more speech, not enforced silence. Only an emergency can justify repression. Such must be the rule if authority is to be reconciled with freedom. Such, in my opinion, is the command of the Constitution. It is therefore always open to Americans to challenge a law abridging free speech and assembly by showing that there was no emergency justifying it.

Moreover, even imminent danger cannot justify resort to prohibition of these functions essential to effective democracy, unless the evil apprehended is relatively serious. Prohibition of free speech and assembly is a measure so stringent that it would be inappropriate as a means for averting a relatively trivial harm to society. A police measure may be unconstitutional merely because the remedy, although effective as means of protection, is unduly harsh or oppressive. Thus, a State might, in exercise of its police power, make any trespass upon the land of another a crime, regardless of the results or of the intent or purpose of the trespasser. It might, also, punish an attempt, a conspiracy, or an incitement to commit the trespass. But it is hardly conceivable that this Court would hold constitutional a statute which punished as a felony the mere voluntary assembly with a society formed to teach that pedestrians had the moral right to cross unenclosed, unposted, waste lands and to advocate their doing so, even if there was imminent danger that advocacy would lead to a trespass. The fact that speech is likely to result in some violence or in destruction of property is not enough to justify its suppression. There must be the probability of serious injury to the State. Among free men, the deterrents ordinarily to be applied to prevent crime are education and punishment for violations of the law, not abridgment of the rights of free speech and assembly.

Notes

Source notes for the selections from Brandeis's works appear first, followed by notes referencing the editor's introductory material.

ABBREVIATIONS USED

LDB: Louis D. Brandeis
BP: Brandeis archives, University of Louisville
BP-HLS: Louis D. Brandeis papers, Harvard Law School Library
FF-HLS: Felix Frankfurter papers, Harvard Law School Library
FF-LC: Frankfurter papers, Library of Congress
Letters: Melvin I. Urofsky and David W. Levy, eds., *Letters of Louis D. Brandeis*, 5
   vols. Albany: State University of New York Press, 1972–1978

CHAPTER 1: INTRODUCTION

Considering savings bank life insurance his greatest achievement: See Alpheus
   Thomas Mason, *The Brandeis Way* (Princeton, N.J.: Princeton University
   Press, 1938).
LDB "dwarfed the Court": William Hitz to Felix Frankfurter, December 17, 1914,
   BP, Addendum, Scrapbook.
Letter about law school: LDB to Otto Wehle, March 12, 1876, BP, M 1–2.
Impact of Homestead strike: Livy S. Richard, "Up from Aristocracy," interview
   with LDB in the *Independent*, July 27, 1914, BP, Clippings II.
Company of labor men: LDB to Alfred Brandeis, June 18, 1907, BP, M 2–4.
"The Practice of the Law," BP, NMF 85–3.
"Important public work": LDB to Edward F. McClennen, February 17, 1916, BP,
   NMF 76–2.
Declining fees for public service: Edward A. Filene, "Louis D. Brandeis as We
   Know Him," *Boston Post*, July 14, 1915.
Public service a joy: LDB, "The Spirit of Get-Together," *American Cloak and Suit
   Review*, January 1911, p. 159, reprinted in LDB, *The Curse of Bigness*, ed. Osmond
   K. Fraenkel (New York: Viking Press, 1934), p. 266.
Berating politicians: Speech in Brighton, Massachusetts, December 2, 1904. Type-
   script, BP, Clippings I.
Senate Committee on Interstate Commerce, *Hearings on Control of Corpora-*

tions, Persons, and Firms Engaged in Interstate Commerce, 62d Cong., 2nd sess., 1911.

Avoiding socialism: LDB to Dix Smith, November 5, 1913, BP, NMF 47-2.

Cooperatives: Interview, *Boston Post,* February 14, 1915, BP, Scrapbook II (see ch. 4). See also LDB to FF, September 30, 1922, in Melvin I. Urofsky and David W. Levy, eds., *"Half-Brother, Half-Son": The Letters of Louis D. Brandeis to Felix Frankfurter* (Norman: University of Oklahoma Press, 1991), pp. 114–115; to Frankfurter, April 6, 1923, FF-HLS; LDB to Elizabeth B. Raushenbush, August 7, 1923, Brandeis Papers, SUNY–Albany.

"Optimist": Dean Acheson, *Morning and Noon* (Boston: Houghton Mifflin, 1965), p. 102.

"Hyphenated Americans": LDB in the *Jewish Advocate,* December 9, 1910, reprinted as "Jews as a Priest People" in Jacob deHaas, *Louis D. Brandeis: A Biographical Sketch* (New York: Bloch Publishing Company, 1929), pp. 151–152.

Aaronsohn: LDB to Alfred Brandeis, January 7, 1912, BP, M 3-3.

Dembitz and the Athenians: LDB to Stella and Emily Dembitz, April 22, 1926, BP, M 4-4.

Contribution for playground: Louis E. Levinthal, *Louis Dembitz Brandeis* (Washington, D.C.: Zionist Organization of America, n.d.), p. 12.

Story of the nomination: Alden Todd, *Justice on Trial: The Case of Louis D. Brandeis* (New York: McGraw-Hill, 1964). To Taft: G. J. Karger, quoted in Arthur Link, *Confusions and Crises* (Princeton, N.J.: Princeton University Press, 1964), p. 347. Mrs. Brandeis: to Alfred Brandeis, January 31, 1916, quoted in Alpheus Thomas Mason, *Brandeis: A Free Man's Life* (New York: 1956), p. 466. Senator Walsh: Todd, *Justice on Trial,* p. 189. Berle: letter to Senator William E. Chilton, February 18, 1916, BP, NMF 75-1.

Norman Hapgood, *The Changing Years* (New York: Farrar & Rinehart, 1930), p. 97.

Justice Marshall in *McCulloch v. Maryland,* 17 U.S. (4 Wheat.) 316, at 409 (1819).

Jay Burns Baking Co. v. Bryan, 264 U.S. 504, 517 (1924).

Clerks and opinions: Paul A. Freund, "Justice Brandeis: A Law Clerk's Remembrance," *American Jewish History* 68 (1978): 7–18, at 11; Acheson, *Morning and Noon,* p. 94; Thomas H. Austern, interview with author, October 22, 1978, Washington, D.C.

Delivering an opinion orally: Reported in an article entitled "Justice Brandeis," no author, *St. Louis Post-Dispatch,* and reprinted in a Louisville newspaper, November 13, 1931. Cutting in Louisville Free Public Library, Kentucky Authors Scrap Book Part I # 8, referring to the case of *St. Louis & O'Fallon Railway* v. *United States,* 279 U.S. 461, 488 (1929) (dissenting).

Citing law reviews: the first case in which he did so was *Adams* v. *Tanner,* 244 U.S. 500, 597 (1917) (dissenting).

Suggesting topics for articles: Philippa Strum, "Louis D. Brandeis: The People's Attorney," *American Jewish History* 81 (forthcoming 1994).

Boulder Dam case: *Arizona* v. *California,* 283 U.S. 423 (1931).

Associated Press case: *International News Service* v. *Associated Press,* 248 U.S. 215, 148 (1918) (dissenting).

Stock dividends case: *Eisner* v. *Macomber,* 252 U.S. 189, 220 (1920) (dissenting).

Erie Railroad v. *Tompkins,* 304 U.S. 72 (1938).

Schechter v. *United States,* 295 U.S. 553 (1935). Brandeis in oral argument, quoted in Mason, *Brandeis*, p. 618. The cases were *Panama Refining Co.* v. *Ryan* and *Amazon Petroleum Corp.* v. *Ryan*, 293 U.S. 388 (1935).

Brandeis to Corcoran: quoted in Arthur M. Schlesinger, Jr., *The Politics of Upheaval* (Boston: Houghton Mifflin, 1960), p. 280.

Arizona restaurant case: *Truax* v. *Corrigan*, 257 U.S. 312, 354 (1921) (dissenting).

"Mind of one piece": Paul Freund, "Mr. Justice Brandeis," in Allison Dunham and Philip B. Kurland, eds., *Mr. Justice* (Chicago: University of Chicago, 1956), p. 118.

Brandeis as a democrat: Alvin Johnson quoted in Alexander M. Bickel, ed., *The Unpublished Opinions of Mr. Justice Brandeis* (Cambridge, Mass.: Harvard University Press, 1957), p. 163; Donald Richberg, "The Industrial Liberalism of Mr. Justice Brandeis" in Felix Frankfurter, *Mr. Justice Brandeis* (New Haven, Conn.: Yale University Press, 1932), p. 137.

Chronology

LDB, "Liability of Trust-Estates on Contracts Made for Their Benefit," *American Law Review* 15 (1881): 449–462.

LDB, "Experience of Massachusetts in Street Railways," *Municipal Affairs* 6 (1903): 721–729.

LDB, "The New England Transportation Monopoly," address to New England Dry Goods Association (Boston), reprinted in LDB, *Business—A Profession* (Boston: Small, Maynard, 1914), pp. 255–278.

CHAPTER 2: DEMOCRACY AND PUBLIC SERVICE

Selection Sources

"True Americanism," lecture delivered at Faneuil Hall, Boston, on July 4, 1915, published in *Harper's Weekly*, July 10, 1915, p. 31; reprinted in Solomon Goldman, ed., *Brandeis on Zionism* (Washington, D.C.: Zionist Organization of America, 1942), pp. 3–11.

Speech to the Good Government Association, December 11, 1903, Boston, BP, typescripts, Clippings I.

Address to the New England Civic Federation, Boston, January 11, 1906, quoted in Alfred Lief, ed., *The Brandeis Guide to the Modern World* (Boston: Little, Brown and Co., 1941), pp. 36–37.

"Efficiency and Social Ideas," statement in the *Independent*, November 30, 1914, p. 327, reprinted in LDB, *The Curse of Bigness*, ed. Osmond K. Fraenkel (New York: Viking Press, 1934), p. 51.

Letter to Robert W. Bruere, February 25, 1922, BP, NMF 15, printed in LDB, *The Curse of Bigness*, ed. Osmond K. Fraenkel (New York: Viking Press, 1934), pp. 270–271.

"An Interview," *American Cloak and Suit Review*, January 1911, p. 159, reprinted in LDB, *The Curse of Bigness*, ed. Osmond K. Fraenkel (New York: Viking Press, 1934), p. 266.

Interview in the *New York Times Annalist*, January 27, 1913, p. 36, reprinted in

LDB, *The Curse of Bigness*, ed. Osmond K. Fraenkel (New York: Viking Press, 1934), pp. 40–42, at p. 41.

"The Greatest Life Insurance Wrong," article in the *Independent*, December 20, 1906, pp. 1475–1480, reprinted in LDB, *The Curse of Bigness*, ed. Osmond K. Fraenkel (New York: Viking Press, 1934), pp. 18–24.

The question of land use: LDB to Alice Brandeis, July 28, 1911, Brandeis Family Letters, Goldfarb Library, Brandeis University; LDB to Robert M. La Follette, July 29, 1911, BP, SC 1–2; LDB to Robert M. La Follette, July 31, 1911, BP, NMF 39–1; LDB to Amos Pinchot, August 2, 1911, BP, NMF 39–1.

Headnote Sources

Corresponding regularly: In addition to the five-volume *Letters*, see Urofsky and Levy, *"Half-Brother, Half-Son."*

CHAPTER 3: THE LIVING LAW

Selection Sources

LDB to William H. Dunbar, February 2, 1893, FF-LC.

"The Opportunity in the Law," address to the Harvard Ethical Society, May 4, 1905, printed in LDB, *Business—A Profession* (Boston: Small, Maynard, 1914), pp. 314–331.

"The Living Law," address before the Chicago Bar Association, January 3, 1916, published in *Illinois Law Review* 10 (February 1916): 461–471, and in *Harper's Weekly*, February 19 and 16, pp. 173–174, 201–202; reprinted in LDB, *The Curse of Bigness*, ed. Osmond K. Fraenkel (New York: Viking Press, 1934), pp. 316–326.

Oral Argument in *Stettler* v. *O'Hara*, 243 U.S. 629 (1914), published as "The Constitution and the Minimum Wage" in the *Survey*, February 6, 1915, pp. 490–491, 521–524; reprinted in LDB, *The Curse of Bigness*, ed. Osmond K. Fraenkel (New York: Viking Press, 1934), pp. 52–69.

Headnote Sources

LDB's income: Mason, *Brandeis Way*, pp. 103, 691.

"Rather have clients": quoted by Ernest Poole, "Brandeis," in LDB, *Business—A Profession*, pp. 1–li.

Enjoying litigation: LDB to Alfred Brandeis, October 31, 1884, *Letters*, 1:66; to Alfred, March 21, 1887, BP, M 2–4.

Holmes on the "man of statistics": Oliver Wendell Holmes, "The Path of the Law" in Holmes, *Collected Legal Papers* (New York: Harcourt, Brace, 1921; New York: Peter Smith, 1952), p. 187.

Address to the Harvard Law Review Association, June 22, 1907, quoted in Alfred Lief, ed., *The Brandeis Guide to the Modern World* (Boston: Little, Brown and Co., 1941), p. 171.

Letter to wife: Oct. 18, 1912. Brandeis Family Letters, Goldfarb Library, Brandeis University.

Description of oral argument: Charles Warren to Felix Frankfurter, April 6, 1939, referring to a "contemporary note made by me," FF-LC, Box 127.
Brief in *Muller* v. *Oregon*, 208 U.S. 412 (1908), reprinted as LDB, assisted by Josephine Goldmark, *Women in Industry* (New York: National Consumers' League, n.d.).
Goldmark's additional findings: Josephine Goldmark, *Fatigue and Efficiency* (New York: Russell Sage Foundation, 1912).
Learning from women in his work: quoted in Alfred Lief, *Brandeis: The Personal History of an American Ideal* (New York: Stackpole, 1936), p. 256; see also Philippa Strum, *Louis D. Brandeis: Justice for the People* (Cambridge, Mass.: Harvard University Press, 1984), pp. 129-130.
On Perkins: LDB to FF, February 23, 1933, FF-LC.

CHAPTER 4: JUSTICE FOR THE WORKER

Selection Sources

"The Incorporation of Trades Unions," debate with Samuel Gompers at Tremont Temple, Boston, December 4, 1902, under the auspices of the Economic Club of Boston, reprinted in LDB, *Business—A Profession* (Boston: Small, Maynard, 1914), pp. 88-98.
Truax v. *Corrigan*, 257 U.S. 312, 354 (1921) (dissenting).
"The Employer and Trades Unions," address on April 21, 1904, to the annual banquet of the Boston Typothetæ, printed in LDB, *Business—A Profession* (Boston: Small, Maynard, 1914), pp. 13-27.
Dorchy v. *Kansas*, 272 U.S. 306 (1926).
"Hours of Labor," address on January 11, 1906, to the first annual meeting of the Civic Federation of New England, printed in LDB, *Business—A Profession* (Boston: Small, Maynard, 1914), pp. 28-36.
"How Far Have We Come on the Road to Industrial Democracy?—An Interview," *La Follette's Weekly Magazine*, May 24, 1913, reprinted in LDB, *The Curse of Bigness*, ed. Osmond K. Fraenkel (New York: Viking Press, 1934), pp. 43-47.
Testimony before the United States Commission on Industrial Relations, January 23, 1915, Senate Document, 64th Cong., 1st sess., 26:7657-7681, reprinted in part in Alfred Lief, ed., *The Social and Economic Views of Mr. Justice Brandeis* (New York: Vanguard Press, 1930), pp. 380-385, and in LDB, *The Curse of Bigness*, ed. Osmond K. Fraenkel (New York: Viking Press, 1934), pp. 70-95.
"Laborers as Directors with Boss Possible, Says Louis D. Brandeis, Who Heard Carnegie and Rockefeller," interview, February 14, 1915, *Boston Post*, BP, Scrapbook II.
Hitchman Coal & Coke Co. v. *Mitchell*, 245 U.S. 229, 263 (1917) (dissenting).
Duplex Co. v. *Deering*, 254 U.S. 443, 479 (1921) (dissenting).
Bedford Cut Stone v. *Journeymen Stone Cutters' Association*, 274 U.S. 37, 64 (1927) (dissenting).

Headnote Sources

Labor hire capital: Interview, *Boston Post*, February 14, 1915, BP, Scrapbook II.
Beatrice Potter, *The Cooperative Movement in Great Britain* (London: Swan Sonnenschein, 1899). Sidney and Beatrice Webb, *The Consumer's Cooperative Movement* (London and New York: Longmans, Green, 1921); *The Decay of Capitalist Civilization* (New York: Harcourt, Brace, 1923). Recommendations to daughter and Frankfurter: LDB to Frankfurter, April 6, 1923, FF-HLS; LDB to Elizabeth B. Raushenbush, August 7, 1923, Brandeis Papers, SUNY-Albany. See LDB to FF, September 30, 1922, in Urofsky and Levy, *"Half-Brother, Half-Son,"* pp. 114–115. Interest in Denmark: LDB to Norman Hapgood, March 2, 1915, BP, NMF 62-1; Alice Brandeis and Josephine Goldmark, *Democracy in Denmark* (Washington, D.C.: National Home Library Foundation, 1936). LDB on worker-management: see Strum, *Brandeis*, ch. 10.
Comment by biographer: Mason, *Brandeis Way*, p. 585.

CHAPTER 5: BUSINESS AND "THE CURSE OF BIGNESS"

Selection Sources

"Business—A Profession," address delivered at Brown University Commencement Day, 1912, and published in *System*, October 1912, pp. 365–369, as "Business—the New Profession"; reprinted in LDB, *Business—A Profession* (Boston: Small, Maynard, 1914), pp. 1–12.
"Big Business and Industrial Liberty," address given at Ethical Culture Meeting House in Boston, February 10, 1912, printed in LDB, *The Curse of Bigness*, ed. Osmond K. Fraenkel (New York: Viking Press, 1934), pp. 38–64.
"Trusts, Efficiency and the New Party," published in *Collier's Weekly*, September 14, 1912, pp. 14, 15; reprinted as "Trusts and Efficiency" in LDB, *Business—A Profession* (Boston: Small, Maynard, 1914), pp. 205–224.
"The New England Railroad Situation," *Boston Journal*, December 13, 1912, reprinted in LDB, *Business—A Profession* (Boston: Small, Maynard, 1914), pp. 286–312, as "The New Haven—An Unregulated Monopoly."
"Interlocking Directorates," in LDB, *Other People's Money and How the Bankers Use It* (New York: Stokes, 1914), pp. 36–37. The passage quoted here was from an article originally published as "Endless Chain" in *Harper's Weekly*, December 6, 1912, pp. 13–17, and reprinted under the title "Interlocking Directorates" in *Other People's Money*.
New State Ice Co. v. Liebmann, 285 U.S. 262, 280 (1932) (dissenting).
Liggett Co. v. Lee, 288 U.S. 517, 541 (1933) (dissenting).

Headnote Sources

Interview in the *New York Times Annalist*, January 27, 1913, p. 36, reprinted in LDB, *The Curse of Bigness*, pp. 40–42.

CHAPTER 6: ZIONISM: PROGRESSIVES
AND PILGRIMS IN PALESTINE

Selection Sources

"The Jewish Problem: How to Solve It," address to the Eastern Council of the
Central Conference of Reform Rabbis, April 25, 1915, published as a pamphlet by
the Zionist Essays Publication Committee, June 18, 1915; reprinted in LDB, *The
Curse of Bigness*, ed. Osmond K. Fraenkel (New York: Viking Press, 1934), pp.
218-232, and Solomon Goldman, ed., *Brandeis on Zionism* (Washington, D.C.:
Zionist Organization of America, 1942), pp. 13-35.

"A Call to the Educated Jew," address delivered at a conference of the Intercolle-
giate Menorah Association, January 1915, and published in the first issue of the
Menorah Journal that month. The reference is to Ahad Ha'am, "Flesh and
Spirit" in *Selected Essays*, trans. Leon Simon (Philadelphia, 1912), pp. 146-147.

"An Essential of Lasting Peace," address to the Economic Club of Boston, February 8,
1915, published in *Harper's Weekly*, March 13, 1915, and reprinted in LDB, *The Curse of
Bigness*, ed. Osmond K. Fraenkel (New York: Viking Press, 1934), pp. 267-269.

"Palestine and the Jewish Democracy," originally given as an address entitled
"Democracy in Palestine" in Washington, D.C., sometime in November 1915
and published in the *Independent*, November 22, 1915, p. 311; expanded as "Palestine and the Jewish Democracy," *Outlook*, January 5, 1916, pp. 36-40; reprinted
in LDB, *The Curse of Bigness*, ed. Osmond K. Fraenkel (New York: Viking
Press, 1934), pp. 238-245.

Pittsburgh Platform, adopted at convention of Federation of American Zionists,
June 25, 1918, Pittsburgh: published in Jacob deHaas, *Louis D. Brandeis: A Biographical Sketch* (New York: Bloch Publishing Company, 1929), pp. 96-97.

Letters from Palestine: to Alice Goldmark Brandeis, July 10, 1919, BP, M 4-3; to
Chaim Weizmann, July 20, 1919, Chaim Weizmann Papers, Library of Yad
Chaim Weizmann, Rehovot, Israel; Letter to Alice Goldmark Brandeis (from Al-
exandria, Egypt), July 6, 1919, BP, M 4-3.

Messages to Zionist workers: to Benjamin Perlstein, September 19, 1914, BP, Z 3-2; to
Richard Gottheil, October 2, 1914, Richard James Horatio Gottheil Papers, Central
Zionist Archives, Jerusalem, Israel; to Louis Lipsky, October 3, 1914, BP, Z 1-4; to
Israel J. Biskind, November 6, 1914, BP, Z 1-2; to Benjamin Perlstein, November 9,
1914, BP, Z 3-2; to Max Mitchell, November 17, 1914, BP, Z 1-2; to Jacob deHaas, Jan-
uary 25, 1915, BP, Z 6-1; to Louis Lipsky, January 27, 1915, BP, Z 1-4; to Henrietta
Szold, March 4, 1915, BP, Z 12-1; to Joseph L. Cohen, May 1, 1915, BP, Z 10-2; Note to
Morris Rothenberg, February 18, 1917, in Solomon Goldman, ed., *Brandeis on Zion-
ism* (Washington, D.C.: Zionist Organization of America, 1942), p. 112; to Robert
Szold, August 19, 1930, Jacob deHaas Papers, Zionist Archives and Library, New
York City; to Maurice B. Hexter, September 7, 1930, BP, Z 42-1; to Bernard Flexner,
April 8, 1940, Robert Szold Papers, Zionist Archives and Library.

Headnote Sources

LDB, Zionism and ancient Greece: Strum, *Brandeis*, pp. 237-243; Philippa Strum,
Brandeis: Beyond Progressivism (Lawrence: University Press of Kansas, 1993),
pp. 103-104.

LDB's tour of Palestine: deHaas, *Brandeis*, pp. 115–117; Strum, *Brandeis*, pp. 243–246.

CHAPTER 7: GOVERNMENT IN A DEMOCRACY

Selection Sources

Myers v. *United States*, 272 U.S. 52, 240 (1926) (dissenting).
Ashwander v. *Tennessee Valley Authority*, 297 U.S. 288, 341 (1936) (concurring).
Letter to Elizabeth B. Raushenbush, November 19, 1933, Brandeis Papers, SUNY–Albany.
Harry Shulman, "Memorandum of Talk with L.D.B.—December 8, 1933," written February 1, 1934, FF-HLS 188–8.

Headnote Sources

NIRA: *Panama Refining Co.* v. *Ryan*, 293 U.S. 388 (1935); *Schechter* v. *U.S.*, 295 U.S. 495 (1935).
Brandeis's involvement with policy: Strum, *Brandeis*, pp. 381–384, 387–390, 393.

CHAPTER 8: THE RIGHT TO BE LET ALONE

Selection Sources

Letters to Felix Frankfurter, November 26, 1920, July 2, 1926, FF-HLS.
Burdeau v. *McDowell*, 256 U.S. 465, 476 (1920) (dissenting)
Casey v. *United States*, 276 U.S. 413, 421 (1928) (dissenting).
Olmstead v. *United States*, 277 U.S. 438, 471 (1927) (dissenting).

Headnote Sources

Samuel D. Warren, Jr., and LDB, "The Right to Privacy," *Harvard Law Review* 4 (1890–1891): 193 (quoting Thomas M. Cooley, *Cooley on Torts* [Chicago: Callaghan, 2d ed., 1875], p. 29).
Roscoe Pound to Senator William Chilton, included in letters printed in U.S. Congress, Senate, Committee on the Judiciary, *Nomination of Louis D. Brandeis*, 64th Cong., 1st sess., 1916.
Letters to Alice Goldmark, November 29 and December 28, 1890, collection of Alice Brandeis Popkin.
Cases: see, e.g., *On Lee* v. *United States*, 343 U.S. 747 (1952); *Griswold* v. *Connecticut*, 381 U.S. 479 (1965); *Katz* v. *United States*, 389 U.S. 347 (1967); *Roe* v. *Wade*, 410 U.S. 113 (1973); *Cruzan* v. *Director*, 497 U.S. 261 (1990); *In re President of Georgetown College*, 331 F.2d 1000 (D.C. Cir. 1964); *In Re T. W.*, 551 So. 2d 1186 (1989); *Stall* v. *Florida*, 470 S. 2d 257 (1990); *American Academy of Pediatrics* v. *Van De Kamp*, 214 Cal. App. 3d 831 (Ct. App. 1989).
Constitutions: see, e.g., the constitutions of Alaska, Arizona, California, Florida,

Hawaii, Illinois, Louisiana, Montana, South Carolina, and Washington. In many instances the writers of the constitution's privacy provision credit Brandeis directly. See Patricia Dore, "Of Rights Lost & Gained," *Florida State University Law Review* 6 (1978): 652–653.
Citation from *Truax v. Corrigan*, 257 U.S. 312, 376 (1921).
To niece: Fannie Brandeis's notes of a 1931 conversation, BP, Addendum, Box I.

CHAPTER 9: THE RIGHT TO FREE SPEECH

Selection Sources

Schaefer v. United States, 251 U.S. 466 (1920) (dissenting).
Pierce v. United States, 252 U.S. 239 (1920) (dissenting).
Gilbert v. State of Minnesota, 254 U.S. 325 (1920) (dissenting).
Milwaukee Social Democratic Publishing Company v. Burleson, 255 U.S. 407, 417 (1921).
Letters to Felix Frankfurter, June 25 and July 16, 1926, FF-HLS.
Near v. Minnesota, 284 U.S. 697 (1931).
Whitney v. California, 274 U.S. 357 (1927) (concurring).

Headnote Sources

Holmes's statements about free speech: *U.S. v. Schwimmer*, 279 U.S. 644, 653 (1928) (dissenting); *Abrams v. U.S.*, 250 U.S. 616, 624 (1919) (dissenting); *Gitlow v. New York*, 268 U.S. 652, 672 (1925) (dissenting); *Commonwealth v. Davis*, 162 Mass. 510 (1895); *Patterson v. Colorado*, 205 U.S. 454 (1907); *Fox v. Washington*, 236 U.S. 273 (1915); *Schenck v. United States*, 249 U.S. 47 (1919); *Debs v. U.S.*, 249 U.S. 211 (1919); *Meyer v. Nebraska*, 262 U.S. 390 (1923) (dissenting).
LDB's first speech case: *Schenck v. United States*, 249 U.S. 47 (1919).
Holmes to Judge Learned Hand, printed in Gerald Gunther, "Learned Hand and the Origins of Modern First Amendment Doctrine: Some Fragments of History," *Stanford Law Review* 27 (1975): 719–773, at 757.
LDB on expression of differences: "Jewish Unity and the Congress," address delivered in Baltimore, Maryland, September 27, 1915, and published as a pamphlet by Jewish Congress Organization Committee.
LDB on citizen's engaging in political discussion: *Gilbert v. Minnesota*, 254 U.S. 325, 335 (1920) (dissenting), at 338, and "Jewish Unity and the Congress."
David Riesman, "Notes for an Essay on Justice Brandeis," May 22, 1936, FF-LC Box 127, p. 2.
LDB to Frankfurter on "things that are fundamental": Felix Frankfurter, "Memorandum" of conversations with Brandeis during the 1920s, BP-HLS Box 114-7, pp. 19, 20–21.
Governor's pardon of Anita Whitney: Vincent Blasi, "The First Amendment and the Ideal of Civic Courage: The Brandeis Opinion in *Whitney v. California*," *William and Mary Law Review* 29 (Summer 1988): 653–697, at 696–697.

Additional Reading

In addition to the collections of LDB's works cited in the notes, the interested reader might also look at LDB, *Scientific Management and the Railroads* (New York: Engineering Magazine, 1911). The books and articles about him cited in the notes are all recommended, as are the following:

Bickel, Alexander M., ed. *The Unpublished Opinions of Mr. Justice Brandeis.* Cambridge, Mass.: Harvard University Press, 1957.

Flexner, Bernard. *Mr. Justice Brandeis and the University of Louisville.* Louisville, Ky.: University of Louisville Press, 1938.

Goldmark, Josephine. *Pilgrims of '48.* New Haven, Conn.: Yale University Press, 1930.

Konefsky, Samuel J. *The Legacy of Holmes and Brandeis.* New York: Macmillan, 1956.

Levy, David W. "The Lawyer as Judge: Brandeis's View of the Legal Profession," *Oklahoma Law Review* 22 (1969): 374–395.

New Palestine 32 (November 14, 1941): entire edition devoted to articles about Brandeis.

Mason, Alpheus T. *Bureaucracy Convicts Itself: The Ballinger-Pinchot Controversy of 1910.* New York: Viking Press, 1941.

Staples, Henry Lee, and Alpheus T. Mason. *The Fall of a Railroad Empire: Brandeis and the New Haven Merger Battle.* Syracuse, N.Y.: Syracuse University Press, 1947.

Urofsky, Melvin I. *A Mind of One Piece: Brandeis and American Reform.* New York: Scribners, 1971.

Index